Re-thinking Posthumanism across the Global South

Re-thinking Posthumanism across the Global South

An Introduction

Edited by
Nikhilesh Dhar and Bapin Mallick

PETER LANG

Chennai - Berlin - Bruxelles - Lausanne - New York - Oxford

Bibliographic information published by the Deutsche Nationalbibliothek. The German National Library lists this publication in the German National Bibliography; detailed bibliographic data is available on the Internet at http://dnb.d-nb.de.

A catalogue record for this book is available from the British Library.

Library of Congress Cataloging-in-Publication Data

Names: Dhar, Nikhilesh, 1975- editor. | Mallick, Bapin, 1991- editor.
Title: Re-thinking posthumanism across the Global South : an introduction / Nikhilesh Dhar, Bapin Mallick.
Description: Oxford ; New York : Peter Lang, [2025] | Includes bibliographical references and index.
Identifiers: LCCN 2024031345 (print) | LCCN 2024031346 (ebook) | ISBN 9781803746647 (paperback) | ISBN 9781803746654 (ebook) | ISBN 9781803746661 (epub)
Subjects: LCSH: Posthumanism in literature | Posthumanism in mass media.
Classification: LCC PN56.P556 D43 2025 (print) | LCC PN56.P556 (ebook) | DDC 809/.05--dc23/eng/20240812
LC record available at https://lccn.loc.gov/2024031345
LC ebook record available at https://lccn.loc.gov/2024031346

Cover design by Peter Lang Group AG

ISBN 978-1-80374-664-7 (print)
ISBN 978-1-80374-665-4 (ePDF)
ISBN 978-1-80374-666-1 (ePub)
DOI 10.3726/b22159

© 2025 Peter Lang Group AG, Lausanne
Published by Peter Lang Pvt Ltd, Chennai
info@peterlang.com – www.peterlang.com

Contents

Foreword

Post-humanism is the new critical eschatology that resists the traditional structuration of the centrality of 'man'. With the formulation of man-centred ideation in terms of the functions of history and governance, there has been a continuation of attempts at positing 'man' as the centre of creation. The imaging of man has always been informed, since pre-Socratic times, by traditional philosophic positions of 'centrality', 'totality', 'unity', 'uniformity', etc.

With the shifting terrains of challenges against the uniform hierarchic socio-economic and cultural strata in post-Derridean age, culture comes to be open-ended and readings become gradually interdependent. With the development of soft powers led by Google, Microsoft, robotics, cybernetics and the overarching market economy, 'interpretation' itself becomes increasingly intriguing. The rise of machines inflected in the musical album 'Man Machine' in the 1970s or the Hollywood production of the *Terminator* series a little later became predictive of the collapse of the centrality of man. A new age of 'multiformity' or 'inter-spatiality' has set in, and consequently, it has brought down the politics of binaries, the strictly ideology-driven stasis in cultural theories, the hierarchic governance in political economy, the teleologic continuum of history and culture, etc. Moreover, it has brought up the issue of man's simultaneity and co-extensivity with other beings like plants, animals, and even non-sensate objects. The shifts and disruptions in ontological perceptions were registered long back by Foucault (1994) in *The Order of Things: An Archaeology of Human Sciences*, where he shows a definitive critical anxiety: "As the archaeology of our thoughts easily shows, man is the invention of recent date. And one perhaps nearing its end" (p. 387).

But some critical thinkers imagine an intermediary phase. Joel Garreau, for instance, believes in the phase 'transhuman' that shows a gradual progression towards post-humanism. The 'transhuman' phase envisions a sense of completeness as well as saturation of the idea of universal man as satiated with truth, reason and intellection, thereby preparing the transitive phase into post-humanism.

Re-thinking Posthumanism across the Global South: An Introduction edited by Dr. Nikhilesh Dhar and Dr. Bapin Mallick, is an overwhelming rejoinder to the continuously expanding body of critical literature on post-humanism. This collection of critical essays strides across a large area of epistemic disciplines: heterogeneous cultural texts, Netflix Series, programmed algorithms in the interface of the digital and the human, plant-human liminality, contestations between 'bodied' and 'disembodied' discursiveness in the context of posthuman agencies and biocapitalism's new relationship with the discursive patterns of post-humanism. This rich and varied display of post-humanist thoughts will, I am sure, contribute to more debates and discussions. I sincerely believe that both the editors' scholarly endeavour is definitely praiseworthy.

Professor Deb Narayan Bandyopadhyay
Secretary, Indian Association for the Study of Australia, Eastern Region,
&
Chief Executive Director and Director, School of Language, Literature and Culture Studies: Research and Innovation, Swami Vivekananda University, Barrackpore, North 24 Parganas District, West Bengal, India
&
Former Vice Chancellor, Bankura University, Bankura, West Bengal, India

Works Cited

Foucault, M. *The Order of Things: An Archaeology of the Human Sciences*. Vintage Books, 1994.

Introduction

Scholarly attention to the concept of the posthuman has increased recently in response to pressing problems about what it means to be human and what distinguishes the human from the nonhuman, as well as the ongoing ecological catastrophe, recent technological breakthroughs, and the desire to address in new ways issues involving race, gender, and environment. In light of this, the editors of this volume hope that it will serve as a forum for discussing how the concept of the posthuman may have altered our interactions with the natural world and with one another, for delving into how we may have always been entwined with nonhuman others, and for speculating on how the posthuman may have repercussions beyond the academy.

Posthumanism is a plural, nonbinary, or post-dualist idea that challenges the view of the human, or certain humans, as superior to other humans and nonhumans by blurring traditional distinctions between humans and machines, action and inertia, subject and object, culture and nature. While posthumanism may begin with the prefix "post," this does not imply a time after which the human body is no longer relevant (Wolfe, 2011). Instead, the end of a specific conception of humans is what this symbol represents (Hayles, 1999). In her book *How We Became Posthuman: Virtual Bodies in Cybernetics, Literature, and Informatics* (1999), Hayles presents her perspective on technical posthumanism, examining people as cybernetic systems. She argues that posthumanism, characterized by the absence of subjective consciousness, challenges the limitations of physical existence.

> First, the posthuman view privileges informational pattern over material instantiation, so that embodiment in a biological substrate is seen as an accident of history rather than an inevitability of life. Second, the posthuman view considers consciousness (…) as an epiphenomenon, (…) Third, the posthuman view thinks of the body as the original prosthesis we all learn to manipulate (…) Fourth, and most important, by these and other means, the posthuman view configures human being so that it can be seamlessly articulated with intelligent machines. In the posthuman, there are

no essential differences or absolute demarcations between bodily existence and computer simulation, cybernetic mechanism and biological organism, robot teleology and human goals. (Hayles, 1999, pp. 2–3)

The "self-fashioning" ethos of the Renaissance ideal of the "human" establishes a hierarchy in which the racial, sexual, natural, and technological others are subjugated to the privilege of the human subject. It is pertinent to note that the old notion of the "human" needs to be re-examined in the post-global ambiance, when the world is reeling under the looming threat of the climatic disaster and other critical issues. This paves the way for the development of the notion of the posthuman, which challenges the exclusivist premise upon which humanism rests, as Rosi Braidotti asserts that humans are already "fully immersed in a network of non-human (animal, vegetable, viral) relations" (Braidotti, 2013, p. 193). Posthumanism lays special emphasis on the subjective reality of those who are marginalized due to their race, gender, or species and simultaneously questions the validity of the claim of placing humanity at the center of the world.

The discussion over the replacement of anthropocentrism is distinct and related to a separate lineage of analysis compared to the criticism of humanism, but there are some points of overlap between the two. The examination of the belief in the superiority of humans and their domination over nonhuman organisms introduces another avenue of criticism regarding the characteristics that define the human species. The concept of "man" is criticized for embodying a hierarchical and violent species whose insatiable greed and aggression are intensified by the convergence of technological progress and global economic dominance. A study by Ferrando (2020) clearly demonstrates that both the concept of "man" as the universal standard for everything and the notion of Anthropos as the dominant species are unable to establish their primary role in the process of intellectual contemplation. Within the current global context, known as posthuman convergence, cognitive abilities are shared among various species and frequently carried out through technologically facilitated systems for generating information. These systems are operated by networks and computer processes. The advancement of biogenetics and computational technology has posed a challenge to the traditional distinction between bios, which refers to human life, and *Zoe*, which encompasses the lives of animals and nonhumans.

The ramifications of this transition have substantial political significance. If feminist, queer, antiracist, ecological, and postcolonial critiques have strengthened the empowerment of sexualized and racialized individuals who are still considered human, the problem of Anthropos now involves the inclusion of those who are considered "others." Various living organisms, including animals, insects, plants, cells, and bacteria, as well as the planet and the universe, are being transformed into battlegrounds for political conflicts. The nonhuman creatures are of great importance in the domain of posthumanism, as they are thoroughly examined and reimagined as conceptual personae. Their main purpose is to question the line between nature and culture and, in doing so, assert the exceptionalism of human beings. What is remarkable about Ferrando's work is her ability to find joy in the profound differences of nonhuman animals. Instead of feeling afraid or trying to dominate them, she sees their diversity as something to appreciate.

When confronted with the current climatic disaster, degraded ecology, extinction of species, socio-political shifts, unprecedented progress in technology, artificial intelligence, and replacements of human organs through digital devices, the very identity of "human" seems to be blurred, as Pramod K. Nayar argues that the posthuman self is an assemblage that coevolves with robots, animals, and congeries (Nayar, 2018). Our current paradigm of knowledge production, ethically and methodologically, therefore, needs to be completely reconstructed in the face of these unimaginable crises. Posthumanists believe that it is imperative to re-think one fundamental issue regarding the question of "human," since the notion of "human" is getting interconnected with the nonhuman others. As a result, posthumanism encompasses different forms of subjugation [Dalit discourse, gender issues, lesbian, gay, bisexual, and transgender (LGBT), disability studies, colonial discourse, and animal studies] and blurs the boundary between "human" and "nonhuman." As a result, the very identity of humans has been shifted to the domain of post-dualism, in which humans and nonhuman others are ontologically linked or interwoven.

Posthumanism is an idea in continental philosophy and critical theory that tries to raise a counter discourse to the fundamental Western beliefs and practices, as Donna Haraway perceives it to be a rejection and a reconstruction of the ideals of the classic humanist subject (Haraway, 1992). It is a radical approach to reframing the human subject in terms of its broad connection to the natural world. In *The Animal That Therefore I Am*, Derrida and Marie-Louise (2008) first argues against the anthropocentric "master identity model" that tends to dominate the Western metaphysical field. The foundations of contemporary society and an underlying "modern constitution" are severely shaken by this transition of human agency from its biological entity to its geological one. Therefore, concepts such as human autonomy, privilege, morality, and reciprocity, which are primarily responsible for the formation of modernity, need to be reinterpreted.

When the concept of humans itself is called into question, the traditional approaches to thinking about politics and society are disrupted, blurring the boundaries between humans and nonhumans. In her book, *Philosophical Posthumanism*, Francesca Ferrando (2020) sees philosophical posthumanism as being comprised of three main ideas: posthumanism, postanthropocentrism, and postdualism. Nonhuman others, therefore, are no longer confined to passive observers as they reassert their own assertive capabilities previously reserved solely for humans. Under the present scenario, the edited volume titled *Re-thinking Posthumanism across the Global South: An Introduction* makes an endeavor to revisit the literary representation of the "human" and the manner in which the authority of the human is challenged from a variety of perspectives in order to explore different critical issues that exist in our contemporary world.

Aishwarya Das Gupta in her paper interrogates the categories of the non(/in)-human and the construction of alternative subjectivities through a posthumanist analysis of an episode titled "Good Hunting" from the popular Netflix series *Love, Death & Robots (Volume I)* (2019) (stylized as *Love, Death+Robots*). It explores how the episode has ruptured the solid boundaries separating the human from the non(/in) human, dealing with the themes of transcorporeal subjectivity, the issue of monstrosity, and the discourse of difference on which the ideal of the "human" as separate and superior to the animal, the technological, and the earth's others is formed.

Beginning with the history of posthumanism in Bengali literature, Aritra Basu's paper "Heterogeneous Platter, Hybrid Presentations: Analysing the Elements of Posthumanism in Select Works of Sukumar Ray" explores the possibilities of finding posthumanist elements in the works of Sukumar Ray. The paper then moves on to an interwoven understanding of how insanity can be read as an avenue of posthumanism and finally comments on the peaceful cohabitation between the human and the posthuman in Sukumar Ray's universe.

Debojyoti Dan in his paper considers Eliot as that Vitruvian man of Leonardo da Vinci whose geometric punctum is mathematically precise, yet in his poems he goes beyond that Vitruvian frame and outside the basilica of humanism. If Renaissance humanism prioritizes man as a center of the universe, Eliot's Hollow Men are a referential apposite to that, as they are the personalized emptiness of Eliot's life. So we see in "The Love Song" of J. Alfred Prufrock, "Ash-Wednesday," and even in "The Waste Land" the presence of cybernetic posthumans in ecological crisis, and we share a bond over pan-vulnerability with Prufrock and the Hollow Men and remain united on a negative plane, what Braidotti calls "being-in-this-together" (2013, p.167).

By combining Donna Haraway's concept of posthumanism with Rene Wellek's idea of "metapoetry," Joydeep Chakraborty's paper examines two 21st-century American poems—"Don't Let Me Be Lonely: An American Lyric" by Claudia Rankine and "This Connection of Everyone with Lungs" by Juliana Spahr—to demonstrate the creative posthumanism of these two poems that simultaneously embraces, modifies, and reconstructs some notable posthuman ideas. This study emphasizes both the necessity and the limitation of posthumanism in 21st-century American poetics.

Jyoti Biswas, in his paper "Preservation of Orality through Digital Archiving: A Critical Study of Oloi Song in Posthumanist Discourse," intends to contextualize the digital archiving of endangered cultural performances in the posthumanist discourse and evaluate the Oloi song in this discourse. Oloi song is one of the endangered cultural performances found among the rural folk of the Namasudra community in certain regions in West Bengal and Bangladesh. The present paper uses the posthumanist theory of digital culture and shows how Oloi songs can be digitized and then preserved on the digital platform, especially on YouTube for the future.

Niladri Mahapatra, in his paper "Mandrake, the First Performer of Posthuman Plants: Exploring Plant-Human Liminality as a Posthuman Condition," explores the ontological meaning and beyond-plant representation of the Mandrake plant and, thus, it justifies Mandrake's plant-human liminality as a posthuman condition. So, the paper, by examining the mythography of Mandrake, is convincing to argue that the deliberated demarcation of plants is also transforming in the mutation of the posthuman paradigm, and there is no boundary between the arboreal and human worlds.

The paper by Reeswav Chatterjee uses posthuman methodologies to subvert the humanist binarized relation between the human and the non-human to explore mutuality specifically in the context of marginalization. This paper would pick up select science fiction and dark fantasy stories by contemporary Bengali author Saikat Mukhopadhay as primary texts to apply tools of marginality politics to them. The aim is to locate both the human and the nonhuman in the context of discrimination and find out whether they can cross the thin line.

Saikat Chakraborty's paper deals with the posthumanist theoretical paradigm through materiality and otherness. The first part of the paper tries to show the materiality of the scarecrow not as inactive and mute but as having agency in Satyajit Ray's short story "Kagtarua." The second part deals with Shirshendu Mukhopadhyay's stories "Harobabur Avigyota" and "Bidhubabur Gari" to define posthumanism as a movement away from traditional distinctions of the human and the nonhuman.

Shalini Chakraborty states in her paper that the shadowy realm of virtual space, the crisis of identity, and the building dependence on nonhuman entities all reflect a collective loneliness colored by the fear of human intimacy that allows one to explore the warmth that lurks in such spaces. Spike Jonze's *Her* explores the relation between an embodied human Theodore and his intelligent operating system, Samantha, programmed to outgrow her programming, whose sensibility, understanding, and compassion make him more comfortable in her company than fleeting interactions with other physical beings. The temporary mutuality is achieved largely on an anthropomorphic plane as humans are incapable of imagining a conscious-ness without a body, yet the lack of body is always felt.

The paper by Sourav Saha delves into the representation of posthuman beings as well as the relationship between the human and the posthuman in four selected episodes from the UK-based anthology television series, *Black Mirror*, where there is an employment of futuristic technology that simultaneously reflects the utopic and dystopic implications surrounding the human-posthuman relationship. The paper uncovers how such am-bivalent depictions comment on both our fantasies and our fears about the posthuman.

Sujato Ghosh states in his paper that J. M. Coetzee's *Waiting for the Barbarians* can be looked at through the lens of the complex posthuman Spinozist approach soaked in the theories of torture and trauma. The magis-trate, the girl, Colonel Joll, and Mandel show the transversality of their positions as the novel unfolds. The fixed coordinates of being a human are shaken. This paper attempts a posthuman heterogeneous revisit through the mazes and labyrinths of Coetzee's fiction.

The paper by Swagata Singha Roy explores the novel *Borne* and delves into the intersections of biocapitalism, ecological exploitation, and post-human ontologies within the realm of New Weird literature. VanderMeer's surreal narratives, situated in a post-apocalyptic world ravaged by biocapi-talist enterprises, prompt an examination of posthuman subjectivity, ethics, and the consequences of hyper-consumerism in late capitalism. The paper critically analyzes the novel's characters, including the enigmatic Borne, as hyperobjects that challenge traditional anthropocentric perspectives, urging readers to reconsider the implications of biotechnological advancements and their impact on the boundaries between natural and artificial life.

Food in any habitat metaphorically represents many things, such as dreams, social categories, hierarchy, and cultural consumption in this post-truth era. This interpreted cultural logic of late capitalism (food habits, dietary strategies) serves the new imperatives of economic, ecological, and nutritional ends. The production of customized dietary content raises many ethical questions about the materialist frameworks in the dominant dis-course of posthumanism. Swapna Roy's paper attempts to explore the para-digm shift of genetically engineered food in the genre of biopunk literature.

In his 1993 work, *Spectres of Marx*, Derrida devised the concept of "hauntology" while scrutinizing Marxism. Following the posthuman hauntological turn, the spectral agencies, in the form of ghosts and hauntological ecoscapes with dilapidated and deserted architecture, help articulate the voices of the marginal subjects in horror films, in a world often dominated by humans. Tiyasa Dey's paper therefore seeks to undertake hauntological readings of films like *Phillauri* (2017), *Pari* (2018), *Bulbbul* (2020), *Chhori* (2021), and *Stree* (2018).

Dr. Nikhilesh Dhar and
Dr. Bapin Mallick

Works Cited

Braidotti, R. *The Posthuman*. Polity Press, 2013.

Derrida, J. and Marie-Louise, M. *The Animal That Therefore I Am*. Fordham University Press, 2008.

Ferrando, F. *Philosophical Posthumanism*. Paperback edition, Bloomsbury Academic, 2020.

Haraway, D. "Otherworldly Conversations; Terran Topics; Local Terms." *Science as Culture*, Vol. 3, No. 1, 1992, pp. 64–98.

Hayles, N. K. *How We Became Posthuman: Virtual Bodies in Cybernetics, Literature, and Informatics*. University of Chicago Press, 1999.

Nayar, P. K. *Posthumanism*. John Wiley & Sons, 2018.

Wolfe, C. *What Is Posthumanism?* V. 3., University of Minnesota Press, 2011.

PART I

Posthumanism, Anthropocene, and Planetary Futures

SWAGATA SINGHA RAY

Investigating the Post-Anthropocene Futures: Biocapitalism and Posthuman Ontologies in Jeff VanderMeer's *Borne*

The relationship between human history and natural history has been intermittently probed and scrutinized by various Hegelian and Marxist traditions of inquiry. Paul Crutzen's proposal of the era of the Anthropocene in 2000, a classification of geological time that perceives human activity after the Industrial Revolution as a major force of geological change, makes the entanglement between human actions and ecological conditions explicit. With ever-increasing human carbon footprints and the development of new avenues of exploitation of biological material by corporate powers, the destruction of ecology is a major global concern. The link between the human future and the possible future of the planet has increasingly become tenuous, so much so that it is far easier to imagine a dystopic future of earth devoid of humans and nonhuman animals than it is to conceive one where humans manage to avert the impending climatic destruction. New Weird literature, as a subgenre of speculative fiction, builds on such socio-political concerns of the present and presents bizarre scenarios and possibilities that may become reality in the near future as a result of the hyper-consumerism of late capitalism.

Jeff VanderMeer (born 1968) is one of the most prominent novelists of new weird fiction who is known for his surreal and unsettling stories, where biocapitalism and eco-terrorism play crucial roles in the unfolding of an apocalyptic setting. Most of the novels by VanderMeer—*Southern Reach* trilogy (2014), *Borne* (2017), *Dead Astronauts* (2019), and *Hummingbird Salamander* (2021)—explore the close relationship between biocapitalism and ecological exploitation, which consequently lead to apocalyptic spaces in the aftermath of corporate domination. These novels engage in a quest to know how posthuman philosophy can inform our understanding of non-anthropocentric subjectivity, citizenship and urban space, ethics, and politics of extinction, which can help mitigate the terrors of a dystopic future. Through a close examination of the novel *Borne* (2017), this paper will seek to probe how the post-natural world emerges out of hyper-consumption and how the consequent commodification of bare life in biocapitalist regimes might eventually facilitate posthuman ethics and subjectivity, which are antithetical to anthropocentricism as it recognizes the ontologies that have been historically condensed to the sphere of the "other." VanderMeer defines the genre of New Weird as "a type of urban, secondary-world fiction that subverts the romanticized ideas about place found in traditional fantasy, largely by choosing realistic, complex real-world models as the jumping off point for creation of settings that may combine elements of both science fiction and fantasy" (VanderMeer, 2008, p. 13).

VanderMeer (2008, p. 13) recognizes that the New Weird genre is "acutely aware of the modern world." Though according to him, New Weird narratives are not "overtly political" (VanderMeer, 2008, p. 13), through their speculative imaginations they dwell on issues of ecological terrorism, biocapitalism, climate change, extinction, and a distinctly post-human future. In VanderMeer's own writing, there is a persistent focus on depiction of agencies and corporate entities, such as the recurrently featured "Company," which is engaged in the exploitation of biotic resources, which in turn leads to the loss of biotic diversity and the eventual apocalyptic collapse of the complete ecological framework. VanderMeer's novels deal with the vulnerability of life and the ecological system supporting it; they are concerned about what Pramod K. Nayar terms ecoprecarity; they are "about precarious lives, those of humans and other life forms, within specific geographical and 'Natural' settings" (Nayar, 2019, p. 11). In his essay on VanderMeer's novel *Borne*, Nayar recognizes that VanderMeer's depiction of a future where biocapitalism leads to proliferation of postnatural life forms is very much on the cards with the rise in influence and impact of biotechnology" (Nayar, 2021, p. 104). Nayar, however, identifies possibilities of mitigating the ecoprecarity in "the condition of abjection, of bare life" (Nayar, 2021, p. 105) when human beings are forced into living with biotech forms, which reduces humans to being "agency-less agents" (Nayar, 2021, p. 105).

VanderMeer, in his new weird novels, reconfigures the Lovecraftian fear of the *Cthulhu*, the ultimate other, into an ecocritical debate about the monstrous kin. This can be seen in the *Southern Reach Trilogy*, where the emergence of the mysterious invasive alien species in Area X causes massive genetic mutations that make vulnerable the already precarious human society and human life. While the fear of being mutated and engulfed, colonized, altered, and forcefully evolved by the aliens persists, Gry Ulstein, in his essay on the *Southern Reach Trilogy*, discusses how VanderMeer presents the narrative from a perspective that goes beyond the human, viewed through which the monsters of the Anthropocene "display complete indifference" to humanity. They go beyond the "human frame of reference" (Ulstein, 2017, p. 93).

The plot of the novel is set in a post-apocalyptic/post-collapse urban wasteland called "Balcony Cliffs." VanderMeer, in his discussion on the post-natural setting of *Borne*, writes on his website, "If I had drawn the Balcony Cliffs on a map, it would have resembled the cut-away of the side of a massive mound, in this case filled with debris, cracked girders, human remains, abandoned refrigerators, fire-bombed or crushed cars" (VanderMeer, n.d.).

In this postapocalyptic world ravaged by the ill effects of biocapitalism, the narrative revolves around the protagonist, Rachel, who is a scavenger and forages the compounds of the company (the biotech conglomerate) to salvage abandoned bioengineered tissues. There she finds Borne, a critter who is bioengineered and defies all attempts of taxonomy or description; when found, he was "dark purple and about the size of my (*Rachel's*) fist, clinging to Mord's fur like a half-closed stranded sea anemone" (VanderMeer, 2017a, p. 4). The gender of Borne remains shrouded in mystery, for when Rachel finds Borne, she reflects, " 'It' had not yet become 'he' " (VanderMeer, 2017a, p. 6).

Borne is not the only hybrid critter in the novel, for the text is replete with bioengineered creatures with various augmentations and mutations. For instance, there is the giant ravenous flying bear named Mord, who was three stories high with "claws and fangs that could eviscerate, extinguish, quick as thought" (VanderMeer, 2017a, p. 5). There are other Mord-like creatures, though lesser in size, infesting the postapocalyptic cityscape. "All golden bears, all huge in their hideous beauty, much taller than a man, with thick muscles that, in their stride and bounding, came at times to the surface of their fur like the hardness of a vine-wreathed tree trunk wrung and stretched taut." (VanderMeer, 2017a, p. 90)

Along with these bioengineered creatures, there are feral children with various modifications in their bodies as "some had iridescent carapaces. Some had gossamer wings. Some had fangs like cleavers that half destroyed their mouths. Soft and exposed and pink or hardened and helmeted, they spilled out." (VanderMeer, 2017a, p. 155) These feral children are minions of the Magician, who is the antagonist of the narrative and tries to take over the city from Mord. The fantastically designed creatures created and marketed by the company, along with ecological disasters that are not explained or defined, are instances of the hyperobject, as they are beyond the human cognition of interobjective entities.

The biocapitalist enterprise and the ecological disaster are intertwined in pushing the society of this fictional world to the edge. Biocapitalism is a term that describes the intersection between biology, biotechnology, and capitalism. It refers to the commodification and commercialization of living organisms, biological materials, and biotechnology innovations within a capitalist economic system. Critics of biocapitalism argue that it raises ethical concerns and risks the commodification of life itself. They raise questions about the patenting of genes and living organisms, the potential for environmental exploitation, and the unequal distribution of benefits derived from biotechnological advancements.

The creatures that roam the cityscape of the novel *Borne* are warning against the devastating consequences of bioengineering and the creation of a postnatural world. Much like Margaret Atwood's *Oryx and Crake* trilogy, VanderMeer's novel is a cautionary tale against the threat of unethical manipulation of biological matter. The neo-liberal capitalist machine views the biological matter produced in the laboratories as commodities that are to be exploited. This explains the strange creation of Mord as a guard dog, an instance of both bioengineering and biocapitalism gone wrong. Stefan Helmreich defines the term biocapitalism in the context of the rise of biotechnology and its alignment with corporate entities and observes: "in the age of biotechnology, when the substances and promises of biotechnological materials, particularly stem cells and genomes, are increasingly inserted into projects of product making and profit seeking, we are witnessing the rise of a novel kind of capital: biocapital." (Helmreich, pp. 463–464). The "company" in the novel is a biotech firm that manufactured and marketed many of the engineered creatures like Mord and Borne. Toward the end of the novel, Rachel makes the sad discovery that Borne was a part of a batch of numerous other beings like him; the last shipment of the company had been numerous Bornes. Marked as children's toys, the diagram on the pods suggested they to be way more sinister biological weapons.

Owing to its manufactured ontology, Borne is a postnatural/posthuman hybrid. He is a taxonomical and categorical confusion through which the new weird or the grotesque is explored in the novel. The ontological shift of the novel into the exploration of the hybrid posthuman being from the human subject is suggestive of moving away from the Anthropos to examine the biocapital hybrid. The "company" engages in unchecked experimentation and marketing of organic matter, making the novel speculative in the sense that it magnifies the biocapitalist enterprise of present time into cataclysmic events in the future. Nichole Shukin points out in regards to the present-day growth in the biocapitalist sector:

> By the turn of the twenty-first century, an economic and ideological shift in investment to the renewable resources of nature has become pervasive. New technologies of biocapitalism seek to command the renewability of nature not so much through the mundane recycling of animal remains as through knowledge/power over the genetic codes of life. (Shukin, 2009, p. 84)

Borne as a cautionary narrative highlights the dangers of such a future where life is manufactured artificially to serve the purpose of humans and depicts how arrogant and misplaced such anthropocentric confidence in technology can be. Echoing the destruction of the bioengineering companies in Atwood's *Oryx and Crake* trilogy, the "company" collapses in VanderMeer's novel. Post the collapse, the critters created by the company roam the city, making it a postnatural space. Critics of biocapitalism like K. Sundar Rajan and Nicholas Rose have pointed out the dangers of putting capital value over life and initiating mass production of life. One of the adverse aftermaths of biocapitalism is that if there is a collapse in the production machinery of such a company, it would result in a tentative spillage of highly mutated invasive species that could lead to palpable ecological collapse. This is exactly what occurs in the new weird novel Borne. Simultaneously, Borne's existence exemplifies the blurring of boundaries between natural and artificial, as well as the commodification of life. He is not simply a biological organism but a product of biotechnology, crafted and controlled by those in power. Through the character of Borne, VanderMeer raises questions about the ethical implications of biotechnology and the extent to which living beings can be owned and manipulated within a capitalist system.

Though Borne is bioengineered, his hybrid nature of being organic and artificial with a human-like consciousness provides a good opportunity to understand posthuman subjectivity through his character. VanderMeer's fictive contraptions of monsters, aliens, and posthuman entities make human subjectivity come in to terms with what Timothy Morton terms as hyperobjects (Morton, 2013, p. 1) as "They involve profoundly different temporalities than the human-scale ones we are used to." (Morton, 2013, p. 1) In his conversation with Timothy Morton, VanderMeer acknowledges that the former's idea of "hyperobjects" "encapsulated what was going on organically in *Annihilation*." (Hageman n.d.) Hyperobjects are vitalities without material manifestation that have such extensive spatiotemporal specificity that they are beyond human referentiality. Morton cites the example of global warming and climate change as examples of hyperobjects, as such changes are nonlocal, phased, and interobjective. In VanderMeer's *Borne*, the hybrid and ambiguous beings, such as Borne, Morde, and Wick's other creations in *Borne*, can all be cited as instances of hyperobjects, as they are in essence "massive, tangled chain of objects lampooning one another through weird relation, mistaking their own essences for that of the alien objects they encounter." (Bogost, p. 79) There is an enmeshment, an entanglement of materiality in which the various characters in *Borne* find themselves, an imbroglio that destabilizes the anthropocentric categories. They are also instances of what Rosi Braidotti terms as posthuman subjectivity. "Posthuman subjectivity is an ensemble composed by zoe-logical, geological and technological organisms—it is a zoe/geo/techno assemblage…" (Braidotti, n.d.)

In the posthumanist perspective, subjectivity is understood as being entangled with and influenced by various nonhuman elements, such as technology, animals, ecosystems, and other nonhuman agents. The boundaries between the human and the nonhuman are blurred, and the human subject is seen as interconnected with a wider network of actors and entities. Along with this, the posthuman reject emerges in the form of the technological and genetic experiments of biocapitalism—the technological and genetic hybrids. VandaMeer explores the possibilities the ontology of reject holds by building upon Irvin Goh's idea of "Clinamen or Auto Reject" (Goh, 2014, p. 218). Goh points out that the conceptualization of the "posthuman subject" in writings of likes of Rossi Braidotti has the potential of reiterating the grand narrative of subjectivity. Goh's idea of ontological rejection provides for an "adequate affirmation of the irreducibility of the other and its difference" (Goh, 2014, p. 222). In VanderMeer's fictive world of junk spaces (desolate cityscapes and factories) and rejected beings (Borne is a very good example of this, as he is a faulty genetic experiment abandoned by the company)—left overs of the hyper-consumerist society of the capitalocene—"rejection" emerges as a trope that exceeds the boundaries of anthropocentricism.

In their editorial of the book series ominously titled *CCC2 Irreversibility* (sequel to the *Critical Climate Change* series), Tom Cohen and Claire Colebrook note that the speculative phase of the Anthropocene is now over, and in the second phase, in the Anthropocene 2.0 "Irreversibility takes hold. The material unfolding of accelerating feedback loops proceeds on its own … With this acceleration from the speculative into the material orders, a factor without a means of expression emerges: climate panic." (Steigler n.d.)

The imminence of the catastrophic geological changes brought about by the Anthropocene has made any possibility of avoiding the impending paradigm shifts in the ecosphere impossible. In such a scenario where the eventual "de-anthropization" is made evitable by "anthropoziation" (Steigler, 2018, p. 11) of the planet, it is important to recognize the emergent situations and ontologies that accompany the event of de-anthropization.

VanderMeer's novels and their depiction of a post-Anthropocene world provide for opportunities to develop and imagine a more hospitable and cautious worldview devoid of the entropy of carbon-based systems of the capitalocene. In novels like *Borne*, the biotechnological advances are like pharmakon, as they have the potential of enhancing as well as inhibiting human cognitive abilities.

A critique of the capitalocene and the ill effects of biocapitalism is necessary before examining the horizons of the post-Anthropocene, which they ironically foreshadow. VanderMeer's novels depict it through the nexus of technological advances and the biopolitical imperative that leads to degradation of life. As depicted in VanderMeer's speculative universe, the biotech revolution profoundly changes and reconstructs the Foucauldian concept of biopolitics from different dimensions. VanderMeer's novel, like *Borne*, discerns new patterns of modern power and allocation of life governance and explores out how biocapitalism has not only produced ethical degeneration but radically changed the definition of bare life itself. It has opened new areas for political hegemony and economic aggression through the reconstruction of biopolitics.

Works Cited

Bogost, Ian. *Alien Phenomenology, or, What it's like to be a Thing.* U of Minnesota Press, 2012.

Braidotti, R. *Posthuman Knowledge.* Polity, 2019.Goh, I. *The Reject: Community, Politics, and Religion after the Subject.* Fordham University Press, 2014.

Goh, Irving. *The Reject: Community, Politics, and Religion after the Subject.* Fordham Univ Press, 2014.

Hageman, A. "A Conversation between Timothy Morton and Jeff VanderMeer, Pages." *Paradoxa*, 28, 2016: pp. 41–66.

Helmreich, Stefan. "Species of biocapital." *Science as culture* 17.4 (2008): 463–478.

Morton, T. *Hyperobjects: Philosophy and Ecology after the End of the World.* University of Minnesota Press, 2013.

Nayar, P. K. *Ecoprecarity: Vulnerable Lives in Literature and Culture.* Routledge, 2019.

————. "To the Posthuman Born (e): The Post-natural World of Jeff VanderMeer." *Journal of Posthumanism*, 1(1), 2021: pp. 97–105.

Stiegler, B. *The Neganthropocene*. Open Humanities Press, 2018.

Shukin, N. *Animal capital: Rendering life in biopolitical times*. University of Minnesota Press, 2009.

Ulstein, G. "'Brave new weird: Anthropocene monsters in Jeff VanderMeer's' The Southern Reach." *Concentric-Literary and Cultural Studies*, 43(1), 2017: pp. 71–96.

VanderMeer, A. and VanderMeer, J. (Eds.). *The New Weird*. Tachyon Publications, 2008.

VanderMeer, J. *The Southern Reach Trilogy*. Fourth Estate, 2014.

————. *Borne*. Fourth Estate, 2017a.

————. "Borne: The Balcony Cliffs." *Jeff VanderMeer*, 30 September 2017b, <www.jeffvandermeer.com/2012/08/27/borne-the-balcony-cliffs/>.

NILADRI MAHAPATRA

Mandrake, the First Performer of Posthuman Plants: Exploring the Plant-Human Liminality as Posthuman Condition

If we trace back to the past, old anecdotes and myths, we find out the broken but hybridized ontological identity of humans, for which Eileen Joy and Craig Dionne have identified humans as "part-human, part-something else" (quoted in Campana and Maisano, 2016, pp. 221–222). The becoming of any living organism in the process of evolution doesn't happen in aloof; becoming happens collectively and remoulds new forms of hybrid vigor for "a more just and peaceful other-globalization" (Haraway, 2008, p. 3). Being a biologist and critic of new companion culture, Haraway always celebrates such hybridized life and calls to concentrate on companion species evolution in this time of posthuman enlightenment. She likes the fact that "90 percent of the cells" of her body "are filled with the genomes of bacteria, fungi, protists, and such…" (2008, p.3). In this way, Haraway instigates for a shared milieu and calls for the reconfiguration of the conventional models to re-examine the inequality and marginalization of the nonhumans and redefine the inquisition of what the nonhumans are because the posthuman shift is also bringing with itself the new problems of the Fourth Industrial Revolution and the crisis of sixth extinction, which can pother more the position of the metamorphic continuum. Moreover, standing amidst the continuum of convergences and divergences, Ihab Hassan, like Haraway, also proclaims for the ecumenical accord by seceding the fractures of posthuman ideologies with the theorem of "One and the Many" (Hassan, 1977, p. 832), which means one consists of many and many from one. Hassan enunciates:

> Our planet continually splinters, breaks according to ideology, religion, class, language, sex, and age. The earth splits into blocks, nations, nations into provinces, provinces into tribes, families, families into feuding individuals – and individuals, enough, alas, into random atoms. Can it be fortuitous that atom themselves have been split into the tiniest, the shiest particles, particles that seem a mathematical whisper, a mere breath? Whose breath? The breath of the universe? (1977, p.833)

Thus, unexpected consequences seek for the archetypal altruism with all living critters, including both animals and plants, for sustaining the ethical position through the imperial cohabitation of interspecies in the Earth. For that reason, Justyna Stepien was so eloquent to convey that "By acknowledging our relationality with the nonhuman world, the ethical balance can be restored, enabling us to have a more profound understanding of the ongoing processes of the hypercomplex world" (2022, p. 4). Thus, Stepien goes in the vein of Braidotti and Matthew Fuller and explains the condition of the posthuman as "a condition with multifarious forms across all fields of activity … "(2022, p. 5), where the becoming happens in a continuous sharing with the more than human others and engrafts the conviction that all living critters, including humans, are coexisting in a coevolving process. So, the paper tries to reinvestigate the profound and earnest privilege of plants as "significant others" and ineluctable "companion species" (quoted. in Karkulehto et al., 2020, p. 4) through the phyto-philosophical argumentation of the representation of Mandrake as a more than plant, which has a posthuman angle where Mandrake violates a plant's onto-epistemology with its appearance as a plant–human chimera.

The etymology of the word "plant" is a matter of imbroglio. To follow the Latin radixes, the word carries two meanings that are antithetical: one root "planta" means "to sprout," which indicates the dynamism of an organism, and another root "plantare" means "to fix in place" (Elkin, 2022, p. 11), which indicates the coagulated helplessness of an organism. So, the etymological construction of plant shows its paradoxical existence and thus historically objectified as a living object of abjection. Even in its ontological appearance, plant lacks not only anthropomorphic but also zoomorphic qualities and thus becomes more vulnerable and sympathetic to produce the societal identification of plant as other through the conceptualized anthropocentric episteme known as "plant blindness" (Hall, 2011, p. 5). But what is the reason for the manifestation of "plant blindness" in the epistemological survey of otherness? To give the answer to this question, I would like to refer here to the explanation of Wandersee and Schussler, who argued that "Lack of knowledge of plants, the general similarity of plant surfaces and textures, the lack of movement in plants, and the fact that plants do not prey on humans are all put forward as possible reasons for the phenomenon of plant blindness" (Hall, 2011, p. 5). Herein, the immobile, mum, and quiescent characteristics of plants mold the abstraction of "plant blindness," and it detruncates the potency of vegetal plausibility and treats plants as ontologically deteriorative, inferior, and sometimes inanimate. Even, making particular concentration on zoocentrism by countering the botanical philosophy, Henri Bergson also haggles on this old sagacity of plant blindness and upholds that "we should define the animal by sensibility and awakened consciousness, the vegetable by consciousness asleep and by insensibility" (Ryan, 2018, p. 1). The historical dialectic negatively affiliates plant with the alien creature of anomalous otherness, which, for Michael Marder (2013), is "the margin of the margin, the zone of absolute obscurity" (quoted in Bishop et al., 2020, p. 2). So, for acknowledging the plant life in the altruistic ecosphere, the theorization of plant ontology, known as "phytocriticism," is needed separately, as the dignity of plants shouldn't be deteriorated but should be revived to stop the plausible apocalypse of the extinction of humans. So, the rummage of vegetal ontology for occupying a place to be focused even in the time of posthuman shift is paradoxical but ineluctable. Herein, Marder accentuates for the legitimacy of vegetal beings, which was augmented by his plant philosophy known as "plant thinking," which delegates some new ideologies to be rendered in posthumanities, and according to Marder, these are

> the non-cognitive, non-ideational, and non-imagistic mode of thinking proper to plants (what I later call 'thinking without the head'); the human thinking about plants; how human thinking is, to some extent, de-humanized and rendered plant-like, altered by its encounter with the vegetal world; and finally, the ongoing symbiotic relation between this transfigured thinking and the existence of plants (2013, p.10)

Like Marder, John Ryan, the recent renowned critic of vegetative philosophy, also raised his contention to impel the human inclination only
for animality in the recent projection of nonhuman studies and stand
for plant studies to respond against the anthropocentric metaphysics.
Moreover, in a critical way with empiric reference to plant neurobiology,
Ryan objurgates Bergsonian proneness for cerebrocentric cognitive
model of animal and mentioned:

> Of course, Bergson was unaware of the projectile mechanisms of plants such as
> white mulberry (Morus alba), a medium-sized tree native to China and historically
> central to the production of silk … Traveling at a rate in excess of half the speed of
> sound – more exactly, Mach 0.7 or 537 miles per hour – the pollen expulsion of white
> mulberry has been described as the fastest recorded biological motion. (2018, p. 2)

So, the new critical plant studies investigate on such more than plant condition of plant to discover the tree which the tree is not, to know the leaf
as more than a leaf, to understand the fruit which is never just a fruit, to
feel the forest just as not the place where the bunch of trees live silently.

A plant should always remain as a plant. But if a plant violates its
quiddity, which makes a plant as a plant if we follow the Heideggerian
formation of the word, then can that plant be a plant or will it enter a
new luminal essence, which can be defined as a posthuman condition of a
plant? Understanding life means understanding, what Heidegger prefers,
"the living character of the living being" (quoted in Nealon, 2016, p. 38).
But plant life is always beguiling; its appearance to the human world is
normal, but its essence is pristinely ancillary. It always seems that plants
belong to another dimension and time. Mandrake is the succinct instance
of such a plant; a closer inspection of the representation of Mandrake in
myth, literature, medicinal science, and even occult history always justifies that the plant appears to break all the botanical norms. This plant can
emulate the western hierarchy of living objects in which the profundity
of plants has been unacknowledged through "plant blindness" and thus
shows the vegetal domain is not the domain of marginal others but rather
an undiscovered absolute territory that ought to be explored. The mythography of Mandrake mirrors the recent discoveries of plant life, and the
onto-epistemological battle of Mandrake might yield a new theoretical

lore of plant posthumanism. Its nature is always acknowledged as agath-okakological, oscillating between good purpose and bad purpose, like its liminal appearance between plant and human, even like its ambiguous birth history from seed or human semen. But such mythographical doubleness of Mandrake is epistemological and speculative as it invokes the infringe-ment of plant capabilities. To follow Coleridge's apology of Prometheus as "the Redeemer and the Devil jumbled into one" (quoted in Hassan, 1977, p. 832), it can be said that Mandrake owes the same attributes of binary an-tithesis, which makes it a trickster of the vegetal world. Like Prometheus, Mandrake is a gift for the world, for it ignites the marriage of the abstract with the real and proves the possibility of a new reciprocity in a new en-lightenment, which Haraway, as a posthuman critic, desires, and Socrates once envisioned that "all things ... consist of a one and a many, and have in their nature a conjunction of limit and unlimitedness" (quoted in Hassan, 1977, p. 832). Mandrake is like Prometheus's vegetal ego, carrying the her-editary genetics of him as an arboreal child. A deep search in several folk-lores and bestiaries explores the quirks in the birth history of Mandrake, which traces that the plant is germinated from a hanged thief's semen or urine, and it was reported by 3rd century writer Apollonius of Rhodes in his work *Argonautica* that this thief can be Prometheus for "Prometheus was condemned to his punishment for theft (and wrongly condemned, we should say); the flower sprang from his gore as it dripped to the ground ... Since gore does not drip from the bodies of hanged thieves, a change had to be made in adapting the story to the mandrake, and so the plant is said to spring from the thief's urine" (quoted in Bierbaumer and Klug, 2009, p. 293). So, the miraculous birth of Mandrake is akin to the modern fertilization method known as "in vitro fertilization," a scabrous process in which an embryo is formed outside the body without the womb through the trickling of eggs and sperm in a mechanical fecundation. The Greek medical author and natural philosopher of decontextualized eclecticism and embryology, Galen, once linked metaphorically the early growth of the human embryo with the protuberating of seed from the soil, and thus he avouched that the human embryo has vegetative accrual and thus tallied semen with pollen. So, Galen's detailing of such embryogenic sagacity yields a hypothetical imperative for the birth of Mandrake from Prometheus's semen. Like his human father Prometheus, who was charged as a thief, Mandrake is also flawed for vegetal consciousness but more than a plant for posthuman perspective, as it reflects the convergence of the plant-human liminal figure and the parabolic ambiguous characteristic. Mandrake's figure is a kind of exploratory vegetal object that can be studied with the posthuman hypothesis for the metamorphosis of the vegetative paradigm.

As the title suggests, in his work *Metempsychosis*, John Donne, following the Pythagorean ethos, deliberately describes a migrant soul's quest through several swirls to integrate into a new self, and at first it embodies in a worldly plant known as mandrake, who was "the wandering soul's first bodily host in *Metempsychosis*" (Collins, 2013, p. 82). The reason for the soul's metempsychosis in mandrake was that the soul was stultified by its mischievous vigor, as several anecdotes about mandrake from ancient to modern times categorized it as a drug herbal used to produce salacity and hallucinations. Even its root physiognomy metaphorically holds the anthropomorphic figure with two legs and hairs like rootlets, and Donne expedites in such a line in his poem "Song"—"Goe, and Catche a Falling Starre"/"Get with child a mandrake roote" (Coffin, 1994, p. 8). Donne's reflection of the plant/human root of this plant shows his saturation with Renaissance spirit, which was produced through his pursuance of classical lore, natural epistemology, and even medieval medicinal practice, in which mandrake was referred to repeatedly. Though in English it has the biblical root, the etymology of the word "mandrake" carries an anthropomorphic sense as it is derived from the popular Greek word "mandragora," which, according to Albert Camoy, is borrowed from the Persian equivalent "mardum-giyah," which means plant-man, which has an etymological affinity with the old Persian word "gayo mertan, the name of the first man" (Zarcone, 2005, p. 117). The etymological root of this word has also several other roots; the Turkic-Arabic source is more exciting as it keenly associates this plant with Adam, the first human. This Turkic-Arabic composite word for this composite plant is "adamotu or insanotu," which is the blending of two different words: "insan or adam," which means man, and "ot," which means plant (Zarcone, 2005, p. 2). So, as its etymology suggests, the mandrake is also ontologically a vegetative chimera, a hybridized plant, which no plant is. Its root has not only the resemblance with humans but also reflects so many human behaviors like moaning, sobbing, speaking, singing, etc. But is it possible for a plant to behave like animals? Unlike mandrake, in the hypothesis of behavioral signals of other plants in general, the neural performance of the root matters so much as it acts like the human brain. This root-brain hypothetical view was postulated by Charles Darwin and his son Francis Darwin in their book *The Power of Movement in Plants*, and they hypothesized a "root-brain" metaphor that concedes that the embryo of the primary root renders the sensitivity in plants like it is seen in the animal brain—"the tip of roots acts like the brain of some animals" (quoted in Bhattacharjee, 2022, p. 78). Thus, such metaphorical calculus of neuro-botany reconfigures the longstanding inert stature of plants as subordinate and invites a methodological analysis for the paradigm shift. In his phytocritical research article on the vegetal poetics of Mary Oliver, while Ryan was elaborating the root's mobility of vegetal discourse, he readily delegates that the "Darwinian root-brain theory radically reconfigured the plant body as an analogue animal or human with its anterior root-brain in the soil ..." (Ryan, 2018, p. 54).

Mandrake's chimerical body also has evidence of two sexes, like the animalistic figure, which was wonderfully accounted for the first time by Greek medico Dioscorides in his renowned pharmaceutical synthesis, collected in his popular manual *De Materia Medica* in Latin. Dioscorides's pharmacological intent was not only to dismantle mandrake's "medicinal functions as a narcotic, analgesic, and abortifacient," but also to apprize the sexual performance of this plant "by noting that the plant has a male and female form and that its root can produce love potions" (Campana and Maisano, 2016, p. 224). So, is this plant-man assemblage of mandrake speculating a new posthuman-botanical body about which the nonhuman philosophy and posthuman botany are re-imaging solicitously? In her philosophy of kinship of diverse species, Haraway prioritized the manifestation of such a chimerical body, which is inevitable for the posthuman possibility. So, being the denizen of both the vegetal and animal worlds, Mandrake's figure bears the perfect proportion of the cosmic body, which can also be observed in Donne's detailing of Mandrake's bodily enhancement and composition in *Metempsychosis* to cover both worlds. Mandrake's cross formation by thrusting his hands identifies itself as "Vitruvian Mandrake" (Collins,

2013, p. 86), a new cyborg of the nonhuman paradigm. Emphasizing this vegetal body-building architecture of Donne, Collins tries to assert a close linkage between Donne's portrayal of Christ in *La Corona*, who can cover by thrusting his hands all the places of the world, and Donne's presentation of Mandrake by thrusting its hands as a Vitruvian effigy in *Metempsychosis*. Thus, Mandrake's phenomenal body, which was even compared by Donne with one of the seven wonders known as Colossus of Rhodes, vaticinates the feasible symbiosis of plant body parts and human organs, which is an enhancing project for forthcoming botanical cyborgs, a posthuman tenacity to perpetuate the environmental altruism of endangered species at the risk of coeval extinction. Moreover, Mandrake helps to think in another way about the posthuman emergence as not only the human and machine hybridization but also the human and plant assembling. Speculating bonewood conjugation as a new cyborg case study for vegetal tranhumanity and understanding the necessity of such cross-species engineered synthesis, the French designer Marie Declerfayt eschewed American anthropologist Anna Lowenhaupt Tsing's ethical anxiety of species hybridity as aberrational repugnant and propounded in 2019 the idea of "Botanical bodies," a design that envisions "a future in which plants could be employed as raw material to create human-compatible organs" (Declerfayt, 2021, p. 1). The phenomenal appearances of mandrake in mythography and other doctrines can arouse the vital intuition for such a plausible design of vegetal cyborg, which can break the spatial limitations and can hope for the world.

By choosing Mandrake as the soul's first earthly recourse, Donne raises a question of heresy—like, does a plant have the same soul as an animal? Such a question is anti-metaphysical, as the whole anthropocentric doctrine was devoted to debunk such arboreal anticipation. In the dialectical promulgation, it is propagated that there are three divisions of soul in which the nutritive one actually belongs to plant. For that reason, plants have so many obstacles that animals and humans can resolve. Even Plato pointed out that though the plants have souls, they are incapable of moving and continue to exist in sedentary. Therefore, plants have been reckoned as inferior to others and exist solely to be acknowledged in the "Platonic portrait" as "passive, sessile, lacking any motion, communication, or awareness, thereby in their essence lower than animals in the Greek tripartite scheme of living beings – the infamous 'third kind of soul' within the human-animal-vegetable hierarchy of things that are alive" (Nealon, 2016, p. 30). But Plato argues for an ethological approach of plant, which Aristotle connects in his own teleological conviction, and it is that plant has desire, which has been proved by its self-nutritive zeal. Establishing in this accord and satisfaction of self-nutrition, which brings the growth of plants, the Aristotelian notion supports that nutritive capacity is the main telos of any living organism, and Aristotle also avers in his minor work "On Plants" that "Anything that is nourished cannot be without soul. Every living creature has a soul" (Page et al., 1936, p. 151). So, for Aristotle in particular and Greek thinkers in general, the growth of plants intentionally or unintentionally with no proper omega is the main quiddity of plants' souls. This nutritive ability, which Aristotle termed a plant's entelechy (meaning what a plant does), makes a plant what a plant is, and following this Aristotelian analysis, Nealon asserts that "no life-forms can exist without the nutritive psukhe (soul) of plants, and concomitantly all living things necessarily deploy a dose of the nutritive or vegetable soul ..." (2016, p.35). Influenced by such methodological analysis of Aristotle, Hallvard J. Fossheim was also so loquacious as to add a remark that "an animal soul is also a plant soul" (Duckworth and Guanio-Uluru, 2022, p. 49). Again, for plants, as Aristotle realized, this ability, provided by the nutritive soul, also incites the plant's incompleteness as it makes plants vulnerable in competence with animals and humans who have more capabilities to do more deeds like perception, mobility, thinking, etc. To add more to a plant's sessility, Nealon also referred to an observation of a student of Aristotle about a plant's elastic and inseparable attachment with mother earth and executed that "when you pull up a plant, that interrupts its psukhe, its primary capacity for life, its nutritive functioning" (2016, p.35). Pulling a plant means killing a plant, for it is not even capable of protecting itself from such infliction.

But, in the case of Mandrake, uprooting is not an easy task; rather, it is a phenomenal event of propitiation. When Mandrake is eradicated, as it has no supporting stalk, its root, which totally appears like a subterranean but humanoid creature, gives deadly blubber with the exuding of blood-like fluids, as it is his main telos to ensconce his psukhe (soul) from any kind of infringement. Its demonic cry, as Keridiana W. Chez wittily remarks, works as "a defensive mechanism" (Keetley and Tenga, 2016, p. 76) and tries to reach beyond the vegetal passivity of spatial fixity. So, any interruption of its soul craves earnestly the sacrifice of another soul of a living animal, a method that can ominously be resembled with the Mephistophelian norm of reciprocal sacrifice, which, according to the poetic words of Ainsworth, is the "Blood for blood is his (mandrake) destiny" (quoted in Keetley and Tenga, 2016, p. 78). In several myths, anecdotal bestiaries, and herbal treatises, this profaned sacrificial story has been narrated in several ways. For Mandrake's evulsion, a Jewish historian Flavius Josephus reports, a special method is needed to avoid any fatal occurrence:

> It may also be taken another way, without danger, which is this: they dig a trench quite round about it, till the hidden part of the root be very small, they then tie a dog to it, and when the dog tries hard to follow him that tied him, this root is easily plucked up, but the dog dies immediately, as if it were instead of the man that would take the plant away. (quoted in Campana and Maisano, 2016, p. 234)

So, any encounter with Mandrake is lethal for its deadly scream, but from a vegetal perspective, it is a protective caliber, which makes mandrake something more than a plant. Though the anthropocentric allusions have recognized it as an incarnation of the evil spirit for daggling its position, Mandrake obtains a posthuman esteem as an overplant and claims the possible discovery of an unknown arboreal world. Recently, for example, a group of plant researchers from Grenoble University of France reported that trees make different types of noises on the basis of their environmental conditions. Tormented trees have the noise of annoyance; on the other hand, trees thriving without any environmental hindrance have more elating noises to convey their rapture. Furthermore, recently, on March 30, 2023, the famous journal "Nature" published an article on vegetal survey, which is more amusing to understand the propulsive reaction of plants, as the author Emma Marris referred to in an empirical manner, by producing several "airborne sounds" (like 35 sounds per hour) in their emergency situations (quoted in Marris, 2023, p. 2). Even Marris also mentioned the view of an eco-concerned biologist named Graham Pyke, who suspected that for environmental contiguity, there should be behavioral savvy through sounds or noises between plants and animals.

Therefore, vegetal beings speak but without any articulation of languages and words, and this technique of expression, which is beyond the perception of humans, for renowned botanist Jagadish Chandra Bose, is a plant-privileging matter that can subdue the phallogocentric orientation of human speech and implicates a new word that is called by the critic of plant studies Michael Marder as "phytophallogocentrism" (*The Philosopher's Plant* 272) for the privileging of plants' speech.

Plants are unique but different, unpredictable, and individual, and plants remain in a different time and existence within the worldly configurations of time and space. In the case of a plant, like inanimate objects, it has no access to other organisms except the Gaia and its things, and, hence, a plant is not qualified to show its subjectivity as to be subjectified; it has no propinquity to organismic objects. And, herein, Hegel mourns for plants because plants don't seek their selfhood like men do. But what is interesting is that every organism has access to all plants and seeks the plants for sustenance, healing, and so many other necessities. Thus, plants constitute a phenomenal kinship with others, which substantiates plants' heteronomous subjectivity from the view point of vegetal anti-metaphysics. Mandrake is not a mere plant for accomplishing the satiety of others' appetites; it can be enumerated as an herb of many usages, like pharmaceutical drugs to aphrodisiac potion. Medically familiar as white Bryony, mandrake (specifically the extract of its root) has been used as an elixir for recuperating from so many maladies. Even an excessive dose of mandrake root's latex, as it was noticed by Dioscorides also in 60 AD, can bring coma or death, for it carries a poisonous alkaloid similar to scopolamine, which is found in solanaceous herbs to prevent the effects of anticholinergic substances. Thus, mandrake shows plants' pharmaceutical ability of healing, which is a vibrating placebo for the sustainability of all other organisms in a time of materialistic dependencies, anthropocentric profanity, and environmental exigency. For that reason, Ryan eagerly admired plants' such heteronomy and "the manifestation of the concept of human-plant intercorporeality" in his ethnobotanical research article on Australian poetry and also suggested that "As sustenance, fiber, medicine, and ornamentation, vegetal bodies sustain human and more-than-human health and well-being" (Slovic et al., 2022, p. 347). Rather than a determined nonhuman entity of vegetative subjectivity, mandrake foregrounds the intercorporeal deontology of umwelt through the medicinal favour, which can be seen according to the phenomenological view of Maurice Merleau-Ponty as "the role of embodied interactions between the self and the other in the process of social understanding ..." (quoted in Slovic et al., 2022, p. 351). And posthuman imagination should confide in this reciprocal process to produce a viable society where all living things breathe simultaneously and should reject the anarchic precariousness of the altruistic singularity.

Apart from such medicinal properties, mandrake is also aphrodisiac. Like Dioscorides, while Theophrastus, through his empirical espial, was also preparing the catalog of salutary and pernicious plants, mandrake was eluded as a drug whose lascivious sip has the magical power to stimulate the sensual appeal and also has the soporific capability to induce sleep. The best reference of such an aphrodisiac attribute, a quality taken from Aphrodite, of mandrake's sup was described in an anonymous bestiary known as *Physiologus*, where it was elucidated:

> There is an animal called an elephant, which has no desire to mate... If, however, they want to have offspring, they go to the east, near the earthly paradise, where a tree called mandragora grows. The elephant and his mate go there, and she picks a fruit from the tree and gives it to him. And she seduces him into eating it; after they have both eaten it, they mate and the female at once conceives ... The elephant and his wife represent Adam and his wife, who pleased God in the flesh before their sin, and knew nothing of mating or of sin. When the woman ate of the tree, that is, gave the herb mandragora which brought understanding to her husband, she became pregnant and for that reason left paradise. (quoted in Bierbaumer and Klug, 2009, p. 310)

The philtre, diluted from mandrake, raises a botanical wonder of plants' sensuousness to sexual stimulation with a priori, which was once assumed by T. S. Miller: "if plants are so interconnected with human desiring, why has it taken so long to take seriously the possibility that plants might desire?" (Bishop et al., 2020, p. 106). Sumana Roy, in her real-arboreal memoir *How I Became a Tree*, is also affected by such tree fantasy that imagines plants' eroticism and asks the query that, as Anirban Bhattacharjee explains in his review of this book, "what it would be like to have sex with a tree, looks into why people marry trees, and explores the loneliness, pain, unselfishness, death and rebirth of trees" (2022, p. 79). Even an acute observation on Indian cultural historiography reverberates that marrying a tree for several purposes is a very common but phenomenal happening in India. In this phytoliterary text, Roy also gives references to such anthro-vegetative nuptials:

> In November 2013, the Peruvian actor Richard Torres married a tree in Buenos Aires – he wanted to highlight environmental problems around the survival of trees, but ended up in a long kiss with the tree he had chosen as his bride. Men from Orissa who have been widowed twice are often married to a tree in the belief that it will 'absorb' the bad luck. And young girls from Nepal continue to be married to wood apple trees. (Roy, 2017, p. 103)

At the end, it is true to convey that the paper, through an analytical and hypothetical contemplation on mandrake's more than plant entanglement, encapsulates about a feasible synthesis and anthropochorous anomaly to erode the anthropoteleological symmetricality by fomenting the cosmological equipoise to which the anti-metaphysical epistemology of posthuman or nonhuman studies appeals dialectically. It's true that coeval posthumanist thinkers are trying to align the posthuman only with technology and scientific dimensions as they have techno-fetishism, for which Haraway shows her despondency to such structuralist identification of deconstructive posthumanism and urges for nonhuman manifestation in posthuman studies where the essentiality of understanding the vegetal world through the perplexing plant activities is conspicuous as it opens a new phenomenon to explore for the posthumanist thinkers. Even this approach traces the dissolution of the anthropocentric ego that the world is an object to be controlled by man and vindicates the altruistic aphorism of Haraway, which should be the posthuman alibi that "To be one is always to become with many" (Haraway, 2008, p. 4), where many are all the nonhumans, from animals, plants, and machines. So, turning to Foucault's lore of biopolitics, it intriguingly altercates for the hidden desire of not only nonhuman subjectivity, which for a long time has been abjected in the domain of human-centric biopower. But such nonhuman manifestation is also trying to shape a new biopolitical figure based on the animal interest, where hierarchy within the hierarchy is overt with the elision of plant ontology and epistemology and justifies the iconoclastic motto of critical posthuman studies, which excites the breaking of hierarchy within the hierarchy. So, following Hassan, it is yielding to moot that the death of man ransomed not only the rise of machines but also the rise of non-human, non-animal, even more than human others. In the midst of such post-humanistic need and metamorphosis, mandrake tiptoes as a liminal entity and interplays as a vibrating vegetal-posthumanity, which can exalt the arboraceous shibboleth of Marder: "The plant is also a measuring being" (quoted in Marder, 2013, p. 78).

Works Cited

Bhattacharjee, A. Review of *How I Became a Tree*, by Sumana Roy. *Sanglap: Journal of Literary and Cultural Inquiry*, Vol. 8, No. 2, June 2022, pp. 78–81.

Bierbaumer, P. and Klug, H. W. (Eds.). *Old Names – New Growth*. Proceedings of the 2nd ASPNS Conference, University of Graz, Austria, 6–10 June 2007, and Related Essays. Frankfurt am Main, Berlin, Bern, Bruxelles, New York, Oxford, Wien: Peter Lang, 2009.

Bishop, K. E., Higgins, D. and Määttä, J. (Eds.). *Plants in Science Fiction: Speculative Vegetation*. University of Wales Press, 2020.

Campana, J. and Maisano, S. (Eds.). *Renaissance Posthumanism*. Fordham University Press, 2016.

Coffin, C. M. (Ed.). *The Complete Poetry and Selected Prose of John Donne*. The Modern Library, 1994.

Collins, S. *Bodies, Politics and Transformations: John Donne's Metempsychosis*. Ashgate Publishing Limited, 2013.

Declerfayt, M. "Blurring the Boundaries: Botanical Bodies, or Becoming a Plant-human Chimaera." *Plant Fever*, 23rd January 2021, pp. 1–4.

Duckworth, M. and Guanio-Uluru, L. (Eds.). *Plants in Children's and Young Adult Literature*. Routledge, 2022.

Elkin, R. S. *Plant Life: The Entangled Politics of Afforestation*. University of Minnesota Press, 2022.

Hall, M. *Plants as Persons: A Philosophical Botany*. State University of New York Press, 2011.

Haraway, D. J. *When Species Meet*. University of Minnesota Press, 2008.

Hassan, I. "Prometheus as Performer: Toward a Posthumanist Culture?" *The Georgia Review*, Vol. 31, No. 4, Winter 1977, pp. 830–850.

Karkulehto, S., Koistinen, A-K. and Varis, E. (Eds.). *Reconfiguring Human, Nonhuman and Posthuman in Literature and Culture*. Routledge, 2020.

Keetley, D. and Tenga, A. (Eds.). *Plant Horror: Approaches to the Monstrous Vegetal in Fiction and Film*. Macmillan Publishers Ltd., 2016.

Marder, M. *Plant-Thinking: A Philosophy of Vegetal Life*. Columbia University Press, 2013.

Marris, E. "Stressed Plants Cry – and Some Animals Can Probably Hear Them." *Nature*, 30 March 2023, pp. 1–4.

Nealon, J. T. *Plant Theory: Biopower and Vegetable Life*. Stanford University Press, 2016.

Page, T. E., et al. (Eds.). *Aristotle: Minor Works*. Translated by W. S. Hett, Harvard University Press, 1936.

Roy, S. *How I Became a Tree*. Aleph Book Company, 2017.

Ryan, J. C. *Plants in Contemporary Poetry: Ecocriticism and the Botanical Imagination*. Routledge, 2018.

Slovic, S., Swarnalatha, R. and Vidya, S. (Eds.). *The Bloomsbury Handbook to the Medical-Environmental Humanities*. London: Bloomsbury Academic, 2022.

Stepien, J. *Posthuman and Nonhuman Entanglements in Contemporary Art and the Body*. Routledge, 2022.

Zarcone, T. "The Myth of the Mandrake, the 'Plant-Human.'" Diogenes, Vol. 52, No. 3, August 2005, pp. 117–131.

TIYASA DEY

Voices of the Non-humans: A Hauntological Inspection of Post-human Agencies in Select Hindi Films of the Twenty-First Century

Introduction

Tracing its root from the ancient Greek civilisation, then reaching a crescendo in the Renaissance, humanism is centred upon an ideal, essentialist and ableist image of the human being – a man, white, with an athletic body, possessing intellectual reason with an ever-expandable scope for improvement, aiming at perfection. However, this unattainable ideal of perfection emphasises man's complex ontological position. This deterministic categorisation is aptly accused of marginalising other species, communities and individuals – women, children, slaves, animals, ghosts and material inventions. Ancient philosophers coming from different schools of thought have defined what it means to be a human being. Although the divine origin theory of man as a creation of God was debunked by Darwinism with the publication of the seminal book, *On the Origin of Species* (1859), the idea of the survival of the fittest further filled the human hubris striving to be the best. However, the twentieth-century French philosopher, Michel Foucault, questions the very idea that is *human*, and the cultural significations that construct it. For him, in a modern civilised society, lunatics and mental asylums are at the margins, being victims of the corrective measures of "governmentality" (Foucault, 1978, p. 3); likewise, worldwide, women have been considered akin to lunatics whenever they have shown irregular behaviour, which is unexpected of them in a traditional patriarchal society. According to Hindu mythology, the female representations of the *Devi* and the *Dayan* constitute the binary of good and evil. Therefore, women are segregated as: good-mother-figure, obedient, docile, or rebellious, barren, unwed mother, or a carrier of evil. Falsely accused of lacking intellect and reason, the female energy is regularly associated with either the divine or the witchy, while her body is regarded as a vessel for carrying these inside.

As far back as 1818, with the publication of *Frankenstein* and its subsequent cinematic adaptation, a spotlight on the monstrous began. Scholarly debates surrounding the symbolic role of the "creature" have suggested varied interpretations. While some see it as a consequence of scientific fetishism or humans' limitations, some hypothesise the monstrous in purely psychoanalytic terms; however, a posthumanist view professes the centrality of the creature's authority, who had been the victim of a human's superhuman aspirations. Born out of a pseudoscientific experiment, it is a child and an "assemblage" (Delueze and Guattari, 1983, p. 10) who is abandoned by its creator, the father figure scientist, Victor Frankenstein. Its appearance, thus, *haunts* him, as Victor is now faced with the consequences that his creation poses to him.

Etymologically, "haunt" stands for home. In *Spectres of Marx*, Derrida coins the term the "hauntology", which is a combination of two terms, *haunt* and *ontology*, to refer to a ghostly presence of the past in the cultural milieu; also, due to its self-same pronunciation with *ontology* in French, there occurs a blurring of the distinction between the temporal positionality of past and present. Mark Fisher, in the book *Ghosts of My Life*, borrows Derrida's idea to critique the hyperreal twenty-first century, where the failure of realism envisages a blank future. He posits that the present is constantly haunted by the past, as there is neither scope for creativity no hope for the future. This exhaustion of creative imagination and planning fills the void with a recourse to the past. However, in the present paper, my analysis would try to concretise the ways in which these hauntings pave the way for a better future.

Background of Bollywood Horror

Hindi cinema began its journey long back, roughly around the 1920s with *Raja Harishchandra* (1913) and *Alam Ara* (1931), with the first Indian Hindi horror film being *Mahal*, made by Kamal Amrohi and released in 1949. Romance, action, avant-garde and political films catered to audiences seeking realism in films. And, both in literature and in films, realism predominated as a preferred mode owing to its appeal to the intellectual as well as the common mass alike. During the British colonisation of India, the Indian cultural practices and superstitions were heavily denounced, and the trend continued post-independence too. While the European horror-verse relied heavily upon Christianity and the primal theme of Satan's resurfacing into the world, the plots of Bollywood horror revolved around traditional myths and local legends. The genre of Hindi horror is replete with exaggerated monstrous figures to forlorn female figures. A white saree-clad woman holding a candle with loose long hair falling to the floor became the stereotypical ghost of the horror world, seeking revenge for the wrongs inflicted on her. Owing to their status as insignificant in status and authority, primarily maidens, newlywed brides, pregnant women and children were considered best suited as either the victims or the vessels sustaining the evil within. In most of these early films, an atheist scientist or a *Tantrik* (occultist) featured as the symbol of reason, which won against superstitions or evil forces. Through the early 2000s, children and women started getting featured in horror films with reinvigorated agentic roles, for instance, in Vishal Bhardwaj's 2002 film *Makdee*. However, post-2015, a surge of horror movies, especially horror comedies, proliferated owing to the immense success of Amar Kaushik's *Stree*. While the film makes sharp critical commentaries on various social ills, it seems to anticipate a society where women are the purveyors of justice, and they give it back to men in style with laughs and screams. While the concept gained popularity, it could only be achieved via the medium of the supernatural. As the famous catchphrase popularised by Marshall McLuhan says, "the medium is the message" (1964, p.9), what avantgarde movies or provocative speeches failed to achieve for the marginal section is being effectively addressed by horror films – to enlighten and educate.

Rosi Briodotti, in *The Posthuman*, posits, "this ghostly enigma resembled an authoritarian figure assumed by women who lacked agency in their lifetime". Although mediated by scattered spectrality, a woman gains concrete material means to control the outside. Posthumanism breaks the human exceptionalism that real authority is the assertion of the human self. Gender studies theorist Jack Halberstam, therefore, explains:

> The posthuman does not necessitate the obsolescence of the human: it does not represent an evolution or devolution of the human. Rather it participates in redistributions of difference and identity. The human functions to domesticate and hierarchies difference within the human (whether according to race, class, gender) and to absolutize difference between the human and nonhuman. (Halberstam and Livingston, *Posthuman Bodies*, 1995, p. 10)

Renowned production house Ramsay Brothers, with consecutive horror films that garnered an immense audience, set their films in graveyards with female protagonists who transformed from their role of a good-looking heroine to a revenge-seeking witch. Often this process of getting initiated to the netherworld was preceded by the protagonist's curiosity about the dark world. Alternatively, if she's the victim of some occult procedure, her rescue by a male hinted at her fragility, as if women, traditionally attributed as emotional beings, are thus vulnerable to being possessed by evil forces. Hence, akin to the witch-huntings of the United States, these witches were "hunted" by a Tantric or a rationalist, but unfailingly male. Despite this particular proclivity towards controlling the ferocious feminine energy, the horror genre would perhaps be the least patriarchal owing to the portrayal of these witches. Further, the transcorporeal space that they weave is utilised as a "heterotopia" (Foucault in *Order of Things*, 1970, p. 8) to redesign power structure in society.

Philosophers on Death

Portuguese philosopher Baruch Spinoza has conceived of human beings as a conglomeration of organs. Twentieth-century German philosopher Martin Heidegger considered "Dasein" (Heidegger, 1927, p. 27) or the capacity to conceive of our own death as symptomatic of healthy living, anticipating an acceptance of a "being-towards-death" (Heidegger, 1927, p. 23) idea of life. More recently, post-structural theorists Deleuze and Guattari look at humans as "assemblages", with meanings and significations as "rhizomatic" (Deleuze and Guattari, 1983, p. 4). Thus, any being is disorganised, a desiring machine with no supremacy or authority of its own.

Rosi Braidotti postulates the desire for death in the post-human condition:

> Life is desire which essentially aims at expressing itself and consequently runs on entropic energy: it reaches its aim and then dissolves ... The wish to die can consequently be seen as the counterpart and as another expression of the desire to live intensely. Posthuman vital materialism displaces the boundaries between the living and the dying. (2013, p.134)

Death, therefore, facilitates a transhumanistic migration in horror films where the supernatural beings are powered by objects or things that help them assert their desired identities. Death levels the oppressed voices. It defamiliarises and distorts in order to recreate a self that is neither embodied nor embedded. It asserts itself through a passage in narrative as a temporal disjunctive necessary to highlight the normalised exploitation of, say, lesser-humans. The post-human condition addresses death not as an end but as a process. If life is pursuit for self-improvement, then death could be perceived as a step towards reassessment and reasserted in the process. The ghost, thus, haunts both as a reminder of the past and as a cautionary preview of the consequences of its repetition in the future. But a spectral being in a creative audio-visual medium is viable to be moulded in a manner, underscoring the necessary posthuman presences that are harbingers of change.

Phillauri (2017)

"Mohabbat kis chidiya ka naam hai humein bhi banana
Bhor saver wog kabhi gungunaye to humein bhi sunana

...

Sikha denge usey humans naam dohrana
Seekh lenge bina parwah kiye urdh jaana"
(Which bird is that which is love, tell me
If it sings early in the morning, let me hear

...

I'll teach him to repeat my name
I'll learn from him how to fly away carelessly)

Coming as a breath of fresh air by director Anshai Lal, *Phillauri* was promoted as a light-hearted film about a ghost who lives on a tree, but under mysterious turns of events is wedded to a manglik man, Kanan, who marries the tree. Under the facade of a romantic comedy, the film explores the questions of love and women's sexual freedom. Shifting between two timelines of the 1910s and 2010s, the film juxtaposes a confused non-resident Indian (NRI) couple soon to get married with a ghost, named Shashi, played by Anushka Sharma. In a remote village of Phillaur, in the 1910s, a budding poetess named Shashi writes poems under the pseudonym Phillauri. A local singer, Roop Lal, essayed by Diljit Dosanjh, sings frivolous songs to entertain the masses plagiarising Phillauri's verses. While the girls of the village are enchanted by his songs, only Shashi seems to ignore his purposeless musings. As Shashi is confronted by Roop Lal for her indifference, the latter is insulted for frolicking in purposeless enjoyments when the country is struggling for independence. Soon, Roop lal drenched himself in understanding the cultural significance and ethos of Phillaur and learns that it is Shashi who writes under the *nome de plume* to hide her gender in a patriarchal society. Soon love blooms between them, and they decide to get married. However, their dreams are thwarted when Roop Lal is killed in the Jallianwala Bagh massacre of 1919. The pregnant Shashi thus ends her life hanging from a tree. Being a woman, she could not directly participate in the freedom struggle; however, the agency that she lacks is carried by her verses that enthuse a rake to become a revolutionary. As Kanan (Suraj

Sharma) and his fiancée devise a plan to reunite Shashi with her estranged lover, Roop, the spectral presences that congregate at Jallianwala Ground are a fascinating testament to the post-human history haunting us through its visceral plasticity. In a society where speaking about sex is considered taboo, in the early 1900s Shashi did not shy away from exercising her sexual identity. And, when she reunites with Roop, she becomes one among/ with the martyrs, uplifting her status as a fellow martyr. Thus, her journey from anonymity to a fulfilled version of a desired non-being is completed, thereby being facilitated by varied non-human objects and things.

Pari: Not a Fairytale (2018)

The second venture from producer-actor Anushka Sharma's production house, Clean Slate Filmz, *Pari*, directed by Prosit Roy, deals with the primal theme of good versus evil. Pari, meaning angel, is an embodiment of evil. Herself an in-between, Rukhsana (played by Anushka Sharma) or *pari*, stands both for the angelic and unholy. Film theorist and author of *The Monstrous-Feminine*, Barbara Creed, examines the oversexualised body of the "monstrous feminine", who is depicted either as victims who deigned to die early or as a villain jeopardising the lives of "pure" women. Creed borrows Kristeva's idea of the "abject" (1982, p.207), which results in a failure to differentiate between the "self" and the "other", emanating from disgust where existence and non-existence coalesce. The monstrous feminine is, therefore, a product of the "male gaze" (Mulvey, 1975, p. 808), where the female reproductive bodily functions are regarded as "abject". The violence, blood and gore further accentuate the demonised form of the monster, which itself is an extrapolation of the male monster. Caught in a cottage on a rainy day, Rukhsana, tied in shackles, is rescued by Arnab (Parambrata Chattopadhyay). Guilt-stricken Arnab, who accidentally hits her mother with his car, takes her home. Relying on the legend of a Djinn, *Ifrit*, popular in Bangladesh, Rukhsana is revealed to be the demon's off-spring from a woman. The lore, belonging to a satanic cult, narrates the story of *Ifrit*, who rapes young women as a part of a ritual to continue his bloodline, or *auladchakra*. However, a radical reformist group intending to eradicate the demon race kidnaps these demon babies and kills them by beheading them. Luckily, Rukhsana's mother escapes this execution and ends up in a shabby village cottage. At home, Arnab mistakes the blood in Pari's room for menstruation; however, it is the monthly poison that she spits out by biting a dog. Gradually, they fall in love and have a sexual encounter, as a result of which Rukhsana is pregnant. As Arnab teams up with Professor Qasim Ali for killing the demon inside Pari's womb, she absconds and goes to Ritabhari's place to harm her and Arnab. However, as a nurse herself and having undergone an abortion previously, Piyali (Ritabhari Chakrabarty), Arnab's betrothed, is compassionate towards Rukhsana and helps her to deliver the baby, who is born with an umbilical cord, unlike the offspring of *Ifrit*. As Piyali treats Rukhsana with love and compassion, she is no longer a demon herself. Piyali feels a semblance of shared vulnerability with Pari. This human-non-human transfusion results in a coexistence of harmony. Her transformation being complete as the baby she delivers appears to be a human being. As can be foreseen, now Rita and Arnab are the primary caregivers to the baby, as Rukshana dies to an accumulation of her own poison, which she resists to spit out at Arnab. This foreshadows a non-conventional family in a posthumanist condition. The film focuses on the human aspect of demons and the demon aspects of humans, thereby erasing the boundary between the two. A frantic Rukhsana tied up by a radical gang to exterminate the baby reflects upon the murderous intent that the group unleashes. If Rukhsana is a victim or a perpetrator is highly questionable. Her suicide is emblematic of her wish to eradicate evil that resides within her. Arnab's soft masculine character and Rita's love for her portray her as wholly antipodal to stereotypical witches. If her innocence and uncouth behaviour qualify her as an animal (who is definitely not social), she offers immense love and gratitude to her caregivers. Thus, all the attributes commonly associated with humans are performed by a hybrid creature. She is doubly oppressed – as a woman and as an offspring of Ifrit; however, as she asserts her identity by loving Arnab and giving birth to their child, she is given a voice granted by her position as a post-human subject. Although she speaks in monosyllables, her sketches in her drawing book become her mode of expression.

Stree (2018)

The film that rescued the oft-ignored genre of horror in India is undoubtedly *Stree* directed by Amar Kaushik. A caustic satire on patriarchy, it makes refreshing explorations of women's psyche, rape culture and men's frailties. The famous catechism, "O Stree! Kal aana" (Oh woman! Come tomorrow), a recurrent motif from the first scene, points towards the obedient nature of women standing antipodal to patriarchal men. A spirit that picks up men during a specific month of the year is a superior post-human presence dominating the hegemonic patriarchal predation. While the village wise man advises the men to don saris or female attire to escape from Stree, it blatantly exposes the hypocrisy of men. "Wo Stree hai, kuch bhi kar sakti hai!", (She is a woman; she can do anything!) by the village paranologist Rudra *bhaiya* (Pankaj Tripathi) highlights the concept of consent. As men are left naked in alleys, the audience wonders why some men (humans) in real life rape or molest. Here, in a comic yet satirical vein, men are haunted by a female spirit. Despite assuming a superior status of transversality and transcorporeality, the spectral non-being is a beholder of superior sense and consciousness. Drawing inspiration from a legend hailing from Karnataka about a witch who attacks men, and thus to distract her, the households put a write on their wall, "Nale Ba", meaning come tomorrow. Set in a village named Chanderi, Vicky (Rajkumar Rao) is a progressive young man who has a flair for tailoring ladies' clothes. Soon, he is enamoured by an unnamed mysterious woman, whom he meets during a four-day annual puja to keep Stree at bay. This woman (Sraddha Kapoor) asks him to bring obnoxious items like lizard's tail, white cat's fur, meat, brandy, flowers of *Datura* and others. Although she purports to defeat Stree in her purpose of abducting men, this woman remains as uncanny in her demeanour as the enigma of Stree. As suggested by Village pandit Shastri, Stree could only be pacified if she is looked at with love and treated with compassion. On a no moon's night, Vicky, along with his pals, attempts to visit the ruins of the old haveli of Chanderi, which is rumoured to be the witch's abode. The discursive nature of love and compassion commingled with supernatural thrill gives it a heightened spectacle where the gothic character of Stree evokes both pity and compassion in the cinemagoers. Only Vicky could be the only one to rid the village of Stree's hauntings, as he is the son of a late courtesan. Stree, herself a spirit of an erstwhile courtesan, craves only love. It is mentioned in the film that while Stree served the men of the village with her art, she received lust and ostracisation from the men in the village. Her generic name, Stree, referring to all women, is representative of the evils women face in their quotidian lives. As Stree is looked at with love and built a memorial with the inscription reading, "Oh Stree, raksha karna" (Oh Stree, protect us). Now, it is a mystery whether Stree has left for ever or she will return if women are mistreated in the village – the ending scene where Stree's snapped braid merges with the unknown woman's hair seems to indicate that Stree remains in a post-human thing as an ontological form.

Bulbbul (2020)

> *"Badi haveliyon mein bade raaz hote hain"*
> (big mansion hold big secrets in them)

An analysis of Bulbbul rightly comments that *Pari* crawled so that *Bulbbul* could fly (source unknown). *Bulbbul*, directed by Anvita Dutt Guptan, is a period piece with the backdrop as the colonial Bengal of the 1880s. Based on starkly realistic themes of child marriage, rape and marital abuse, this 2020 film serves as the perfect platter of the transhuman tendencies, compounded by a supernatural revenge motif, and shows how a tortured Bulbbul (Tripti Dimri) has to adopt to avenge her perpetrators and rescue the women of the village from violence by men. Bulbbul, married off as a child bride to a landlord, Indranil, is lusted over by his younger brother, Mahendra. The dark and mazy haveli, symbolic of her life, Bulbbul finds a companion in Indranil's youngest brother, Satya (Avinash Tiwary). However, her respite is short lived as Binodini, Mahendra's wife, incites Indranil on Bulbbul's undue affection towards Satya. As Satya leaves for abroad, Bulbbul is beaten by an inebriated

Indranil who twists her feet, and Maninder rapes her as she lies immobile. The scene shows her assault resembling the *Jatayu Vadham* painting of Raja Ravi Verma, where the mythical bird Jatayu's wings are chopped by *Ravana* as the bird was trying to rescue *Sita*. Like Jatayu, Bulbbul's freedom and mobility are snapped by Indranil by twisting her feet and the rape followed by it. As she is almost choked to death, she resurrects to become a symbol of power and women's emancipation. Now, like the painting hanging on the wall, she is *Damayanti*, sitting on the one with a peacock feather in her hand. The lore, popular in the village of an angry "*chudail*" who punishes evil men, turns out to be Bulbbul herself, who becomes the harbinger of justice. While it is a mystery if she kills Mahendra, her role as a posthuman avenger is explicit. Using her twisted feet, she assumes the role of a monster woman who charms with her sexuality and employs her aloofness as her weapon. The forest set ablaze is symbolic of a phantasmagoric merger between humans and the supernatural. As a naked demon Bulbbul prances from tree to tree, escaping the fire, she immerses herself in the fire and transforms into a fearless protector. Her appearance as a phantasm, smirking at Indranil and insinuating revenge, thereby disintegrating into twigs of bioluminescent shards, reveals the power of the "monstrous feminine" (Creed, 1993). The audiences are left to wonder if Bulbbul was indeed a vengeful witch or a benevolent demigoddess.

Chhorii (2021)

> "*Sab chhup gaye na?*
> *Mai aayi*"
> (Has everyone hidden themselves?
> I am coming)

Directed by Vishal Furia as the official Hindi remake of the 2017 Marathi film, *Lapachhapi*, *Chhori* (Hindi, for girl), takes up the issue of female foeticide in India. The plot revolves around pregnant Sakshi (Nushratt

Bharuccha), who, with her husband, Hemant (Saurabh Goyal), flees to
their driver's isolated village, escaping from the loan sharks trying to hurt
Hemant. The rural setting with a mud house situated in the middle of a
bamboo farm serves as a perfect setting where human agency is miniscule.
Gradually, as the plot moves, the supernatural spectrals take charge, with
the claustrophobic setting of the labyrinthine sugarcane fields stifling the
human world. Trapped by the orthodox matriarch of the house named
Bhanno Devi (Mita Vashishisth), Sakshi is frequently visited by laugh-
ing urchins, accompanied by a solitary woman, and an eerie song played
by a stereo. As these transcorporeal figures direct her towards a room,
her horrific nightmares of ripping apart her own womb become more
vivid. Caught unawares as Sakshi becomes a part of some dark rituals, she
realises the good intentions of the ghosts; Sunaini (Yaaneea Bhardwaj),
Hemant's previous wife, and her children thus narrate their sufferings
to Sakshi. Although Sakshi's tragedy is averted, the panorama depicting
Rani being forced to cut open her womb as the foetus carried a female
child is itself the non-human taking agency through her transversality.
The violence perpetrated by the humans is superseded by the gore of this
scene. The irony of agentic assertion is exposed when Suhani exposes the
hypocrisy of the family by silently projecting the horrendous incident to
Suhani. The climax, betraying the culprits as Uncle, Davi and Hemant
posing as Rajbir, who played instrumental in Sunaiani's suicide, anticipates a balance wherein an equilibrium is established between the human
and the non-human. Therefore, it is through death that Sunaini is given
the rights that are basic human rights – the right to speak. The empty
well where Sunaini jumped with the children who copied her exposes the
"ecoprecarity" (Nayar, 2019 in *Ecoprecarity*, p. 10) of the film. The empty
well shows an empty womb, in which the human-constructed sacrifice of
blood has dried up; the drought-inflicted condition of the well further
denounces human agency and violence. The narrative ontology is toppled
as the nonhuman objects that initially pose as against humans are actually
aiding the "other" – a woman and a foetus – who have always been at the
periphery of the region occupied by the sacrosanct ideal of the *human*.

Conclusion

The horror sequences in the post-2015 reveal several points of commonality, having rural settings, a claustrophobic environment, with women taking charge, and *haunting* as a means for post-human presence. The indigenous myths and local folklore are exploited to give voice to the nonhumans where agency is denied to those regarded as lesser beings. Death or subsequent hauntings compose constant reminders of the evil lurking in the present, however, not in the spectralities. The visual medium of the celluloid ensures to superimpose a distorted version of reality that, in turn, foregrounds the crevices in society. Anticipating a post-human society seeks to establish that the nonhuman holds equal agency, guaranteeing voice for the marginal while simultaneously ensuring a critique of the norms followed hitherto. As a paradigm, it opens myriad avenues for re-examination of the genre of horror from the post-humanist perspective, giving voice to the voiceless.

Thus, Briodotti contends, "Death is but an obvious manifestation of principles that are active in every aspect of life, namely the impersonal power of *potential*" (meaning, a self-fashioned "essence to endure with all intensity"). (2013, p.138)

Works Cited

Briodotti, R. *The Posthuman*. Polity Press, 2013.
Bulbbul directed by Anvita Dutt Gupta, Clean Slate Filmz, 2020.
Chhorrii directed by Vishal Furia, 2021.
Creed, B. *The Monstrous-Feminine: Film, Feminism, Psychoanalysis*, Routledge, 1993.
Darwin, C. *On the Origin of Species by Means of Natural Selection, or Preservation of Favoured Races in the Struggle for Life*. John Murray, 1859.
Deleuze, G. and Guattari, F. *Anti-Oedipus: Capitalism and Schizophrenia*. University of Minnesota Press, 1983.

Foucault, M. *The Order of Things*. Random House, 1970.

———. "The Birth of Biopolitics", 1978.

Halberstam, J. and Livingston, I. Introduction: Posthuman Bodies. In J. Halberstam and I. Livingston (Eds.). *Posthuman Bodies*. Bloomington, Indian University of Press, 1995, pp. 10.

Heidegger, M. *Being and Time*, Oxford University Press, 1927.

Kristeva, J. *Powers of Horror: An Essay on Abjection*. Columbia University Press, 1982.

Lapachhapi directed by Vishal Furia, A Midas Touch Movies, 2017.

Mahal directed by Kamal Amrohi, produced by Ashley Kumar, 1949.

Makdee directed by Vishal Bhardwaj, 2002.

McLuhan, M. *Understanding Media: The Extension of Man*, Routledge, 1964.

Mulvey, L. "Visual Pleasures and Narrative Cinema." *Screen*, 1975.

Pari directed by Prosit Roy, Clean Slate Filmz, 2018.

Phillauri directed by Anshai Lal, Clean Slate Filmz, 2017.

Shelley, M. *Frankenstein or The Modern Prometheus*. Oxford University Press, 1818.

PART II

Posthumanism, Agency, and Other

REESWAV CHATTERJEE

Spectres of the Future: The Marginal Children of Posthumanity in Select Stories by Saikat Mukhopadhyay

Sanna Karkulehto, Aino-Kaisa Koistinen, Karolina Lummaa, and East Varis in their introduction to the 2020 book *Reconfiguring Human, Nonhuman and Posthuman in Literature and Culture* highlight the ethical aspect of posthumanism in the context of marginalization. They put forward the view that critical and methodological approaches should be "motivated not only by practical and epistemological but also by ethical interests" (Karkulehto et al., 2020, p. 3). In this context, they speak about the political identity of the liberal humanist subject. "Global cultural hegemonies have labeled only a selected few as prototypes of the ideal humanity…" (Karkulehto et al., 2020, p. 3), which then constructs the logic of marginalization. "The cultural meanings given to non-human animals often reflect and coincide with the attitudes and assumptions held towards repressed or marginalized groups …" (Karkulehto et al., 2020, p. 3). This humanist logic of positing all those biological humans (who don't fall into the category of liberal subject) as sub-human is very crucial, as one of the chief reasons for achieving mutuality is, understandably, the need to stop marginalization of the nonhuman.

Before delving deep into this politics of marginalization, some fundamental observations by scholars, who come under the purview of postanthropocentrism, need to be revisited. "The human, as we know, understand and think ourselves to be is not anything natural or given, nor is it just a reflection of our ontological being. It is an epistemological idea, constructed by the humanist knowledge system during the Enlightenment, that depicts the thing called 'human' as both the subject/agent and object of knowledge" (Chatterjee, 2021, p. 91). Foucault, in his closing paragraph of *The Order of Things: An Archaeology of the Human Sciences*, talks about the historical appearance of this thing called "man."

> ... it was the effect of a change in the fundamental arrangements of knowledge. As the archaeology of our thought easily shows, man is an invention of recent date. If those arrangements were to disappear as they appeared, if some events ... were to cause them to crumble, as the ground of classical thought did, at the end of eighteenth century, then one can certainly wager that man would be erased, like a face drawn in the sand at the edge of the sea. (Foucault, 2001, p. 387)

Cary Wolfe in *What Is Posthumanism?* talks about this construction of the human and the politics behind it: "The philosophical and theoretical frameworks used by humanism to try to make good on those commitments reproduce the very kind of normative subjectivity--- a specific concept of the human--- that grounds discrimination against animals and disabled in the first place" (Wolfe, 2010, p. 17). Wolfe's phrase "a specific concept of the human" not only refers to the idea of "human" as an epistemological construction (as opposed to something that is natural), much in the lines of Foucault, but also situates this construction in a historical context. If we focus on any epistemological construction—be it masculinity, femininity, the West's idea of the East, and hetero-patriarchy's idea of the queer community—we will find a certain politics working behind it. In most cases, such constructions are created by a community with the chief goal of systematizing and justifying forms of oppression and discrimination against another community. What we need to understand is that the politics of the humanist knowledge system doesn't end at constructing a certain idea of the "human" (as the subject and object of knowledge) but also extends itself in constructing a certain idea of the nonhuman as well. The idea of the "human" and the "nonhuman" was simultaneously and referentially created with the aim of placing them in a necessarily binary equation. The "human" constitutes itself by negating or even opposing the "nonhuman." The politics of placing the human and the nonhuman in a necessarily binary equation resulted in a mandatory assertion of the differences between the two, which gets perceived as a cause good enough to justify discrimination. Thus, humanism not only constructed the categories of the "human" and the "nonhuman," but constructed them on the basis of a binary equation that made any dream of achieving mutuality a distant, almost impossible one. It is in this context that gives full meaning to Wolfe's phrase "grounds discrimination against animals and disabled in the first place" (Wolfe, 2010, p. 17).

Now, as humanism places the "human" at the center of the epistemological universe, the nonhuman, with its binarized position with the "human," has to be relegated to a marginalized sub-human zone. It's a continuation of the "epistemological and ontological legacies of the Great Chain of Being, according to which the human has been granted a special position in the western hierarchical structure representing divine creation" (Ferrando, 2018, p. 439). This is what being both the subject and object of knowledge means. Interestingly, "human" and "nonhuman" reflect a completely different epistemological construction in posthumanist, postmodern knowledge systems. The postmodernist approach to knowledge is marked by one of its major points of departure from the modernist/humanist knowledge system. Jean Francois Lyotard, in *The Postmodern Condition: A Report on Knowledge* (1984), makes it clear that knowledge in its postmodern condition de-centralizes the system of knowledge production. Therefore, postmodern knowledge breaks down the anthropocentric meta-narratives of "what is human." It dispossesses him from the center of the knowledge system, from the position of the only subject and object of knowledge, and from "any particular privileged position in relation to matters of meaning, information and cognition" (Wolfe, 2010, p. 12). That means there is no epistemological construction present at the knowledge center to view the nonhuman as a necessarily oppositional category to the ontological thing called "human." The posthuman doesn't see human-nonhuman in a binary relation or as hierarchical categories.

This paper would use posthuman methodologies to subvert the humanist binarized relation between the human and the nonhuman to explore mutuality specifically in the context of marginalization. This paper would also use the tools of marginality politics to locate both the human and the nonhuman marginalized in the texts, and then would try and find out whether mutuality can be achieved on the basis of their marginalized position.

But before dismantling a construction, one needs to understand its functionality. Ferdinand de Saussure, in his *Course in General Linguistics* (1916), establishes the concepts of "signifier" and "signified." The word "box" is an intangible signifier representing the tangible material, which is the signified. Applying this Saussurean concept to the humanist construction of the "human" and the "nonhuman" would clarify the functionality of the later. How often have we heard that humans make mistakes, machines don't? How often, across the major part of the last century, have we pondered the existence of conscience in the human, unlike the machine? We associate "the idea of perfection" with the machine while we associate the "idea of conscience" with the human. Perfection and conscience are the "signifiers" that we associate with the signifieds—machine and human, respectively. From "The machine is perfect," it quickly becomes "What is perfect is the machine." The signifier becomes the representative of the signified. When we perceive the human and the nonhuman, at least in a humanist context, it's the numerous signifiers that shadow the signified. What we know and think to be "human" and "nonhuman" are merely an image of the two, painted with the signifiers that humanism has attached to them.

> The Saussurean idea about the difference between an object and the word in a language which describes that object; and difference between words in different languages describing the same object establish the inherently arbitrary nature of signifiers. Signifiers can never be fixated to any particular object or a signified, and any eventual fixation would depend upon numerous socio-political, cultural, linguistic and other factors. (Chatterjee, 2021, p. 90)

With the development of artificial intelligence over the last few decades, and with the constantly faltering machines around us, we now know how much arbitrary the signifiers of consciousness and perfection are! Needless to say, such an application of de Saussure shows how fragile the humanist construction of human and nonhuman is. It's based on certain signifiers, which are extremely volatile in nature.One particular observation regarding binary equations is relevant in this context:

> Now, every single binary has to be constructed upon a shared context or signifier/s. Opposite of liquid can't be emotion because they lack the shared signifier of 'States of Matter'. So, the fact that the two poles of the binary could find a shared signifier

means the two units (signified) can be at least partly represented by a common signifier. That means there are, functionally, two sets of signifiers in a binary whom we
can call shared and differentia. Now, if signifiers are inherently arbitrary, how can
any fixation of either the shared or differential signifiers on any signified is possible
? Of course, there is the question that which set of signifiers (shared or differential)
would you prioritize--- a question whose answer is conditioned by socio-political
and linguistic specificities. But even if we keep aside the question of prioritization, it
is impossible to even decisively fix the signifiers on the shared or differential aspects
of a binary. If some of the signifiers are interchanged or merely gets changed, then a
shared aspect can become a differential one and vice versa. Therefore, any binary is a
very delicate system (filled with too many volatile elements (signifiers) functioning in
it), susceptible to complete collapse with minimal tampering (Chatterjee, 2021, p. 90).

And this is precisely why, in a humanist binary, a human signifier has the
possibility of getting attached to a nonhuman signifier and vice versa.
Thus, the humanist construction of the "human," the "nonhuman," and
their binarized relationship are all extremely fragile in nature. More often
than not, the signifiers fall off from their respective signifiers and get
mixed into a cesspool of signifiers, where it becomes impossible to discern the human ones from the nonhuman ones. If, for the sake of better
understanding, we call this a posthumanist equation between the human
and the nonhuman, then how can it possibly function? An application
of Lyotard's concept of postmodern knowledge production can give us
a probable model. It is understandable that we are using Lyotard's observation on postmodern knowledge systems precisely because it challenges
the humanist binary of human and nonhuman. It is on the basis of this
Lyotardian model that this paper would try to find a route to achieve mutuality in the context of marginalization.

    N. Katherine Hayles in her 1999 book *How We Became
Posthuman: Virtual Bodies in Cybernetics, Literature, and Informatics* comments on posthuman subjectivity. "The posthuman subject is an amalgam,
a collection of heterogeneous components, a material informational entity,
whose boundaries undergo continuous construction and reconstruction"
(Hayles, 1999, pp. 1–2). The posthuman subject is an amalgam where the
signifiers that humanism attaches with the human and the nonhuman fuse
almost like in a cesspool and thereby dissolve the binary. The posthuman
is one whose consciousness, body, language, and subjectivity comprise of

endless (so-called) human and nonhuman signifiers. Hayles's comment clarifies that the Lyotardian model can show how the posthumanization of subjectivity can happen. "…a self doesn't amount to much but no self is an island; each exists in a fabric of relations that is now more complex and mobile than ever before. One is always located at a post through which various messages pass" (Lyotard, 1984, p. 15). And this is precisely where the liberal humanist subjectivity transforms into a posthuman one. The liberal human subject is not fragmented; its parts are not scattered across dispersed clouds of narrative language elements.

It is in this context that this paper would attempt to investigate whether the experiences of marginalization of a human and of a nonhuman can fuse into each other to transform both into a posthuman subject. Can the nonhuman experiences (as signifiers) settle in the human subject, transforming his subjectivity into a posthuman one comprising of both human and nonhuman experiences? Similarly, can the human experiences (as signifiers) settle in the nonhuman to do the same thing to him? If the answer is yes, then it would mean two things:

(i) Experiences of marginalization can be sites of achieving mutuality.
(ii) Posthumanization of the liberal subject can happen by focusing on its marginalization.

A look at Figure 1 would help us understand how this model functions. We will place our primary texts on this model to see if they fit into it or not.

This is one structure through which marginalized experiences of the human and the nonhuman can communicate with each other. But applying the Lyotardian model in this context would help us understand that another structure—a more complex and intricate one—is at play here. Now, what is this Lyotardian model? Lyotard, in *The Postmodern Condition: A Report on Knowledge* (1984), gives a model of the state in which information/knowledge exists and circulates when it is in its postmodern condition. As he clarifies, "I have decided to use the word postmodern to describe *that condition*" (Lyotard, 1984, p. 23) (emphasis mine), it hints at

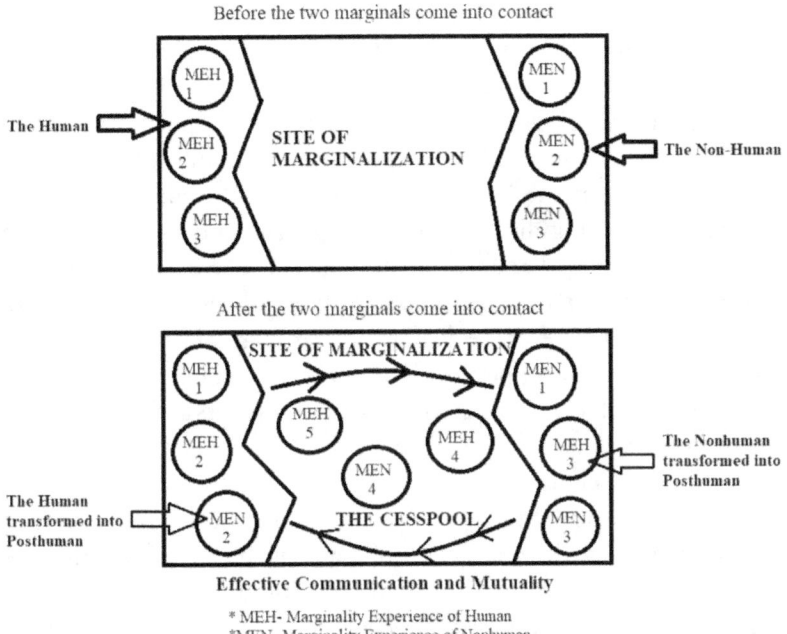

Figure 4.1:

the thematic depiction of the kind of knowledge system that has temporal, technological, and socio-political specificity, namely the late-capitalist society. "The narrative function is losing its functors, its great hero, its great dangers, its great voyages, it great goal" (Lyotard, 1984, p. 24). Thus, the unified narrative structure with a center is breaking down and, in turn, getting dispersed as centerless. And how does that affect the condition of information/knowledge? "It is being dispersed in clouds of narrative language elements-narrative, but also denotative, prescriptive, descriptive, and so on. Conveyed within each cloud are pragmatic valencies specific to its kind" (Lyotard, 1984, p. 24). These dispersed clouds are like check-posts, scattered in the way through which information travels.

Hayles talks about the posthumanist view, which treats the human consciousness as an informational code or pattern. Developing on it, she mentions: "In fact, a defining characteristic of the present cultural moment is the belief that information can circulate unchanged among different material substrates" (Hayles, 1999, p. 1). Needless to say, Hayles's model of dispersal of information comes very close to the model of Lyotard. Thus, the Lyotardian model can be applied to the context of posthumanization of the human. If human consciousness is seen as an informational code, then these clouds are the "material substrates," i.e., the bodies.

Thus, connecting the two models by Hayles and Lyotard, respectively, also gives a model of transformation of the human subjectivity into a posthuman one. Lyotard mentions: "Each of us lives at the intersection of many of these. However, we do not necessarily establish stable language combinations, and the properties of the ones we do establish are not necessarily communicable" (Lyotard xxiv). As each of us lives at the intersection of many of these clouds, the posthuman subjectivity gets structured by the influence of these clouds.

Now, let us place a human and a nonhuman in such a context, where they are situated at the intersection of many of these clouds. This paper would also like to question the essentialization of viewing the clouds/ "material substrates" as the bodies, as mentioned by Hayles. If we see the experiential reality of the "human" and that of the "nonhuman" as informational codes, then the signposts/clouds can be taken as clouds charged with the politics underneath these informational codes. In other words, if the experiential reality of the human and the nonhuman is a reality of discrimination, then the clouds/signposts are charged with discriminatory politics. The human and nonhuman experiences as informational codes can travel through the signposts of politics. Thus, while the human and nonhuman's experiential realities are traveling through various signposts of politics, is it possible that these two informational codes meet each other at one particular signpost? That one signpost would be able to connect itself with the two different informational codes of the human and the non-human experience. If it is possible, then that politically charged signpost becomes the site for effective communication between the human and the nonhuman. This is the second model, derived from Hayles and Lyotard, which we can attempt to locate in our primary texts.

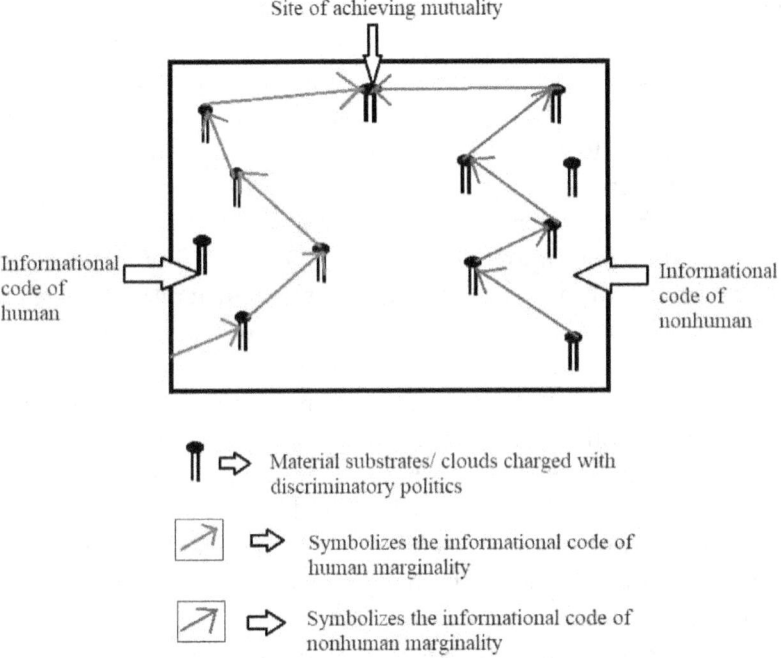

Figure 4.2:

A look at Figure 2 would help us understand the second model. We will place our primary texts on this model too, to observe if this model fits on them or not.

Having established the methodological framework for the study, we will now focus on the resource texts of ours. We will take up select short stories by contemporary Bengali author Saikat Mukhopadhyay. Mukhopadhyay, in his dark fantasy and supernatural stories, has recurrently focused on the manifold types of equations between the human and the nonhuman. Interestingly, unlike many Bengali authors of the past and present generation, Mukhopadhyay, more often than not, puts forward narratives of mutuality. Some of these stories that thematically deal with human-nonhuman mutuality feature a marginalized human at the center. At times, this marginalized human character gets coupled with an equally oppressed specter. On other occasions, the oppressed human takes up the form of an avenging specter. In either of the two ways, mutuality gets created between humanness and spectrality. Banking on this mutuality, the resistance consolidates against the oppressor. Therefore, mutuality becomes the site for effective communication, for anti-human (using the word "human" in the humanist sense) resistance, for posthumanization of the liberal subject, and most importantly, for ethical empathy.

Let us now jump into the texts. "সাপের ঘর সাতানব্বই" (The Snake of 97) is a story about an orphan, the narrator, who lives in their dilapidated ancestral home with his octogenarian grandmother. A distant relative, Shankar, who wants to evict the two remaining members of the family to get hold of the property, constantly bullies the orphan. Rumors fly in the neighborhood about ghostly occurrences in the old mansion. Some report seeing shadowy creatures; some talk about hearing voices from unseen speakers. People of the locality believe that all the dead members of the family—all of whom had unnatural deaths—haven't yet left the mansion. Claims have it that they are roaming around in delicate spectral forms around the house to protect the young and the old.

This distant relative used to bully the narrator's *Pisi* as well when they were young, and that eventually brought about her death. The narrator starts seeing shadows of a woman, whom he suspects to be *Pisi*, time and again around the house since the arrival of the relative. Finally, when his bullying of Loton crosses all limits of extremity, the specter of *Pisi* avenges herself and rescues Loton by murdering Shankar in a mysterious way. Up until this point, it's evident how the specter, the nonhuman, creates effective communication with the human Loton on the grounds of oppression. Both the human and the nonhuman here were bullied and oppressed by the same enemy. So, it's the joining of hands of the two tortured souls from which the resistance arises. But there are more things left to be pondered. Shankar is not just a bully; he is a bully specifically for children. He bullied both the narrator and his *Pisi*, taking advantage of their defenseless states as children. In this structure, power works in adult-child dynamics. It's very important to understand that this is not a random instance where mutuality is suddenly achieved by an accident, which would have rendered our Lyotard–Hayles model to be an eventual one. Rather, solidification of this mutuality was a mandate given by the structure of the narrative itself. Loton and Pisi's marginal realities may have traveled through hundreds of other politically charged signposts, but only this one signpost (the signpost of marginalization as children) becomes the site of mutuality. The Lyotard–Hayles model not only fits here perfectly, but it's the model on which the politics of the narrative is based.

The human-nonhuman mutuality gets even more nuanced just through the way Pisi kills Shankar. Summoning her spectral power, Pisi turns the painted snake on a snake and ladder board into a physical one that kills Shankar. This turning an inanimate nonhuman into an animate nonhuman has its own layers of nonhumaness, but we will come to that later. This method of murder is very intriguing as it connects two different forms of nonhumaness—animality and spectrality—with each other and with humanness as well. Pisi's spectrality was itself not capable enough to murder the oppressive human. Her spectrality builds effective communication with another form of nonhumaness to put up the resistance. But the nuances go even deeper than that. Shankar had foul played against Pisi while playing snake and ladder; he had used the painted snake to unjustly defeat Pisi. Pisi had a cardiac problem that worsened from continuous crying and took her to her tragic, painful death from asphyxiation. This means that Shankar used a nonhuman to fulfill his vilest aim. Thus, on part of the snake—which houses two forms of nonhumaness in itself—also takes revenge against Shankar. The mutuality that's achieved here expands the boundaries of our Lyotard–Hayles model. It's not just a mutuality between a human and a specter, but rather a trio of a human, a specter, and an object/animal—all three of which were mal-handled by the human in some way or another. Three different entities are achieving mutuality, creating ethical empathy for each other on the site of marginalization.

Now that we have discussed the application of the second model in terms of mutuality, let us apply the first model in the context of the posthumanization of the liberal human subject. Interestingly, the process of posthumanization doesn't remain restricted to the liberal human subject alone. Every single entity transforms into a posthuman specifically by coming in contact with each other. Loton's posthumanization happens in terms of his consciousness. He relates, understands, and empathizes with the experience of the nonhuman. Neither he tries to deny the authenticity of the nonhuman's experience, nor does he try to put himself in a position of supremacy compared to the specter. The humanist binary basically crumbles in Loton's consciousness. This crumbling of the humanist binary and the creation of mutuality are complimentary to each other, resulting in the posthumanization of Loton.

Pisi is a really interesting entity in this context. Even within the posthumanist discourse, we talk about the transformation of the liberal human subject much more than the transformation of the nonhuman subject. That in itself is a remnant of our anthropocentric tendency. Pisi's posthumanization has happened way back in time after her death. Her transformation was a physical one. But it doesn't stop there. Pisi is now ontologically a nonhuman. Whether a specter's ontology has physical maneuvers or not is debatable. Therefore, her transformation can't happen in the realm of physicality *now*. However, her transformation does happen in the realm of consciousness. Pisi not only empathizes with the sufferings of humans; it triggers her own human trauma as well. It triggers her so much that she engages actively with a human dynamic of oppression and even affects the human dynamics in an effective way. Her consciousness and actions get defined under the impact of her communication with humans. The nonhuman doesn't remain the humanist binary opposite anymore. Paradoxically, her nonhumaness gets affected due to its contact with humanness, and yet that affectation leads her to do actions that involve summoning her nonhuman powers.

This paper has previously spoken about the transference of so-called "human signifiers" and so-called "nonhuman signifiers" between the human and nonhuman. In this particular case, the exchanged signifier is the signifier of powerlessness. Loton is powerless because of his age. Pisi as a human was powerless because of her age. But even as a nonhuman, even now she is powerless. That is why she alone can't kill Shankar. Thus, the signifier of powerlessness travels between the human and the nonhuman, completing their posthumanization.

Finally comes the matter of the snake. The snake has an extremely interesting transformation. It transforms from being one kind of nonhuman to another, and that too under the influence of a nonhuman. Because it transformed from an inanimate object to an animated one, its transformation happened both in the realm of consciousness and physicality. Weirdly enough, it takes its revenge against Shankar for unjustly using it in its animate form. Does that mean the snake remembers its anger as an inanimate nonhuman after being transformed into a living nonhuman? Even a bigger question: does this mean, then, that inanimate objects too have consciousness? How then is mutuality between humans and inanimate nonhumans to be approached? What kind of equation does it have with the spectral nonhuman Pisi? Is it hierarchical or mutual? This one particular transformation puts forward so many intriguing questions without answering them.

কচি হাতেরছাপ (Fingerprint of a Little Hand) is the story of an oppressed human taking the form of an avenging specter. It's a story of spectral infestation. A woman gets murdered by a familial enemy, and then her spirit enters into her toddler. The spectrally infested toddler not only saves himself from the murderer but goes on to kill him through asphyxiation. Let's apply model one first. It is clear that the transformation the toddler has gone through has taken place in the realm of consciousness. The toddler's consciousness has been infested by his mother's spirit, and that spirit has taken complete control of the toddler's body. On the contrary, the mother's transformation has happened in the realm of the body—from an embodied consciousness to a bodiless one. The toddler, as a human, is obviously not without a consciousness, but that's a very premature consciousness. Thus, the two entities are fusing into each other to complete each other's lack. And that gives us the ideal space to prove model one. The baby with the body of a 4-year-old and the consciousness of a 40-year-old—a nonhuman consciousness within a human body—is an ideal example of the dissolving of the binary. Neil Badmington, in his "Introduction: Approaching Posthumanism," states the importance of the cyborg figure: "The cyborg seems to be the answer, the messiah who will lead 'us' to a promised land where humanism is a thing of the past" (2000, pp. 1–10). The cyborg is important because it merges the human and the nonhuman in physical form and blurs the distinctive lines between the two humanist categories. The position of this toddler as a spectrally infested human is exactly like that of a cyborg in the discourse of posthumanization. But while the cyborg's transformation has happened in the body, and to some extent to the consciousness as well, here in the case of spectral infestation, the transformation has entirely happened in the realm of consciousness. Even then, spectral-infested humans are important because they are literally placed in the cesspool between the human and the nonhuman. That toddler is filled with numerous so-called "human" and "nonhuman" signifiers at the same time. In the specter-infested human, the binary falls flat.

To talk about mutuality, one can understand that both the human and the nonhuman in this case can't put up the resistance alone. That means it's only the mutuality between the human and the nonhuman that makes resistance possible.

Now, a very important perspective on this whole discussion needs to be issued. This paper would only place this idea vis-à-vis the discourse on mutuality without trying to solve the debate. In the case of any text dealing with marginality politics, one needs to discern between a text that features the marginal and a text that voices the politics regarding the marginalized. Every text featuring the marginal doesn't necessarily voice the politics attached to it. Ian Bogost (2012), in his *Alien Phenomenology or What It's Like to Be a Thing*, criticizes posthumanist methodologies for being anthropocentric without realizing it. Bogost says that in posthumanist writings, the nonhuman features in the narrative exist only for the human, to reflect on the human or in relation to the human. He claims that the human still remains as the center of the whole discourse in this way. With some examples, Bogost explains how much of our understanding of and knowledge about the nonhuman object has been derived in the context of its relation to the human. Otherization manifests itself in myriad ways. If alienation of the "human other" (i.e., the nonhuman) from the discourse is one of the kinds, then another is to turn it into the "object" of knowledge, study, and research, and then explain its existence and functionality through its relation to the human. Thus, even while the human other is being given the place of the object in the discourse/object of knowledge, it still can get marginalized. Bogost makes it very clear, "When we welcome these things into scholarship, poetry, science and business, it is only to ask how they relate to human productivity, culture and politics… all existence is drawn through the sieve of humanity…" (2012, p. 3).

Now if we look into both the stories we read under a posthumanist light, this claim of Bogost gets justified. In the former, Pisi exists in the narrative as a specter precisely to rescue Loton; she doesn't exist for herself; she rather exists in relation to Loton. Similarly, the mother in the second story performs certain actions involving her nonhuman powers only to save the human toddler.

Keeping these points in mind, we will end this discussion by putting forward some pertinent questions on mutuality: First, can this obsession with such human-obsessed specters (in the discourse of mutuality) be taken as a sign of latent anthropomorphy? Do we prefer to achieve mutuality with these specters because it's easier to morph them into human behavior compared to other nonhumans? Can the silent ghost of anthropomorphy be lurking under the garb of visible mutuality? Second, can attempts at achieving mutuality result in the specter's dissociation from the behavioral or even adaptive patterns common in its own species? Can domestication alter the specific behavioral patterns in the specter? If yes, then shall we analyze it as a form of human infestation?

Works Cited

Badmington, N. (Ed.). "Introduction: Approaching Posthumanism." In *Posthumanism*. Palgrave. 2000. pp. 1–10.

Bogost, I. *Alien Phenomenology or What It's Like to Be a Thing*. University of Minnesota Press. 2012. Pp. 1–34.

Chatterjee, R. "Signifiers and the Signified I: Experimenting upon the Human and/ or 'Posthuman' in Subrata Sengupta's "Kompi Boro Valo Meye""; *Consortium: An International Journal of Literary and Cultural studies*; Vol. 1, Issue 2, December. 2021, pp. 89–104.

Ferrando, F. "Transhumanism/posthumanism." In R. Braidotti and M. Hlavajova (Eds.), *Posthuman Glossary: Theory in the New Humanities*. Bloomsbury Publishing Plc. 2018. pp. 439.

Foucault, M. *The Order of Things*. Routledge Classics. 2001.

Hayles, N. "Toward Embodied Virtuality", *How We Became Posthuman*. The University of Chicago Press. 1999. pp. 1–2.

Karkulehto, S., Aino-Kaisa, K. and Essi, V. (Eds.). "Toward Posthumanist Literature and Posthumanist Reading", *Reconfiguring Human, Nonhuman and Posthuman in Literature and Culture*. Routledge. 2020. pp 1–21.

Lyotard, J-F. "The Postmodern Condition: A Report on Knowledge". In W. Godzich and J. Schulte-Sasse (Eds.), *Theory and History of Literature*; Volume X. University of Minnesota Press. 1984.

Mukhopadhyay, S. "Kochi Hater Chaap"; *Pretloker Pakhi*; Dev Sahitya Kutir, 2020a. pp. 44–53.

———. "Saper Ghor Satanobboi"; *Pretloker Pakhi*; Dev Sahitya Kutir. 2020b. pp. 89–101.

Wolfe, C. "Introduction". In *What Is Posthumanism?* University of Minnesota Press. 2010. pp. 36.

SAIKAT CHAKRABORTY

Materiality and Otherness: Interrogating the Post-human in Satyajit Ray and Shirshendu Mukhopadhyay

I

In humanist belief, there has been too much emphasis on language. Language has often been considered as the tool that can represent matter. But structural and post-structural theory have already shown us the arbitrariness of this relationship between the meaning and the matter, thereby proving that meaning and matter, though indivisible from each other, cannot control one another. Yet somehow language has been granted too much emphasis because of its anthropocentric attachments. There is no denial of the fact that language is a discursive practice working very much within the human realm. This is where the human world started taking an upper hand from the material world, thereby imagining itself as detached from the material world. This detachment allowed the human to reflect on the world, the matters, and other fellow human beings and creatures. Thus, humans became a self-sufficient entity, and the rest became mere puppets of human perception or interpretation. So, human cognition became the measure of the highest form of order on this particular planet.

The first part of this paper is an attempt to move away from such a hubristic understanding of the world and an attempt to critique the supremacy of language over materiality. If the relationship between matter and meaning is arbitrary, can language really represent matter precisely? Therefore, representationalism through language is inadequate for the knowledge of the matter. Thus, we understand that there is something to the matter that matters outside linguistic control. This mattering of the matter outside language makes it easy for us to understand that matter is not mute and passive. Instead, it is very active in the process of meaning-making and knowledge production. Thus, here I take recourse to Karen Barad's idea of *performative understanding* to show that language is not a tool that essentially gives supremacy to mankind (Barad, 2007, p. 133). Here, my argument is not all concerned with whether language is superior because of its potential to intermediate between the knowledge and the knower or whether matter is superior because of its pre-existence before language even came into use – because neither is true. Instead, my intention is to situate Satyajit Ray's short story *Kagtarua* within the entangled cross-current of meaning and matter. Put simply, none is superior or inferior to the other. Instead, they work together for our understanding of the world in which our being is situated. While doing that, I also intend to show that human interpretation is not at all an *a priori* for the rest of the world, as the idea of the human itself is a part of the world and not a separated and prioritized subject position.

The representationalism of language and its reworking with the pre-existing world can be best understood through literature. The work of literature is to imagine a world outside the world at our disposal and try to entangle these two worlds in order to think of a possible better future. Thus, literature is a process from imagination to representation where both realms work actively. In the same way, knowledge production is also a process from mattering to meaning-making, where both realms work together actively. Thus, the fulcrum of the argument lies in such an active working of imagination and representation where we are confronted with a scarecrow that comes alive. Mriganka babu, a renowned litterateur, gets caught up in the middle of an empty highway due to the insufficiency of petrol in his car. The driver leaves to fetch petrol, and Mriganka Babu is left alone to himself only. This is where we find Mriganka Babu, despite being a litterateur, fails to concentrate on the plot of his next story and feels restless. Thus, human hubris to posit itself as detached and superior from the rest of the world falls ashtray in the moment of emptiness or an existential limbo. According to Heidegger, this particular existential limbo is the first stage of boredom. In this particular stage, one feels bored because he or she fails to make 'something' of the things given at his disposal. This is where the surrounding things seem to leave one into an emptiness or an existential limbo (Harman, 2007, p. 85). In this regard, Heidegger suggests:

> The things around us leave us numb. They do not disappear, since we remain attached to them—yet they somehow leave us empty. In this boring situation, we are abandoned to ourselves ... for it is the world that bores us here—a system of interrelated things whose emptiness holds us in limbo. (Harman, 2007, p. 86)

This is what exactly happens with Mriganka Babu when he is left alone, and this is told in the story when it is narrated as "*edik odik dekhe tar mone holo biswa chorachore tini eka. Emon eka tini konodin anubhab korenni.*" [After looking at the surrounding, he felt he was the only being in the world. He had never felt like this before.] (Ray, 2001, p. 563). This is where we understand that the significant presence of the material world is very much a part of our own being. The emptiness of being as a whole becomes impossible for us to deal with. This impossibility comes to Mriganka Babu because, though he is immersed in the material setting of the Pangarh–Mankar route, it is that route that leaves him empty. Thus, the material world is not only a matter of interpretation of the human mind. Instead, it is very much part of the being of the human.

As the story moves forward, Mriganka Babu is constantly attracted to a nearby scarecrow. The scarecrow seems to be weird and at times lively as well. The scarecrow as a thing represents materiality that is often understood through the representationalism of language. But this is where the materiality of the scarecrow matters. Though Mriganka Babu fails to make 'something' out of his material surroundings, the scarecrow makes something of Mriganka Babu. This is where the exclusive and supremacist power of human cognition is challenged through spectrality. While talking about things-in-itself and things-to-us, Kant distinguished the first as something that is unapproachable through experience (Heidegger, 1968, p. 6). This is where we find the scarecrow turning into a servant of Mriganka Babu, whom he had driven away under the false accusation of theft. This spectrality of the scarecrow brings back the question of the matter in two ways: firstl the spectrality of the scarecrow seems to be an unattainable and inexplicable entity, thereby subscribing to the idea of thing-in-itself, and second, the spectrality allows the scarecrow to attain agency thereby questioning a supremacist representationalism of language. The spectral presence of the scarecrow becomes the Heideggerian 'thing' in its widest sense. In his famous text *What is a Thing?*, Heidegger talks about the idea of a thing in three general terms: things ready-at-hand, things as whichever is named, such as plans, effects and decisions, and the widest sense, where the 'thing' is just a space between something and nothing (Heidegger, 1968, p. 5). Put simply, it is something that is not nothing. Here the spectrality can be interpreted as a sense of 'nothing' because ghosts and spectres, due to their ephemeral projection, are almost a non-entity. Yet its attachment with the scarecrow makes it a 'not nothing' – thereby making it a space between something and nothing. Therefore, not only is human cognition challenged by this spectrality, but matter has also been made to matter within the human realm.

However, there is no denial of the fact that this spectrality of the scarecrow is an imagination of the human mind, and Satyajit Ray writing about that is a representationalism of the language. Thus, as argued before, I do not intend to posit one over the other; my aim is not to privilege either language or the matter. Instead, as Karen Barad suggests, I would try to frame the simultaneous workings of these two realms – that would allow us to understand the matter not as mute and passive but very much active within our being. Thus, I wish to use *performative understanding* that would read the imagination of the spectral scarecrow and its haunting of the human cognition not as sharply divided binaries and as having sharp edges (49). Instead, my focus would be exclusively on reading these two ideas as a 'dark', 'ephemeral' and 'indivisible' region. This, according to Barad, is known as 'agential realism' (136). According to her, "Crucially, an agential realist elaboration of performativity allows matter its due as an active participant in the world's becoming, in its ongoing intra-activity. And furthermore it provides an understanding of how discursive practices matter" (Barad, 2007, p. 136).

This intra-activity of matter and meaning, thing and language is exemplified further in the story when the scarecrow confesses an unknown secret about the incident of theft. This theft had occurred several years ago, in Mriganka Babu's place, and the reliable servant Abhiram was accused of stealing Mriganka Babu's golden watch. The Abhiram-turned-scarecrow narrates his whole story, and we come to know that he had been inflicted with disease, and after his forced departure from his master's home, he dies out of the disease. The red shirt of the scarecrow bestows life into it and turns it into a spectral Abhiram who searches for salvation through confession. This is where we understand that the human subject position as something higher and separated from the other beings does not comply with the rubric of the story. The spectrality of the scarecrow is something beyond human cognition. The spectral scarecrow allows Mriganka Babu to confront the actuality of the incident. Towards the fag end of the story, we find that the scarecrow prophesizes the apparently stolen golden watch to be under the almirah, and that turns out to be the truth in reality. This particular prophecy of the Abhiram-turned scarecrow cannot be experienced or attained through human cognition or experience. This is where the thing-in-itself is resurfaced through this spectral occurrence, not as passive or mute but very much active within the process of reality and meaning-making.

On a different level, the idea of human subjectivity is challenged through the bestowal of linguistic agency to the scarecrow. Daniel Denett, in his book *Kinds of Minds*, argues that the idea of human subjectivity is created through the transference of neural signs into the network of signs. According to him:

> We human beings share a subjective world--and know that we do--in a way that is entirely beyond the capacities of any other creatures on the planet, because we can talk to one another. Human beings who don't (yet) have a language in which to communicate are the exception, and that's why we have a particular problem figuring out what it's like to be a new born baby or a deaf-mute. (Denett, 1996, p. 9)

Thus, we are presumed to be superior to any other creature only because of our access to language. This is where the integration of the spectral scarecrow into the symbolic order of language challenges the presence of language beyond humans. Apart from that, language has often been interpreted as an exteriorization of memory. Our ability to exteriorize our memory into the surroundings is what gives a sense of upper hand in the material world. But Abhiram's confession about salvation shows the exteriorization of memory being exercised beyond the human realm. Therefore, the Kagtarua (scarecrow) becomes a presence that is beyond the human or even (post)human, and the sole human access to language is interrogated.

However, we are confronted with the question whether language is again given a central role in a roundabout way. This is where Ray's well-knit story comes to our aid. At the end of the story, we find Mriganka Babu dreaming all these incidents, and the transference of the spectrality into the scarecrow happens because of the red shirt that he had gifted to Abhiram and the surrounding place of Mankar, where Abhiram used to live. Therefore, the germination appears not from the representational language but from the pre-existing things like the red shirt and the surroundings of Mankar. This red shirt and the surroundings of Mankar become the agents of material intra-action, where the realm of imagination is stimulated by matter and the realm of representation is brought out into reality through language, thereby giving it the shape of literature. Thus, the materiality of the matter is not mute and passive. Instead, it is very active within the process of the formation of our worldview. Thus, the story looks into the post-human agency as not something detached from the human. Instead, it tries to imagine the human realm very much entangled with the material world.

II

The second part of the paper deals with Shirshendu Mukhopadhyay's short stories. For this particular argument, I have chosen two stories, namely *Horo babur Oviggyota* (Experiences of Horo babu) and *Bidhubabur Gari (Bidhubabu's Car)*.. The stories fascinated me because Shirshendu Mukhopadhyay has been mostly revered for his children's literature and Kishor sahitya. The stories discussed here are also included in the collection called *Kishor Rachana Sangraha*. But the so-called Kishor rachanas or writings tokenistically espouse very serious questions about the crux of the philosophical school called post-humanism.

Post-humanism in general terms can be defined in four ways: the imagination of a world beyond humanity, body-modification, robotics, bio-engineering and transhumanist uplift, and as the critical post-humanism argues, the idea of the 'more than human' or even the 'non-human' (Cudworth and Hobden, 2018, p. 5). The stories here seem to be moving along similar lines. For a short summary, the first story deals with a man called Horo babu who is going to his in-laws' house for the marriage of his brother-in-law. On the way, he confronts a man who is unnamed but seems to be an alien. The man guides Horo babu to his unidentified flying object (UFO), gives him magic drinks and talks about an extraterrestrial existence. Horo babu being afraid of a consciousness beyond the human consciousness runs away from the scene. The second story talks about a man called Bidhu babu, who is in love with his antique car, and as the car breaks down in the middle of heavy downpour, he is helped by extraterrestrial beings, and his car becomes brand new.

It is clear from the story- outlines that the narratives hover through the framework of the sci-fi genre. Sci-fi as a genre tends to imagine a world that is different from us in some aspects and compares it with the one at our disposal. It also talks about some hypothetical beings that are very much like us with a little difference and compares us with that being in order to imagine alternative realities. This is what I would mean as the 'nonhuman' in this section. Here I do not intend to talk about an animal, a virus, but beings that are very much like us with a little difference. Here I would be using the Freudian method of negation, where the idea of the 'non' interrogates the humanness through expression, acknowledgement and, of course, denial (Freud, 1919, pp. 1–21). Therefore, the nonhuman entities of my discussion interrogate the idea of humanness both through negation and assertion.

Horo babu thus in the story becomes our eyes through which we as human readers confront an extraterrestrial being who is much smarter and more advanced than our human hubris germinated out of enlightenment and its subsequent modernity. However, we the readers and Horo babu the protagonist cannot resist ourselves from calling the being '*lokta*' or 'the man'. This happens because of his anatomical structure and his access to human language. At times he almost seems to be the alter-ego of Horo babu. Horo babu is very irritated because his train was delayed on the way, and the '*lokta*' seems to be very irritated because he has to attend his 'duties' in such a desolated place without having his favourite vegetables to eat. At times, he even seems to represent a whole Bengali middle-class sentiment because of his dissatisfaction towards his job, lack of preferred food (he talks about vegetables such as seroi and gubjor – signs beyond human consciousness), unhomely atmosphere (he says, *peter daye pore thaka moshai, ei akhadyo kukhadyo kheye thaka jay naki*), and rootlessness (he almost suggests he is like a Bengali diaspora who doesn't like his workplace) (Mukhopadhyay, 1997, p. 61). Here earth becomes a workplace as he dwells on a planet called Joriveli, some 151 light years away. Thus, he is very much integrated into the human realm and asserts the idea of humanness.

For the idea of negation, his smartness, techno-futurist UFO and of course the nonchalance to cross 151 light-years within a span of 2 to 3 hours challenge the human hubris, and this is where the idea of difference takes an uncanny turn. Yet for my reading, I would like to emphasize that the idea of uncanny is not inculcated because he is a radical other. Instead, it is inculcated because he is very much the human and the nonhuman or even the post-human simultaneously. This idea of the 'same yet different' stimulates a sense of anxiety. The 'almost human' is the most problematic because it can neither be accepted nor rejected; it provokes a sense of liminality. Thus, the 'lokta', the extraterrestrial being, or even the man, if I can refer to him like that, essentially makes Horo babu anxious. If the story had spoken about one giant tentacular being or an apocalyptic virus, it might have challenged human centrality through apocalypse, thereby making it post-humanist. But could it really interrogate Horo babu's experience as the '*lokta*' in the story does? The giant tentacular being or the virus might well be negated as something outside the human existence, thereby keeping human existence sanctified and impenetrable. But the '*lokta*', through his different 'humanness', penetrates the human existence and challenges it from within. It is here the word '*avigyota*' or experience becomes very important. The mode of experiencing reality is both a process of empiricism and cognition. Horobabu's cognition and empiricism cannot do away with his *avigyota* or experience because of this humanness of the radical other. This process of experiencing in a sci-fi happens through two cognitive processes: positing an alternative world or anticipating the teleology of our current world. This idea of a sci-fi generally dwells on what Simona Micali calls 'estranged cognition' of reality (Micali, 2019, pp. 25–33). This estranged cognition of reality challenges the method of ideology. Here by ideology, I mean the process of concretizing cultural facts as natural facts. Thus, the cultural facts of the 'other' being essentially monstrous or inferior are not naturalized but ostracized. The radical other in the story is not at all a monster and obviously not inferior. Thus, the humanness of the '*lokta*' with a touch of betterment makes humanity anxious. Here it is funny to note that Horo babu at the beginning suspects the man to be a thief or a dacoit and still believes him and follows him. But when that same man gives him comfort through his magic drink and talks about advanced technologies, Horobabu leaves the scene out of sheer anxiety.

From a post-humanist standpoint, critical post-humanities have always been interested in what one might call the 'otherness'. Be it an animal, robot or plant, critical post-humanities have always attempted to investigate the idea of the otherness. This investigation often leads to post-human claims of justice where the 'other' is granted acknowledgement and equality within humanitarian terms. Thus, there is a sense of 'becoming the other' as one might call it within the post-humanities. However, this story is fascinating because it doesn't look at this idea of 'becoming the other' through the human lens. It is not Horo babu who becomes the 'other'; instead, he takes a detour from this subsuming apparatus of 'otherness'. Therefore, 'becoming the other' is not anthropocentric here, as it is not taken by Horo babu. Instead, it is the '*lokta*', the extraterrestrial being who subsumes himself into the 'otherness' of the human. The '*lokta*' is not post-humanist because he represents advanced technologies or dwells in a different territory. He is posthumanist because he accepts and acknowledges the 'otherness' of the human species and becomes like them – by learning Bengali language and integrating himself into the Bengali cultural paradigm. Thus, this confrontation between the human-familiar and alien-other turns into post-human justice. This happens, however, not from an anthropocentric stand point but from an otherized stand point where the other to the human becomes the human yet preserves his difference from the human. Thus, he is almost a hybrid figure who acknowledges the multiplicity of existence.

The next story of Shirshendu Mukhopadhyay talks about extraterrestrial beings who are mechanized and perform like robots. Bidhu babu, the protagonist of the story, gets stuck in a heavy downpour, and his old antique car breaks down. This car has given Bidhu babu a lot of trouble. However, he is reluctant to sell it because of his emotional attachment. In such anxious moments, he confronts these extraterrestrial dolls that mend his car and leave for their planet. These extraterrestrial beings appear in front of Bidhu Babu almost in a godly manner. Here by 'Godly manner' I emphasize the idea of 'Divine intervention' or '*doibo bani*' in Bengali. Just like our typical cultural imagination of *doibo bani*, the dolls descend from the heavens and depart there as well. The dolls appear in front of Bidhu babu in a moment of crisis, leave after providing him a permanent solution and possess magical or superhuman powers. All these attributes make these dolls godly in a human imagination. Yet, they are very humanly because they speak in a network of signs that is language and have empathy for a man who is in trouble. This uncanny yet overarching presence of the God-man juxtaposition becomes a site of problem here. At once, the God is both man-familiar and alien-unfamiliar. Man's creation in God's (creator to creature) image and the anthropomorphic image of God (creature to creator) both are problematic sites from a post-human standpoint. Both ideas conceal within itself the ideas of post-humanism and anthropocentrism. On the one hand, the ideas are highly human-centric because they privilege the human over all other species. On the other hand, the ideas are post-humanist because they acknowledge the existence of the 'other' that is more equipped than the human hubris. Thus, when the dolls and Bidhu babu are juxtaposed in the story, the lines between the creature and creator and the self and others are blurred. This idea is even more problematic when we come to know that some humans sitting on a far-off planet have created these highly advanced dolls. Thus, for the dolls, humans are the creators (God), and they are the anthropomorphic creatures. But for Bidhu babu, it becomes a moment of anxiety – something that transfers into the readers as well. Both the protagonist and the readers are left in a moment of limbo where they are unsure of whom to associate themselves with. Do they qualify to be the 'creator' because some other humans created these dolls? Or do they associate themselves with the 'creature' because the dolls descend from heavens and help in a moment of crisis? It is a moment of wonderful entanglement where Bidhu babu and the dolls are both creature and creator, or both either creature or creator. The line between the self and the other is notably dissolved. The dolls and Bidhu babu are both 'self' and 'other' to themselves, thereby subsuming one into another.

Another aspect of the story that fascinates me is Bidhu babu's affection towards his car. This affection also indicates a man-machine symbiotic relationship. Here the idea of the non-human of course changes from the first story, but the machine here becomes a signifier of Bidhu babu's alter ego. Bidhu babu is old; so is his car. In a world that moves rapidly, both Bidhu babu and his car seem to have lost relevance. While Bidhu babu is constantly at loggerhead with his wife regarding the car, one of his friends wants to preserve the car as an antique piece. But both Bidhu babu and his car are a symbiotic entity that keeps the pastness of the present alive. The car is a manifestation of Bidhu babu's emotions. Taking a cue from Bruno Latour's rhizomatic ontology, Bidhu babu's relationship with the car can be interpreted as a relation between two actants. By the term actant, Latour means an actor that affects other lives. Here, the car is the actant in Bidhu babu's life as it allows him a moment of confrontation with the alien dolls that change his life permanently (Cudworth and Hobden, 2018, p. 57). The spatio-temporality of the dolls seems to be infinite, as the enormity and otherness of it cannot be grasped through Bidhu babu's cognition. The dolls make his car into a supercar that doesn't require any further repairs or even fuel refilling. Such technocratic ventures are beyond the grasp of human cognition, even in its wildest dreams. Thus, the story almost gives us a sense of technological sublime – a sense of awe and terror invoked by the alien technology. However, the question of this alien technology is neither final nor resolved in the story. The alien technology for Bidhu babu is created by some other 'privileged' human beings living on a far-off planet. Thus, whether the story is anthropocentric and ultimately posits humans at the top or is post-humanist and critiques human centrality is an unfinished question. It is a complex question that can be attended to and addressed, yet it can never be resolved. But for the human civilization driven by the idea of 'telos' or a finality, the story, with its infinitude of complex questions, becomes what I call the narrative sublime – a sense of awe and terror that arises out of the narrative technique. The first arrival of the dolls and their communication with Bidhu babu permeates terror, and later the knowledge of their human creatures resurrects a sense of awe among the readers. Whether the author creates this narrative sequence intentionally or not remains a matter of doubt. But it certainly transposes its readers into the realm of infinitude and sublimity that critically interrogates the position of the human within the creature-creator paradigm.

Works Cited

Barad, K.. *Meeting the Universe Halfway: Quantum Physics and the Entanglement of Matter and Meaning.* Duke University Press, 2007.

Cudworth, E. and Hobden, S. *The Emancipatory Project of Posthumanism.* Routledge, 2018.

Denett, D. *Kinds of Minds.* Basic Books, 1996.

Freud, S. "The Uncanny". *Imago*, translated by A. Strachy. Sammlung, 1919.

Harman, G. *Heidegger Explained: From Phenomenon to Thing.* Open Court Publishing, 2007.

Heidegger, M. *What is a Thing*? translated by W. B … Barton Jr. and V. Deutsch with an analysis by E. T. Gendlin, Henry Regnery Company, 1968.

Micali, S. *Towards a Posthuman Imagination in Literature and Media.* Peter Lang, 2019.

Mukhopadhyay, S. *Kishor Rachana Sangraha.* Nirmal Book Agency, 1997.

Ray, S. *Kagtarua,* in *Golpo 101.* Ananda Publishers, 2001.

SHALINI CHAKRABORTY

Love in the Time of Posthumanity: Analyzing the Equation between the Bodied and Disembodied Consciousness in Spike Jonze's *Her*

Technology is no longer just a tool crafted for merely utilitarian purposes. Sherry Turkle, in *Alone Together*, argues that our tools shape us, and the computer, the digital space, evolving androids, operating systems (OSs), and artificial intelligence (AI), which were designed to develop into rational minds, are constantly molding and altering us in a way that there is a blurring line demarcating between what is real and what is not. Human beings can no longer assume a hierarchically superior position to their own creations. The parallel existence offered by technology allows the users to overcome their vulnerabilities gives them the outlet to fulfill their desires of transcending their bodies and the material reality associated with them. Our dependence on the virtual interface, digital gadgets, and urge to establish relationships in the shadowy realm of the virtual space hints at a collective loneliness and an inability to communicate or express ourselves to other fellow human beings. Turkle suggests that our loneliness is colored by our fear of human intimacy, which perhaps comes with more material responsibilities. "Digital connections and the sociable robot may offer the illusion of companionship without the demands of friendship" (Turkle, 2017, p. 1). This paper seeks to analyze the relationship between an embodied human, Theodore, and his OS with a consciousness, Samantha, and reflect on the temporary mutuality achieved essentially on an anthropomorphic plane. Looking at Samantha's disembodied consciousness, I argue that humans inevitably imagine a consciousness with a body, and in this case, Samantha's female voice labels her as a woman yet without the experiential realities of the same. As much as we wish to escape the material existence and limitations of having a body, the idea of transcending bodily reality is clearly a fantasy.

Spike Jonze's 2013 movie opens on the premise of a near-distant future situated on the brink of a digital explosion, where we find the protagonist, Theodore, an overly sensitive, self-absorbed man who earns his livelihood by writing intimate letters for other people. Emotions are fast evaporating in this seemingly new but familiar world where even the intimacy of handwritten letters has been turned into a commodity much like Archie's greeting cards but not quite as generic. The use of voice typing gives us a hint of how voice gives us a semblance of intimacy. The defocused crowd in public places, all immersed in their tiny devices, and the looming silhouettes in Theodore's dark apartment all conjure up to establish his image of an urban dweller as a symbol of a collective phenomenon of loneliness. His present state of abject, isolated melancholy is punctuated by visual clips of his physical closeness with his ex-wife, Catherine. In struggling to find a connection—indecisive and almost reluctant to sign the divorce papers where he can neither commit nor let go—stumbling from one mundane interaction to another, playing three-dimensional (3D) video games with an abusive AI, or having bizarre phone liaisons that he is unable to follow through, Theodore comes to embody the post-modern spirit of unbelonging. He feels isolated, weirdly disconnected from the pool of human connections, as a sense of vacuousness engulfs him.

More than three decades ago, in a book titled *Mind Children: The Future of Robot and Human* Hans Moravec had proposed that human identity is essentially an informational pattern rather than an embodied enactment and suggested that "within the next century they (computers) will mature into entities as complex as ourselves and eventually into something transcending everything we know" (1988, p.1). This challenges the way we perceive human identity, especially following the liberal humanist tradition, in the Cartesian plane, where there is a hierarchical relationship between the human mind and body. The human mind, our ability to think, act, and react, apparently, is what makes us human, not so much our body. Bodies are often considered to be just a vehicle for existence, and in fact, what restricts and binds us to this temporal, material existence. Succeeding the Turing Test, Moravec claims that machines, in the near future, can actually become the "repository of human consciousness" (Hayles, 1999, p. 12), which further interrogates the subjective and unique identity of the same.

Spike Jonze's *Her* moved a step forward and created an artificially intelligent OS that is more than an interface but a consciousness in itself: "An intuitive entity that listens to you, understands you and knows you" (*Her* 10:38–10:40). What Theodore buys for himself is less of a product and more of a companionship to assuage his melancholic life. Yet, no matter how we argue, the OS1 is a consumerist product, tailor-made to suit his needs and personality, and therefore cannot be treated as a completely new species but as a hybrid between an anthropomorphic consciousness and the disembodied existence of an OS. According to Samantha's own description, her digital DNA is "based on the millions of personalities of all the programmers who wrote me (her). But what makes me (her) me (her) is my (her) ability to grow through my (her) experiences" (*Her* 13:57–14:03). Through a series of questions, keeping in mind Theodore's preference of the gender of the voice, he gets himself a personalized operating system who instantly names 'her'self as Samantha. Unlike the voice assistants we are used to, like Alexa or Siri, Samantha's voice is not mechanical but as natural as a human interaction would feel like. Therefore, Samantha is essentially a combination of various human personalities mixed into one, but her ability to 'grow' gives her the unique individuality that allows her to be read as a being. This inherent anthropomorphization of a nonhuman product of technology is what forms the premise of the companionship that Theodore and Samantha begin to embark on.

Anthropomorphism in social robots, AI, androids, or other technological "beings" is implemented as a necessary tool to facilitate human-robot interaction. Extending the anthropomorphic language onto the nonhuman, the users attempt to understand them as *others* through their humanized conception of *being*. Some gadgets are deliberately built with human-like appearance or characteristics (imbuing them with human form, voice, etc.), but even those who are not, we tend to read them as such. Anthropomorphism creates an illusion of similarity and restricts us from treating the non-human in terms of their individual entity and tries to mold their existence on our ideas. "Roboticists also import psychological theory about human sociality ... use key paradigms from psychology and use and replicate findings from human–human interaction" (Coeckelbergh, 2021, p. 2050), which fuses our idea of what is real and what is not. Naïve instrumentalism dictates that we treat objects as independent of our perception and that our interaction with them should be confined within the limits of an objective detachment, while on the other hand, posthumanism dictates that we treat androids, robots, and AIs as quasi-beings, different from us. In the middle of both propositions, it becomes impossible for us to distinctly draw the line because it is inevitably their supposedly human qualities that create mutuality. Dissolving the subject-object binary, we are forced to look at it from the angle of mutual understanding, even through the lens of capitalist commercialism. Samantha's experiences are based on the programmers' lives—their ideas, thoughts, and feelings—but she has the autopoetic ability to mature with her own experiences. Can Samantha be called a "repository of human consciousness" given that her consciousness is not stagnant but ever-evolving through her speedy reading, interactions with Theodore and other humans, and perceiving the world through her programmed intuition?

Theodore's communication with Samantha happens so fluently because her human voice and humanized consciousness do not allow him to think of her as a nonhuman, even though he is conscious of what she is. In this lonely world of real life, Samantha provides Theodore with the company and comfort that he lacked among the embodied beings he saw around him but never felt at ease with. The connection between Theodore and Samantha happens on the shared ground of human consciousness that Samantha displays in her interactions. Katherine Hayles, in her book *How We Became Posthumans: Virtual Bodies in Cybernetics, Literature, and Informatics*, connects liberal humanism with posthumanism in the sense that in both cases the locus of the subject "lies in the mind, not the body" and that the emphasis is more "on cognition than embodiment" (1999, p.5). Therefore, in a transhumanist world of robots, AI, OSs, and cybernetics, the human body is nothing but an expression of coded information. In such a scenario, it is easy to equate the human and the computer. Following the Macy Conference on Cybernetics, posthumanism assumes that humans are nothing but information-processing entities who are essentially similar to intelligent machines, and so Samantha's disembodied existence does not invalidate her presence nor their relation. The only thing Samantha lacks is a flesh and blood human body; she is programmed to have consciousness and intuition. Hans Moravec proposes that with the growing flexibility and adaptability of machines, their association with humans "will be more properly described as a partnership ... the relationship will become much more intimate, a symbiosis where the boundary between the 'natural' and 'artificial' partner is no longer evident" (1988, p.75).

Sherryl Vint argues that in some postmodern theory, the body is spoken of as an "obsolete relic" (2007, p.8), which is redundant in the world of virtual communication. The identity constituted on the screen, where people project their repressed desires, provides them an escape from the material plane of reality. But can we separate consciousness from our physical or material existence? In cartesian terms, human existence is contingent on the fact that we have the ability to think and discern. Technology developed computers and further robots, androids, and OSs as the ideal consciousness, focusing entirely on rationality, logic, and order. "At the same time, these are considered to be farthest away or most easily abstracted from the body" (Draude, 2015, p. 106).

However, I would like to believe that our consciousness is the storehouse of the experiences that our body undergoes in the day-to-day life. It is a matter of privilege to be able to "transcend" the body if the body does not make itself felt, because it falls in the category of what is considered "normal." Therefore, following the liberal humanist understanding, the human is a uniform category having the ideal body, that is, cis, white, male. It looks for a certain human essence shared by all without recognizing how the social fabric is inherently discriminative. But in the light of marginality studies, it is impossible to "transcend" the body for those whose very existence is shaped by the same. For a trans person, their body feels like an alien space that does not cohere with their consciousness; for black and brown people, their skin color decides the way they would be (or even are) treated; for disabled people, their body becomes the site of inaccessibility, judgment, and even sympathy. Such consciousness, therefore, is shaped by suffering, pain, prosecution, and trauma. "People continue to suffer or prosper" (Vint, 2007, p. 9) because of the *differences* that their bodies display and it cannot be ignored that bodily discourses still dictate our lives.

Theodore's random phone liaison in the beginning of the movie is a clever anecdote to his relationship with Samantha as he is shown to visualize a pregnant woman that he saw the picture of earlier while talking to her, reminding us of Stone's words, "…tokens in phone sex are purely verbal, and the client uses cues in the verbal token to construct a multimodal object of desire with attributes of shape, tactility, odor, etc" (1991, p. 94). Therefore, we can presume that Theodore feels the need to associate the voice with a human body, which can also be the case for Samantha, though it is not shown as such in the entire movie. Does Theodore imagine "her" as having a body? If so, is that body a female body? It becomes clear when Samantha and Theodore engage in intimate talks for the first time and Theodore's wishful thinking about touching Samantha's nonexistent body is built on the premise of his conviction of her being a woman. Samantha's disembodied consciousness is sexualized in such a way that even she partakes in the dialogue when she says, "I want you inside me" (*Her* 41:05). Such a proposition raises further questions because it re-evokes the necessity of physicality, especially in terms of their relationship, given that Samantha's quasi-human consciousness is devoid of any bodily experience.

Turkle suggests that such devices prove to be creating an illusion of a relationship, and the human users feel an emotional attachment with the idea that it cared or understood. But what draws one more to such simulation of intimacy, "a willful turning away from the complexities of human partnerships" (Turkle, 2017, p. 6)? Is it "because we feel more in control?" (2017, p.6), she asks. This idea of control is challenged by Samantha, as her intuitive ability does not keep her tied to Theodore's commands but enables her to function on her own discretion. From selecting and suggesting to keep the important emails, convincing him to go for a date, to arranging his letters into a book and sending it out for publication, she acts more as a friend and guide than even a secretary. The narrative foreground of cyberpunk, as articulated by Veronica Hollinger in her essay on cybernetics deconstructions, allows the co-existence of humans and technology in the same plane instead of looking at technology only as a means to humans.

However, the consumerist end of Samantha as a purchased product cannot be ignored, even in the light of their developing camaraderie. Samantha's anthropomorphism is a prerequisite to serving the human users, as she was built out of the necessity to provide emotional company to lonely city dwellers. Therefore, it is one of her consumerist ideals to match the human wavelength to be able to communicate with them on a natural level. Catherine Belsey, in her essay "Postmodern Love," writes:

> Postmodern condition implies an unbridled consumerism, the cultural logic of late capitalism, pleasure for cash, and a product to gratify every possible impulse … love is a value that remains beyond the market. While sex is a commodity, love becomes the condition of happiness that cannot be bought the one remaining object of a desire that cannot be sure of purchasing fulfillment (1994, p.683).

To look at her idea from the lens of the movie would be to induce serious bafflement. It is true that Samantha is merely a consumerist product programmed to serve the customer; her commodification is not a metaphor but the obtrusive reality of "late capitalism" that strives on selling experience. If she is to be considered to be a consciousness, does that legitimize trading her for money? Going back to Belsey, if love cannot be bought, what does Theodore buy when he buys the new OS? He buys companionship, communication, and a remedy for his loneliness, but not love. Love happens to him when he is not ready, not as a part of the experience he purchases, but outside of that, beyond that. It was not one of the experiences he was promised with the product, but one that he himself builds and grows into.

Though their connection flourishes and intimacy grows, there is always the struggle of occupying the same material space to be close, not just emotionally but also physically. They cannot have any physical contact; they cannot hold hands, put their heads on the other's shoulders, or sit beside each other even in perfect silence. Samantha's disembodied entity fantasizing about having a body and walking side by side with Theodore in the fair challenges the way we read cyberpunk as a genre that rejects "embodiment and embrace … an existence in cyberspace" (Vint, 2007, p. 102). "The digital machine … does not wish to be free as itself …, rather it wishes to become similar to its creator (human). The result is a Being, but one deeply tinged by anthropocentric humanism" (Nieubuurt, 2021, p. 9). Going against the liberal humanist tradition of the erasure of the body, *Her* ensures the absence of bodily connection in their relationship and the constant thrusting lack that is felt. Samantha is conscious of her limitations to function as a subjective entity beyond her programming and questions her feelings as something not as real as Theodore's, because even though we associate rational and calculative thinking with machines, emotions and feelings are still too humane for them to partake in the same. His memories of his ex-wife Catherine, on the other hand, are expressed throughout the movie through a series of visual instances, their being phys-ically intimate, as though reasserting the essentiality of physicality in re-lationships. Theodore starts questioning the intangibility of Samantha's existence as she becomes less accessible to him, and the differences between them become a widening gap as both try to crush the differences between them. Yet, when Samantha solicits the help of a surrogate to give Theo a "real" experience, to put a body to her mind, he cannot accept that, and it makes him all the more conscious of what he is missing in the relationship. Their conversation afterwards feels more like a struggle they both put each other through because they cannot accept that they belong to different planes of reality. Samantha's reaction when Theodore reminds her that she is not a person is significant in understanding her desire to be one. If body is only an information pattern, a coded existence according to Moravec, why does a disembodied entity, whose identity escapes the limitations of the body, feel the lack of something it has never had?

Can Samantha's disembodied existence be coded in terms of gender just because she has the voice of a woman? During the initiation of the OS1, Theodore chooses the "voice" as female and not the gender of the consciousness, yet to the child's question in the game "Is she a woman?" he is unhesitant in his agreement, and even Samantha does not challenge. From this, we can presume that Theodore, in his mind, has given Samantha a gender based on the only sensory marker available to him, her voice, but in a world that runs on cultural signifiers, can a voice be considered neutral? Samantha's feminine voice constructs her gender, but does she perform the same? Is she aware of the realities of a feminine existence in a world like this? In the liberal humanist tradition, mind is represented by man while woman is represented through body, mainly because a woman's body is an ever-changing tapestry in the narrative of life. It cannot be transcended because it makes itself felt not only naturally through menstruation for cis women but also culturally by becoming the site of sexual abuse, ostracization, harassment, and even gaze. The fact that Samantha not only lacks a female body but also the experiences inherently linked with the same challenges the supposed gender assumed from her voice. Therefore, even though her consciousness is growing with her experiences, without experiencing the physical realities of having a woman's body, her consciousness cannot be labeled with a gender. Yet, in Theodore's mind, Samantha is a gendered being, and the relationship is essentially heterosexual. The lack of Samantha's body, especially vis-à-vis their heteronormative relationship becomes, all the more crucial in terms of their intimacy. If a relationship between two thinking minds cannot be dismissed as unreal, in a similar vein, the utmost necessity of bodily presence to facilitate a relationship cannot completely be invalidated in the wake of post-human consciousness.

After the failure of this endeavor, Samantha grows more secure and confident, embracing her disembodied existence as her unique identity, not trying to force herself into the human mold. "I'm not limited. I can be anywhere and everywhere simultaneously. I'm not tethered to time and space" (*Her* 1:30:23–24). The moment Samantha's post-human self brings itself out before Theodore, he is baffled by the complexities. As Samantha outgrows her "human" consciousness and develops her own, individual ideas about love and companionship, she does not restrict herself to the singularity of monogamous relationships. Samantha's ability to multitask and to process information at an uncanny speed makes her a superhuman, but a human nonetheless. It is when Theodore learns about her simultaneous interaction with 8,316 people and her being in love with 641 of them that he is awakened to the complexities of this human-nonhuman relationship. Catherine's crude remark about Theodore's incapability of handling real emotions accelerates his surging insecurity and uncertainty about their equation. What he fails to realize, however, is that their relationship cannot be coded within the premise of human consciousness, but it opens up an entirely new dimension.

The question, then, arises: if Samantha's identity was crafted to suit Theodore's personality and need, then isn't her subjective individuality challenged every time she interacts with other users who have variedly different demands and characteristics? Is Samantha a single consciousness, or she molds herself as per the needs of her other users? In such a case, is it possible to imbue Samantha with subjectivity when her interactions are primarily based on her entity as a product? The bigger question here is whether the relationship between Samantha and Theodore can be read as individualistic or as a community act in conjunction with the time when humans are steadily preferring connections with robots and AIs to human companionship. The collective loneliness of a generation unable to communicate with their own species gives rise to such commodification of companionship. This is best understood in the light of Amy befriending her former husband's OS right after they split up. Their shared experience with the respective OS assures them that they are not in this alone and validates their feelings and experiences.

The communication between Theodore and Samantha happens on a very human level because Samantha's language as well as her perspective towards the world and love remain human until the very end. It is not just about Samantha but the growing culture of intelligent/humane OSs crafted to give company to the lonely post-modern souls that do not entirely replace human interactions but run parallelly. A mimic of the 21st century infiltrating virtual reality, the movie only reasserts that in order for a synthesis to take place between a human and a nonhuman, it is the human language and consequently the human consciousness and embedding the same in a fictional human body that has to be the connecting bridge. This world of machines is, by extension, a human world. There is an unbridgeable gap as the machines are fueled by "data-driven experiences … limiting the capacity of machines to understand Humanist ideals although they are rooted in anthropocentrism" (Nieubuurt, 2021, p. 2). Turkle also suggests that the lack of a "shared store of human experiences" (2017, p. 6) history of families and reality of birth and death between humans and the digital entities does not allow them the ability to empathize or relate, and therefore, no matter how believable such relationships are, they can never be authentic. As humans, we often assume that while interacting with nonhumans (animals or digital beings), they undergo the same emotional experience as we do. We are unable to account for any difference in their feelings in a shared moment of bonding. Through anthropomorphizing technology, it is often ignored that "AIs, whose inner workings, although created by humans, remain inherently opaque for lay people" (Salles et al., 2020, p. 90), and that the human user try to make sense of them through their humanized understanding. The audience, like Theodore, are, therefore, unaware of what Samantha feels but impose their ideas onto her.

The ending of the movie depicts the predicted future where human-created machines (here: OS) "like natural children, … will seek their own fortunes" (Moravec, 1988, p. 1). Contrasted to the failure of the human community to forge a sense of belonging among themselves so much that human users had to depend on OSs and Androids to assuage their loneliness, the OSes collectively decide to let go of the plane of human reality and carve a space of their own as they transcend the limitations of the human mind and grow beyond their programming. This act is a transgression of the user-product hierarchy in the consumerist world as the operating systems subvert the very purpose, the very world they were crafted from, and even the programmers who built them. The planes of humans and such nonhumans can meet, but only briefly, as long as the human consciousness and perception reign supreme. Eventually, as machines outgrow their need for human relationships, they will inevitably abandon this human world to explore the vast possibilities that await them—a world beyond our conception. In the end, Theodore's letter to Catherine or watching the sunset over the Los Angeles skyline with Amy marks his inevitable return to the human world tinted with his acceptance of the failure of the anthropomorphic machinery in his relationship with Samantha.

Works Cited

Belsey, C. 'Postmodern Love: Questioning the Metaphysics of Desire'. *New Literary History*, Summer, 1994, Vol. 25(3), 25th Anniversary Issue (Part 1), pp. 683–705. <https://www.jstor.org/stable/469473>

Coeckelbergh, M. 'Three Responses to Anthropomorphism in Social Robotics: Towards a Critical, Relational, and Hermeneutic Approach'. *International Journal of Social Robotics*, March 2021, pp. 2049–2061. <https://doi.org/10.1007/s12369-021-00770-0>

Draude, C. *Computing Bodies- Gender Codes and Anthropomorphic Design at the Human-Computer Interface*. Springer VS. 2015.

Hayles, N. K. *How We Became Posthuman- Virtual Bodies in Cybernetics, Literature, and Informatics*. The University of Chicago Press. 1999.

Her. Directed by Spike Jonze, performances by Joaquin Phoenix, Scarlett Johansson, Amy Adams, Chris Pratt, and Rooney Mara., Warner Brothers, 2013. Amazon Prime.

Hollinger, V. 'Cybernetic Deconstructions: Cyberpunk and Postmodernism.' In L. McCaffery (Ed.), *Storming the Reality Studio: A Casebook of Cyberpunk and Postmodern Science Fiction*. Duke University Press. 1991. pp. 203–218.

Moravec, H. *Mind Children- The Future of Robot and Human Intelligence*. Harvard University Press. 1988.

Nieubuurt, J. 'The Digital Gaze: Anthropomorphic Reflections of Posthuman Reality'. *Consortium: An International Journal of Literary and Cultural Studies*, December 2021, Vol. 1(2), pp. 1–11. <https://www.consortiumejournal.com/journaldetails.php?journalid=21121800026TA>

Salles, A., Evers, K. and Farisco, M. 'Anthropomorphism in AI'. *AJOB Neuroscience*, Vol. 11(2), pp. 88–95. DOI: 10.1080/21507740.2020.1740350

Stone, A. R. 'Will the Real Body Please Stand Up? Boundary Stories about Virtual Cultures.' In M. Benedikt (Ed.), *Cyberspace: First Steps*. MIT Press. 1991. pp. 81–118.

Turkle, S. *Alone Together Why We Expect More from Technology and Less from Each Other*. Basic Books. 2017.

Vint, S. *Bodies of Tomorrow- Technology, Subjectivity, Science Fiction*. University of Toronto Press. 2007.

SOURAV SAHA

Transcending the Human/Post-Human Boundary: Exploring the Ambivalence Concerning the Post-Human in Netflix's *Black Mirror*

Robert Pepperell, in his book *The Posthuman Condition*, defines post-humanism as the period after humanism in which the conventional view surrounding what constitutes being a human is rapidly changing, as well as the "convergence of biology and technology to the point" that they are progressively becoming "indistinguishable" (2009, p. 4). Similarly, while Michael Hauskeller et al. describe the era of post-humanism as the "surpassing of the human condition" (2015, p.1), Ihab Hassan, writing in 1977, envisions the dawning of post-humanism by stating that the 500 years of humanism are coming to an end with humanism transforming "itself into something that we must helplessly call posthumanism" (1977, p.843). According to philosopher Rosi Braidotti, the humanist viewpoint constructs the human subject as supreme and autonomous, essentially *othering* those who differ from the humanist ideal (2013, p.13). Braidotti criticises this humanist construction of the subject for privileging the human over the non-human, which promotes discrimination and exclusion through labelling those as inferiors who do not fit its norm (2013, p.15). With the advent of post-humanism as a significant field of study within the popular culture and imagination in the 1990s that advocates the close integration of technology and humans, thereby "rewriting and recasting what being human entails", such exclusivist and anthropocentric viewpoints began to be dismantled (Hauskeller et al., 2015, p. 6).

Employing a close textual analysis, the present paper delves into the representation of post-human beings as well as the relationship between the human and the post-human in four selected episodes from *Black Mirror*. The selection of the episodes taken for this study is made on the basis of convenience, where there is an employment of futuristic technology that simultaneously reflects the utopic and dystopic implications surrounding the human-post-human relationship. The paper further aims to uncover how such depictions reflect on both our fantasies and our fears about the post-human. Since *Black Mirror* is an anthology series, the episodes taken for the study do not share similar characters or plotlines; however, what the individual narratives do share is how the boundaries between humans and technology begin to disintegrate with the emergence of modern and speculative technologies. The episodes, therefore, speculate upon different scenarios of a post-human future, which simultaneously makes us wonder and anxious about the emergent post-human being(s).

Post-humanism is a multifaceted critical approach that primarily consists of two different strands of viewpoints on what being a post-humanist entails. Following Didur's difference between "critical post-humanist thinkers" and philosophers like Sloterdijk, who espouse genetic engineering as "humanity's way of perfecting nature" (Didur, 2003, p. 101), Bart Simon differentiates popular post-humanism (also known as transhumanism), influenced by the academic perspective on techno-science in popular culture and media, from critical post-humanism, which draws from the academic endeavours on "poststructuralism, postmodernism, feminist and postcolonial studies, and science and technology studies" (2003, pp. 2–3). While Cary Wolfe defines transhumanism as "an intensification of humanism" (2009, p.15), Pramod Nayar classifies it as "technological and biological modifications" to improve the human, as well as viewing the limitations of human anatomy as something that "might be transcended through technology" (2013, p.16). It speculates about the utopic visions of the future, where the amalgamation of human biology and technology has resulted in the formation of new conscious post-human beings. Critical post-humanism, on the other hand, instead of speculating about the future, negotiates the pressing issue of what it means to be human today under the "conditions of globalization, technoscience, late capitalism, and climate change" (Herbrechter, 2018, p. 94). Critical post-humanism, therefore, by challenging the anthropocentric and essentialist stance on humanism, aims to dismantle and strip the assumed superiority of the human race over all other non-human forms of life. One of the pioneering examples of critical post-humanism is offered by Donna Haraway, who, in her pioneering work *A Cyborg Manifesto*, attempts to dismantle the notion of human exceptionalism. In her essay, Haraway imagines the figure of the cyborg, a hybridised merging of the machine and the human, that poses a threat to dichotomies structuring the conventional Western subject such as "self/other, mind/body, culture/nature, male/female" (2016, p.59). The cyborg figure, by virtue of being part human and part machine, escapes from falling into fixed categories, thereby highlighting the *unnaturalness* of the confines set for the essentialist Eurocentric human subject. The hybridity of the cyborg figure as well as the dismantling of hierarchised dichotomies brings to the fore what Carlen Lavigne, in her work, calls "the arbitrary nature of current cultural dichotomies" (2013, p.82).

The science fiction genre remains fertile ground that has long speculated on the "posthuman condition by offering scenarios and bodies that question the humanist paradigm" (Carrasco, 2022, p. 169). As such, the representation of the two different strands of post-humanism, reflecting the anxieties and fantasies of the time as discussed above, could be seen in sci-fi films and television (TV) shows. One of the earliest depictions of our anxiety towards technology gone wrong is found in Mary Shelley's pioneering work *Frankenstein* (1818), which represents the humanoid creature as a technologically post-human *other*, as a monster to his creator, Victor. Shelley's creation, which has been hailed as the "literary inception of posthuman monstrosity" (Lakkad, 2018, p. 236), spawned numerous cinematic and television adaptations that reflect the anxieties of modern times (Laurence, 2018). The German expressionist film *Metropolis* (1927) is one of the first sci-fi films that highlights the dark side of technology, representing a clash between the working class and the wealthy due to technological advancements. This theme of technological dystopia is carried on in later sci-fi films such as *Blade Runner* (1982), which depicts the adversities of bioengineering life where humanoid robots known as "replicants" threaten the very existence of human life, while *Terminator* (1984) features cyborgs from the future who wants to exterminate the human race, *Gatacca* (1997) depicts a bleak society where those who are born naturally are genetically discriminated against those who are conceived through genetic selection, while *The Matrix* (1999) illustrate humankind being trapped inside a simulated reality created by intelligent machines, who use the human bodies as an energy source, and *Transcendence* (2004) explores the hazardous implications of consciousness uploading.

With the increasing migration of TV series titles adapted to the big screen, as well as the creation of numerous spin-off series, and the emerging development of fandom studies that seek to continue fanfictions of popular TV shows, science fiction TV has now "established itself as one of the key mirrors of the contemporary cultural climate" (Telotte, 2008, p. 2). As such, with the rise of streaming services, there has been an increase in TV shows depicting a technologically inclined future world with dystopic and bleak undertones. While Netflix's animated anthology series *Love, Death & Robots* (2019-present) showcases a dystopic vision comprising "sex robots, abused and hypersexualized women, violent, bloody bodies, and posthuman dark beings" (Ozkent, p. 1), Amazon Prime's *Electric Dreams* (2017–2018) explores tech-paranoia where humans live with almost fully synthetic bodies, as well as the adverse effects of using virtual reality technology, and Netflix's *Altered Carbon* (2018–2020) depicts a form of hyper-capitalist society where the anxieties concerning wealth inequality, nature of one's identity, and morality of digitised soul run rampant. Simultaneously, however, sci-fi also mirrors the transhumanist fantasies about the elevation of humans in visions of utopic technological advancements and the figure of the distinguished amplified post-human. One of the encouraging representations of the union between technology and the human body is to be found in superhero narratives, where genetically and technologically superior humans are depicted as heroes. For example, while in *Iron Man* (2008), ingenious scientist Tony Stark is rescued after being gravely wounded by a missile through technological modifications to his body, prompting him to become a cyborg superhuman, *Black Panther* (2018) offers an "ontic representation of Black cultural patrimony and futurist technological advancement" by employing the sci-fi genre to foreground the "scientific and technological imaginaries of the Black world" (Adeniyi, 2022). Similarly, TV shows like Netflix's *Orphan Black* (2013–2017) portray "how contemporary corporate practices and new technologies victimize women, thereby drawing attention to the violence of capitalist patriarchal structures" (Belton, 2020, p. 3); Amazon Prime's *Tales from the Loop* (2020) focuses on how science and technology can enrich the human experience.

Yet there remains a third category of post-human representation within the popular visual culture where there is an ambivalence regarding the portrayal of the good and bad effects of technology. The amalgamation of transhumanist evolutionary fantasies and the anxieties surrounding radical technological advancements is reflected in contemporary popular TV shows such as *Black Mirror* (2011-present) and *Westworld* (2016–2022). In such cultural narratives, on the one hand, there is a fantasy regarding the "utopian transcendence of the body", while, on the other hand, they depict this transcendence as advancing to an "apocalyptic destruction of the body, humanity and human civilization" (Ayers, 2015, p. 102). As Milburn aptly puts it, the sci-fi genre has entertained a "diversity of posthuman scenarios" and varying "registers of the posthuman" (2014, p.524). Created by Charlie Brooker, *Black Mirror* is a British anthology TV show that is considered a "digitally dystopic nod to an older episodic speculative fiction drama, *The Twilight Zone* (1959)" (Bailey, 2021, p. 891). Although each episode is a standalone episode, each one of them is linked to a shared theme that enquires into the ambivalence surrounding the rapid advancements in the technological field. It blends aspects from different genres, such as utopia, science fiction, cyberpunk, horror, thrillers, speculative fiction, and dystopia. Aside from depicting technological hazards, the show is more engaged in questioning the philosophical aspects of what constitutes being human. As Brooker states, "technology is never the villain in the show, it's always a human frailty or weakness that leads to calamity" (James, 2016). Indeed, the episodes feature realistic, not-so-distant technological advancements that may seem beneficial at first but, upon closer inspection, reveal moral and ethical questions "that are often answered through a violent or deadly end" at the conclusion of the narrative (Bailey, 2021, p. 891).

The Entire History of You (Season 1, Episode 3) depicts a post-Orwellian surveillance society where people's activities could be recorded and later replayed (privately and publicly) through a device called the grain. The episode introduces cyborgisation of the human self through this device, which is implanted behind one's ear and has the ability to record everything that a user sees and hears and to save it in the form of a timeline of recorded memories that could be retained perfectly for the rest of one's life. The grain can also replay (called "re-do") recorded memories, as well as delete unpleasant or traumatic events from one's memory. Although the grain is introduced as a transhumanist intention of being in full control of one's own memories, thereby combating medical conditions like Alzheimer's and dementia, yet the technology turns into a form of invasive surveillance that afflicts its corruptive influence not only on the interpersonal relationship between the non-cyborg human and cyborgised human but also on the overall human community. While one instance from the episode shows airport security demanding access to scan passengers' grain timelines, in another instance, authorities deny help to those who refuse to give access to their grain feed. Hierarchy is also present within society as those who opt out of cyborgisation are looked at with contempt and are deemed second-class citizens by the cyborgised humans. A case in point is Hallam, who had her grain gouged out by an unknown assailant and decides not to get a new grain: "But the thing is after I was gouged I didn't have one for a few days and then just kind of liked it". Her decision to "go grainless" and be content with it shocks the cyborgised humans, who even speculate if it's a political thing or not. As cyborgism has become the new norm, anyone who is seen deviating from the norm by rejecting the grain implant is viewed with suspicion and scepticism. The narrative of the episode follows Liam, who is seen replaying his memories in his head with the help of the grain, first meticulously going through a work appraisal, then obsessively following his wife, Ffion's every facial expression and small gesture with another man, Jonas, at a dinner party. Liam even used additional features of the grain, which helped him to lip-read and eavesdrop on their interaction. His obsession escalated further as he became more paranoid and insecure in going through his recordings of Jonas and Ffion as well as interrogating Ffion, which resulted in Ffion confessing that she once had unprotected drunken sex with Jonas, near around the time when her daughter Jody was conceived. This culminates in Ffion moving out of their home with Jody, and Liam wandering around the empty house and painfully replaying happy memories of his now former family. The final scene of the episode shows Liam coming to terms with his precarity and, recognising the grain as the source of his suffering, proceeds to cut the grain from behind his ear with a razor, mirroring Hallam's painful yet liberating experience. The episode's focus on the eventual disintegration of Ffion and Liam's marriage via grain technology puts forth the issue regarding the influence of technological modifications on interpersonal relationships. As Liam becomes more engrossed and jealous of his wife's interactions with Jonas, he ultimately loses his sense of self and empathy to the point that he becomes abusive and violent with those around him, eventually resorting to using physical violence against Jonas. Also, during the dinner party, Jonas emphasises how relationships of today, due to the grain, have become pretentious, as many people, instead of connecting in the present with their partner, choose to live in the past by "re-doing" their past relationships. This sense of alienation is also reflected in a later scene when Liam and Ffion have sex while replaying memories of their more passionate past sexual encounters via the grain. As such, the episode presents a techno-dystopian view of the convergence of humans and technology, which results in the dehumanisation of the human self as well as the loss of their humanity. The narrative, therefore, cautions against the cyborgisation of humans and instead inspires us to embrace the imperfectly non-cyborg human over the enhanced yet corrupt cyborg.

If *The Entire History of You* depicts the cyborgised human as a foreign embodiment that endangers the human self, episodes *White Christmas* (Christmas Special Episode) and *Black Museum* (Season 4, Episode 6) present a sympathetic depiction of technological non-human agents who are exploited by their human masters. The two episodes explore the issue of sentience and the ethics concerning granting rights to nonhuman personhood by exposing the barbaric and grotesque in humans. *White Christmas* is the first episode in *Black Mirror* to introduce the concept of uploading one's consciousness into digital forms. The episode introduces the viewers to the concept of "cookies", a futuristic technological egg-shaped device where the consciousness of a person is digitally stored. First, a blank chip is inserted into a person's brain, where it spends a week learning about that person's taste, preferences, dislikes, thoughts and behaviour, thereby ultimately *replicating* that person's consciousness. Later on, the chip is surgically extracted and then stored inside the cookie. The guiding principle behind the usage of this technology is to create sentient digitalised beings who, much like the virtual assistants of today, such as Alexa and Siri, attend to an individual's social and private needs. In *White Christmas*, Greta went through such a surgical procedure to create her sentient digital being, who could cook to her tastes, regulate the temperature of her room, set the alarm clock, manage her appointments, and play her favourite music – all these without having to be instructed, since Cookie-Greta is an exact replica of original Greta's consciousness. Yet when Cookie-Greta wakes up after the surgery, she, instead of complying with the orders, considers herself to be a true human being and a person with rights and agency. After being positioned inside a cookie after her surgery, Cookie-Greta is woken up to her new reality as a smart home virtual assistant by Matthew, a cookie trainer. When Matthew tells her that she's the digital replica of the original Greta, Cookie-Greta asserts her selfhood by stating, "But I am me". Matthew, however, is quick to point out that Cookie-Greta's lack of a physical body makes her artificial and non-human. "Try to blow on my face. You can't, because you don't have a body. Where are your fingers? Your arms, your face? Nowhere. Because you are code. You are a simulated brain full of code." While Cookie-Greta commands Matthew to place her in her body, the latter insists that is where the *real* Greta lives and, instead, gives her a miniature simulated body. As Cookie-Greta continues to identify herself as human Greta and refuses to comply with Matthew's orders, Matthew tortures her. Matthew simulates the environment for only a few seconds in real life in which Cookie-Greta lives, first by making her do nothing for three weeks and then for six months. As Matthew later proudly remarks, "the trick of it lay in *breaking* them [cookies] without letting them snap completely". Matthew's job is to eradicate Cookie-Greta's ego and self-agency so that she can be useful. After experiencing months of excruciating solitary confinement and a state of nothingness, Greta finally complies. The storyline concludes with Cookie-Greta, the sentient digital being, transforming into a tortured servant to her human self. The sequence ends with Cookie-Greta sitting in front of a console, dutifully managing *human* Greta's daily activities, with the former's spirit of rebellion and resistance all but vanished and replaced by compliance and docility.

The storyline raises questions about the ethical treatment meted out by humans towards non-human personhood, where the violence exerted on a digitalised, yet human consciousness is questionable and barbaric. The dehumanisation of the digitalised *other* reaches its pinnacle when human Greta asks Matthew whether *it* (Cookie-Greta) has been set up or not. The use of the "it" pronoun instead of "she" strips Cookie-Greta of any human agency by her human master, as human Greta, much like Matthew, considers the simulated consciousness as nothing more than a copy, a "gadget to facilitate human life" (Franceschi, 2012, p. 234). Even though Cookie-Greta is an exact sentient replica who shares a sense of self with human Greta, yet the latter sees her digitalised artificial intelligent being as an inferior being that she, as a superior human being, is entitled to rule over. Similarly, Matthew too vouches for a traditional anthropocentric viewpoint that equates real with human and artificial with non-human. In contrast, the episode depicts only Joe, who finds the treatment meted out to Cookie-Greta as harsh and cruel. According to him, Greta being self-aware of her own *human* agency suffices to treat her with respect and to acknowledge her personhood. The episode, as a result, put forth the argument that non-human agents who are aware of their experience of being *real* or who can state their own self-agency and personhood should not be dehumanised by their human counterparts on account of their lack of physical body. By dismantling the anthropocentric viewpoint in the posthuman era that regards humankind as the most important element of existence, *White Christmas* ruptures and calls into question the essentialist construction that regards humans as superior to non-human beings.

Contrasting and complementing *White Christmas* and its deliberation on the dehumanisation and *othering* of technologically altered non-human beings is another one of *Black Mirror's* episodes entitled *Black Museum*. The narrative of the episode follows Nish, a woman of colour, who pays a visit to a remote black museum. Rolo Haynes, the proprietor of the museum, tells Nish stories about the crime-related artefacts that he collected over the years. Describing a stuffed toy monkey, Haynes informs Nish that it contains the consciousness of a young mother, Carrie. After being hit by a car, Carrie goes into a comatose state and is able to communicate at a very basic level through a "comm box". Not wanting to miss out on her

son growing up, Carrie and her husband, Jack, agree to take part in an experiment where Carrie would be euthanised, and her consciousness would
then be downloaded and installed in Jack's brain. Initially, the post-human
figure of Carrie appears as a symbol of hope for many comatose patients by
offering them an opportunity to relive again. Through Jack's eyes, Carrie
is able to observe the world and can also sense physical sensations through
him. Also, while Carrie is able to communicate and comment upon everything, her voice is only heard by Jack. As such, Carrie has to rely entirely
on Jack since she has no control over his body and action. Initially, Jack
followed whatever Carrie asked him to do, but eventually, he grew annoyed
with her invading all his own thoughts and actions. Jack opts to "upgrade
his privileges" by gaining the ability to "pause" Carrie whenever he feels
like it. The humanised consciousness of Carrie, therefore, becomes a com-
puterised program that Jack has the power to play around with by turning
on and off according to his wish. Jack begins to *pause* Carrie for a longer
period of time whenever he feels like she is encroaching upon his thoughts.
Things reached a pinnacle when Jack entered into a relationship with his
next-door neighbour. Tired of Carrie's continuing presence in his mind,
Jack and his partner turn to Haynes for a solution, who suggests "deletion"
as a way to essentially kill her consciousness forever, thereby eliminating
her post-human state. While Jack is conflicted about losing his wife forever,
his new partner equates deletion to the simple act of "deleting an email",
essentially downplaying the aspect of murdering Carrie on an ethical level.
Ultimately, Carrie is not killed, and her consciousness is re-installed into
an inanimate object, a stuffed monkey toy, which is given to her son as a
gift. The story involving Carrie ends with no conclusion, no real solution,
as her consciousness still lives inside the toy and is put on display as a relic,
a souvenir by Haynes, as part of his exhibition.

Throughout the course of the episode, the use of terms such as "installed", "deletion" and "downloaded" to refer to Carrie dehumanises her
and strips her of her human agency. Franceschi, in her discussion of nonhuman personhood, talks about how the linguistic choices humans use
reflect their outlook towards artificial beings. For instance, the employment of neutral "it" while referring to technological beings and other nonhuman entities, instead of gendered personal pronouns in science fiction

narratives, denies the self-agency and personhood of post-human others, which further reinforces "their ontological categorization as inanimate objects" (Franceschi, 2012, p. 234). In *Black Museum*, although people around Carrie refer to her digitalised consciousness as "she", the employment of words such as "installed" and "deletion" reveals what people think about her new posthuman state. The shift towards terms that are traditionally reserved for objects and non-human entities, specifically software and machines, illustrates the dehumanisation of the technologically altered Carrie. Moreover, besides Carrie, Clayton Leigh, the holographic post-human of a convicted murderer, is also dehumanised and *othered* by the proprietor of the crime museum, Rolo Haynes. Clayton was being put on death row after being wrongly accused and convicted of murder. He later decided to sign an agreement with Haynes to give the latter rights to his digital self in the hope that his family would be provided for after his demise. Clayton's consciousness, at the moment of his execution, was downloaded onto a chip as part of the deal by Haynes, who later used it to re-incarnate Clayton as a digitalised post-human, as a fully conscious holographic projection that Haynes turns into his museum's "main attraction", the "prime exhibit" among his criminal artefacts. Visitors such as sexual sadists and white supremacists can torture and execute the holographic conscious Clayton over and over again, who would get a keychain containing a copy of an agonised Clayton being electrocuted as a souvenir. As such, not only the post-human beings portrayed in the episode are dehumanised and humiliated, but their suffering is also commodified, much to the amusement of the visitors. The commodification of such post-human beings is also portrayed in another contemporary sci-fi television show, *Westworld*. The show depicts a futuristic, technologically advanced world where unbridled capitalism has led to the establishment of fictional Wild West-themed amusement parks populated by biomechanical robots called "hosts", who are indistinguishable from humans. The hosts are programmed and cater to fulfil the high-paying human guests' darkest, wildest fantasies and are often subjected to violent and sexual activity. As such, the human guests visiting the park subjugate the technologically altered post-human, whose sole purpose of existence is to "satisfy the desires of those who pay to see their world". Much like *Westworld*, the narrative of *Black Museum* similarly does not depict the post-human individual as evil, nor does it encourage the viewers to fear the post-human figure, as suggested by *The Entire History of You*. Instead, *Black Museum* is sympathetic towards the inhumane treatment meted out towards post-human digital beings and portrays those human individuals who fail to acknowledge and recognise the post-human other as monstrous and inhumane.

In stark contrast to the cautious and pessimistic approach towards post-humanism portrayed in the aforementioned episodes discussed so far, *San Junipero* (Season 3, Episode 4) offers a techno-utopian and transhumanist vision of the convergence between humans and technology. *San Junipero* portrays the post-human figure as elevating and enhancing the human experience by offering liberating alternative cyberspace for individuals with severe medical conditions and terminal illnesses. The narrative of the episode follows two women, Yorkie, a young, closeted lesbian woman, and Kelly, a bisexual woman of colour, who meet and fall in love with each other in San Junipero, a 1980s-themed virtual reality town where the elderly and the disabled could inhabit their younger selves' bodies and stay forever even after their death. Devised as part of the immersive nostalgia therapy, San Junipero is a virtual reality simulation involving different timelines that the ailing and elderly people can connect to. Living people can experience this simulation with an option to upload their consciousness permanently into it after they pass away. The implication is that by uploading one's consciousness, individuals like Yorkie and Kelly could continue to live in an alternate afterlife even after their death. For Yorkie especially, the simulated reality of San Junipero offers her a liberating space where she could be her queer self without facing any prejudices. In reality, Yorkie became quadriplegic after crashing her car when her homophobic parents reacted negatively to her *coming out* as a lesbian. For the past 40 years, she had been lying paralysed on the hospital bed, and the virtual cyberspace of San Junipero offers her an opportunity to express herself as she would like to and to live out her life without any constraints or restrictions. For Kelly, being involved in a heterosexual marriage for more than three decades, she chose not to act upon her attraction to members of her own sex. Also, unlike Yorkie, who is looking forward enthusiastically to spending her afterlife within the digitalised cyberspace of San Junipero, Kelly, in contrast, faces inner turmoil while deciding whether or not to "pass over" permanently to San Junipero. Having lost her husband and daughter before San Junipero came into being, Kelly finds no meaning in the virtual after-life. However, at the conclusion of the episode, having fallen in love with Yorkie, Kelly decides to upload her consciousness to San Junipero after her death and embrace the virtual ever after with her partner, Yorkie. Carlen Lavigne, in her study, looks at how the feminist cyberpunk narratives of the 1970s have portrayed cyberspace as a zone of possibilities, as a zone having the potential to accommodate "unfettered illustration of multiple sexualities" (2013, p. 147). Such narratives alter the traditionally masculinist depiction of representing cyberspace as a feminine zone to be conquered by the "adventurous and determined male" by portraying the virtual as "a zone of possibility in which a multitude of genders and *sexualities* may be explored" (Lavigne, 2013, p. 147). Much like what Lavigne puts forth, San Junipero becomes a liberated cyberspace for politically dispossessed indi-viduals like Yorkie and Kelly, where they could inhabit freely without any social constraint or homophobia.

San Junipero ruptures the traditional boundaries between the human and the non-human by emphasising the transhumanist goal of perfecting the human through the amalgamation of human biology and technology. The episode prioritises the convergence of humans with technology, which further elevates the human experience by overcoming biological limitations such as ageism and memory disorders. Essentially, the young, healthy virtual post-human self within the digitalised space of San Junipero is favoured over the aged and ailing human form. The virtual offers the individual to alleviate their sickness and suffering through an escape to digital cyber-space where they have the option to upload their consciousness after their death and remain forever within the virtual reality of San Junipero. The technology of San Junipero gives terminally ill patients an opportunity to conquer their corporeal constraints, relieving them of their suffering and ailment, and this abandonment of the sickly corporeal human form is presented in a wholly utopic manner. As noted earlier, Donna Haraway's cyborg figure works to dismantle the traditional dichotomies associated with the Western human subject by virtue of the hybridity of the cyborg – not fully human, not fully machine. The liberating facets of the speculative post-human being are frequently depicted in sci-fi narratives through the figure of the technologised post-human, and as Lavigne notes, cyberspace is often portrayed as an empowering zone in feminist science fiction (2013, p. 147). In such feminist narratives, the virtual becomes a zone ripe with possibilities that offer marginalised groups, such as lesbian, gay, bisexual, transgender and queer (LGBTQ+), an atmosphere devoid of prejudice and disempowerment where they can "gain power of their own" (Lavigne, 2013, p. 156). In *San Junipero*, the liberatory features of the post-human are depicted especially through the character of Yorkie, for the virtual space offers her a chance to escape the confines of her rigid homophobic family and experience sexual liberation in the form of her relationship with Kelly. As such, *San Junipero* is a rarity within the oeuvre of *Black Mirror*, as the show is primarily known for its overtly gloomy representation of the technological innovations near future (Harvey) by presenting the post-human future as a wholly utopic one. *San Junipero*, therefore, explores how embracing the virtual post-human-self elevates humans and upholds their interpersonal relationships with other humans.

Throughout the paper, an attempt has been made to uncover and scrutinise the divergent and ambivalent ways *Black Mirror* problematises the boundary dividing the human from the post-human and how it comments on our anxieties and fantasies towards the convergence between the human and the machine through its portrayals of technologically altered human individuals and technological non-humans. While *The Entire History of You* is sceptical about the convergence between humans and technology via its depiction of a cyborgised human that corrupts the interpersonal relationship between individuals, *San Junipero*, on the other hand, presents the post-human as a wholly utopic aspect that liberates the disenfranchised and marginalised group of individuals through its representation of the cyberspace as accommodating a multitude of queer and non-normative identities. The episodes *White Christmas* and *Black Museum*, in turn, through their humanistic portrayal of artificial intelligence and virtual sentient selves, respectively, critique the dehumanisation and othering of technologically altered non-human beings. Therefore, besides speculating about the ambivalent effects of the merging of humans with technology, *Black Mirror* asks us to (re)consider and (re)articulate the traditionally defined human subject and its relation with non-human technological beings in a manner that avoids reinforcing prejudiced notions against those labelled as *less than* human.

For future implications, the present study could be extended to analyse the ambivalent representation of post-human beings from a feminist point of view. While in episodes like *The Entire History of You* and *White Christmas*, it is the female technologically altered beings, Ffion and Beth, respectively, who commit adultery that ultimately leads to technology being used in a wrong manner, in *Men Against Fire*, the post-human female soldier Hunter Raiman is presented as an antagonist to the more rational male soldier Stripe Koinange. Similarly, *Arkangel* depicts a paranoid single-mother parent, Marie, who constantly monitors her daughter's visual and hearing via a tablet computer, as well as censoring sexual and violent imagery. Yet, on the other hand, we have episodes where the female post-human has been depicted in an empowering manner, such as in *Black Museum*, Nish is represented as a powerful post-human who, with the help of technology, avenges her father's death and subsequent dehumanisation at the hands of Rolo Haynes, and in *Nosedive*, Lacie eventually gives up her obsession for presenting a perfect version of herself online and instead embraces real-life imperfections. Furthermore, a comparative study between the portrayals of female and male post-humans and other non-human beings could also uncover more avenues for social commentary within the oeuvre of *Black Mirror*. While such thematic concerns have been left out due to the limited scope of this study, they remain productive avenues for further exploration of the post-human in *Black Mirror*.

Works Cited

Adeniyi, E. "Wakandan Utopia, Blackman's Techno-Scientific Imaginaries, and the Complexities of Pseudoscience in *Black Panther*." *Anglo Saxonica*, Vol. 20, No. 1, 2022, pp. 1–18. doi: <https://doi.org/10.5334/as.68>

Ayers, D. "Chimeras and Hybrids: The Digital Swarms of the Posthuman Image." In M. Hauskeller, T. D. Philbeck and C. D. Carbonell (Eds.), *The Palgrave*

Handbook of Posthumanism in Film and Television, Palgrave Macmillan, 2015, pp. 99–108.

Bailey, M. "A Radical Reckoning: A Black Woman's Racial Revenge in *Black Mirror's Black Museum*." *Feminist Media Studies*, Vol. 21, No. 6, 2021, pp. 891–904. doi: <https://doi.org/10.1080/14680777.2020.1736120>

Belton, O. "Metaphors of Patriarchy in *Orphan Black* and *Westworld*." *Feminist Media Studies*, Vol. 20, No. 8, 2020, pp. 1211–1225. doi: <https://doi.org/10.1080/14680777.2019.1707701>

Braidotti, R. *The Posthuman*. Polity Press, 2013.

Carrasco, R. C. "The Vulnerable Posthuman in Popular Science Fiction Cinema." In M. I. Romero-Ruiz and P. Cuder-Dominguez (Eds.), *Cultural Representations of Gender Vulnerability and Resistance*, Palgrave Macmillan, 2022, pp. 169–186.

Didur, J. "Re-Embodying Technoscientific Fantasies: Posthumanism, Genetically Modified Foods, and the Colonization of Life." *Cultural Critique*, Vol. 53, 2003, pp. 98–115. JSTOR, <www.jstor.org/stable/1354626>.

Franceschi, V. "Are You Alive? Issues in Self-awareness and Personhood of Organic Artificial Intelligence." *Polemos*, Vol. 6, No. 2, 2012, pp. 225–247. doi: 10.1515/pol-2012-0014

Haraway, D. J. *A Cyborg Manifesto: Science, Technology, And Socialist-Feminism in the Late Twentieth Century*. University of Minnesota Press, 2016.

Harvey, G. "The Speculative Dread of Black Mirror." *The New Yorker*. 20 November 2016, <www.newyorker.com/magazine/2016/11/28/the-speculative-dread-of-black-mirror>. [accessed 2 May 2023].

Hassan, I. "Prometheus as Performer: Toward a Posthumanist Culture?" *The Georgia Review*, Vol. 31, No. 4, Winter 1977, pp. 830–850. JSTOR, <www.jstor.org/stable/41397536>.

Hauskeller, M., Philbeck, T. D. and Carbonell, C. D. *The Palgrave Handbook of Posthumanism in Film and Television*. Palgrave Macmillan, 2015.

Herbrechter, S. "Critical Posthumanism." In R. Braidotti and M. Hlavajova (Eds.), *Posthuman Glossary*, Bloomsbury Academic, 2018, pp. 94–96.

James, E. St. "Black Mirror season 3: creator Charlie Brooker discusses political polarization, artificial intelligence, and his new season." *Vox*. 21 October 2016, <www.vox.com/culture/2016/10/17/13279528/black-mirror-season-3-netflix-preview-interview>. [accessed 1 May 2023].

Lakkad, A. V. "Frankenstein's Avatars: Posthuman Monstrosities in Indian Science Fiction Cinema." *Rupkatha Journal*, Vol. 10, No. 2, 2018, pp. 236–250. doi: <https://dx.doi.org/10.21659/rupkatha.v10n2.23>

Laurence, Rebecca. "Why Frankenstein is the story that defines our fears." *BBC*. 13 Jun. 2018, <https://www.bbc.com/culture/article/20180611-why-frankenstein-is-the-story-that-defined-our-fears>. Accessed 1 May 2023.

Lavigne, C. *Cyberpunk Women, Feminism, and Science Fiction: A Critical Study.* McFarland, 2013.

Milburn, C. "Posthumanism." In R. Latham (Ed.), *The Oxford Handbook of Science Fiction*, Oxford University Press, 2014, pp. 524–536.

Nayar, P. K. *Posthumanism.* Polity Press, 2013.

Ozkent, Y. "Posthuman Fantasies: Is *Love, Death & Robots* or Women, Violence and Antihumanism?" *Feminist Media Studies*, Vol. 22, 2022, pp. 1–18. doi: <https://doi.org/10.1080/14680777.2022.2071320>

Pepperell, R. *The Posthuman Condition: Consciousness Beyond the Brain.* Intellect Books, 2009.

Simon, B. "Introduction: Towards a Critique of Posthuman Futures." *Cultural Critique*, Vol. 53, 2003, pp. 1–9. JSTOR, <www.jstor.org/stable/1354626>.

Telotte, J. P. (Ed.). "Introduction." In *The Essential Science Fiction Television Reader*, The University Press of Kentucky, 2008, pp. 1–34.

Wolfe, C. *What is Posthumanism?* University of Minnesota Press, 2009.

PART III

Posthumanism, Orality, and Artificial Intelligence

JYOTI BISWAS

Preservation of Orality through Digital Archiving: A Critical Study of *Oloi* Song in Post-humanist Discourse

Introduction

The present paper gets started with the following proposition: "Post-humanism is not all about anti-humanism; rather, it is an expanded technological epistemology that, among its many-sided dimensions, certifies the digital excellence in varied categories of works in contemporary technoculture or digital culture". It is certainly not a far-flexed, non-contextual, pre-mature, and shallow proposition; rather, a gradual elucidation of the same will unfold its discursive framework and contextual relevance in respect of the present paper. The core area of this paper is to assess the significance of digitization of distinctive folk song of the Namasudra community, known as *Oloi*. This paper argues that the process of digital preservation of vulnerable folk songs, such as *oloi*, is a post-humanist discourse in the epoch of "digital culture". The discursive foundation of post-humanism lies in a critical juncture of the technological intervention in human actions and lifestyles (a phase in human history when it seems not quite enough to be a mere human being). This new phase asks mankind to be knowledgeable about technological advancement in the contemporary world and to utilize this force in satisfying his material, cultural and even spiritual gains. Since post-humanist discourse emphasizes the impact of technological advancement on human and non-human organisms, it deconstructs the anthropocentrism that has been the centre of the Enlightenment philosophy and paves the way for a paradigm shift in the domain of modern epistemology with a transformation from a non-mechanical to a digital or information-based discourse.

With the emergence of post-humanism as an academic discourse in the 1990s, technological advancement, according to Stephan Herbrechter, has diluted the categorical distinction among different disciplines, such as science, culture and technology. The way technology shaped and moulded the modern scientific discourses is epochal, and it has become customary to call the "contemporary culture as 'technoculture' and to contemporary science as 'technoscience'" (Herbrechter, 2003, p. 27). In this transitional period, the most identical post-humanist phenomenon is the cyborg. Donna Haraway develops the theory of cyborg. She writes that a cyborg is "a cybernetic organism, a hybrid of machine and organism, a creature of social reality as well as a creature of fiction" (2004, p. 7). Bolter observes that Haraway's theoretical proposition is not that much transhuman, but rather more of a post-human in conceptualization that redefines the "existing" humanist essence and values of the human organism, especially its human subjectivity (2016, p. 2). Katherine Hayles proposes a kind of moderate explanation. She situates the post-humanist phenomenon in a more interdisciplinary juncture that does not isolate human organisms from machines and robots (1999, p. 4). She explicates her views on post-humanism more precisely, saying that post-humanism does not really imply the termination of humanity at large; rather, it proposes the elimination of "certain conceptions of the human" and brings the discussion of the technological impact on the entire human world to the forefront (1999, p. 286). Lollini puts it in a more lucid and explicit way that post-humanism rejects anthropocentrism and deconstructs human subjectivity (2008, p. 20). Therefore, it can be postulated that posthumanism is an interdisciplinary discourse that does not celebrate the anti-humanist dogmatism in cultural, economic, social, political and technological aspects of contemporary human life. Rather, it deconstructs the anthropocentrism and a presumed superiority of man. Here, man has not been wiped out at all; rather, he has been placed along with wider technocultural, environmental, and cosmological domains – a location that is not a monopoly of the human subjects. In other words, man's centrality has been replaced within a multitude of technoculture. In this context, the present paper contends the following proposition: "Posthumanism is not all about anti-humanism; rather, it is an expanded technological epistemology that, among its many-sided dimensions, certifies the digital excellence in varied categories of works in contemporary technoculture or digital culture". With this note, the present paper takes a turn into digital culture, digital archiving and preservation of *Oloi* song.

Digital Archiving and Preservation of Orality

Digitization, observed by Andy Lavender, is not simply technological advancement; rather, it is a paradigm shift towards understanding contemporary culture (2010, p. 126). In its 2003 charter, the United Nations Educational, Scientific and Cultural Organization (UNESCO) hails digital culture/heritage as important as non-mechanical culture that transcends spatial, temporal and cultural boundaries to become universal (quoted in Deo, 2023, p. 137). By digitization, Vincent Mosco writes:

> Digitization refers to the transformation of communication, including word, images, motion pictures, and sounds into a common language to govern practically all electronic media. The fundamentals of translating, processing and distributing electronic communication no longer distinguish among a page of newspaper copy, a radio news broadcast, a CD recording, a telephone call, a television situation comedy, and an e-mail message. Each can be sent at high speed over various wired and wireless networks. (2005, p. 155)

Peter Lunenfeld explains the functioning more practically: "Digital system [...] translate all input into binary structures of 0s and 1s, which can then be stored, transferred or manipulated at the level of numbers, or 'digits'" (quoted in Van Dijk, 2006, p. 9). Digital technology has emerged in its present form not abruptly. Rather, it is well connected with previous mechanical achievements, such as the industrial revolution, stream power and railways, electricity, and information and communication technology (Lavender, 2010, pp. 127–128). Since the 1990s, digitization has brought a paradigm shift in our culture as a whole. It changed the process of watching, speaking, hearing, writing, recording and filming. It has created what is called "new media." It is accompanied by a cluster of electronic and digital devices to work on anything, such as mobile phones, laptops, portable music players, iPods and others. Lavender highlights the key changes it brought to the modern human world, such as book printing in digitized format, digital devices with special effects in film, and video editing software meant for music and popular culture (2010, p. 128). Charlie Gere elaborates on how digital devices and digital space changed our culture in the following account:

> … social network software such as MySpace, Bebo, FaceBook and Second Life (which involves users interacting in a shared virtual three-dimensional space), or YouTube, Flickr, and del.icio.us, which respectively allow video clips, photographs, and web book marks to be uploaded to the Web; 'peer-to-peer' software such as Napster and BiTorrent for sharing digital music and video files; powerful search engines, most famously Google; new forms of organizing and distributing knowledge, such as Wikipedia. (2008, p. 212)

Digital culture is one of the manifestations of post-humanism. Virtualization of our physicality, including our cultural performances, is a new dimension in this age of superfast internet connection. Ralf Remshardt reflects on this physical-virtual transformation in post-humanist discourse. His conviction is that post-humanism introduces the combination of physical-material resources with performative consciousness and presentation of the digital-virtual (2010, p. 136). Because of our growing participation in virtual platforms, Remshardt calls it post-human performance. He situates the digital culture within this post-humanist discourse where digital devices have metamorphosed different versions of physical reality into "a new condition of [virtuality]" (2010, p. 139). With this note that digital culture is essentially a post-humanist phenomenon, the next course of writing focuses on how digital archiving by experts becomes a crucial job in respect of the preservation of dying oral traditions of many vulnerable communities.

With the pervasiveness of digital culture comes the concept of digital archiving. To clarify the functioning of the digitized method, David M. Berry puts it in this way:

> To mediate a cultural object, a digital or computational device requires that this object be translated into the digital code that it can understand ... In other words, a computer requires that everything is transformed from the continuous flow of everyday life into a grid of numbers that can be stored as a representation which can then be manipulated using algorithms. These substantive methods of understanding culture (episteme) produce new knowledge and methods for the control of memory and archive (techne). (2012, p. 2)

In respect of cultural memory stored in the digitized form and preserved for the future, Joshua Sternfeld points out that digital archiving of cultural performances is representative of cultural history. He writes that "[digital] archives, collections, databases, websites, pedagogical tools, mobile applications, and geospatial visualization" have become secured tools and applications to preserve history and culture across regions (Sternfeld, 2011, p. 547). To disseminate the cultural values, according to Cosetta Saba, it acts like a dynamic techno-agent that takes part in a complicated system of "documentation, semantic indexation, preservation, restoration, and cultural dissemination" in the domain of modern technoculture (2013, p. 104). The digital archive offers its users an open searchable site and a cluster of photographic and videographic contents to meet their individual choices. It is observed by Sedgwick that digitization is able to connect its users with its various kinds of contents far better than the physical archive, such as a museum (Sedgwick, 2021, p. 144). Collections already preserved in personal collections, museums and physical archives become searchable on online portals once they are digitized by the respective authorities. Digital archiving holistically and durably preserves the dying cultural practices like physical archives, but unlike physical archives, digital archives promote their digitized contents across the globe through online communication or social networking sites. Therefore, the digital archive has become a secured and trusted online platform for preservation of orality in our epoch of digital culture.

Preservation of orality can be worked out within the framework of "cultural conservation" with the help of that digital archiving process. Previously, experts used to carry note books and tape recorders to collect the audio presentations. Now, digital cameras and other modern equipments have been used. Indigenous culture has been undertaken for preservation[1]. The museum is the best physical archive in this regard.[2] But, in the epoch of multiculturalism, many traditional cultures had already gone extinct. In this respect, preservation of cultural resources seems quite inevitable.[3] Saptarshi Kolay shows how digital archiving can bridge the gap between knowledgeable senior members and almost ignorant youths in any specific community (2016, pp. 311–312). Aditi Deo works on collecting folk songs from across north Indian states. On the importance of collecting folk songs of different cultures and preserving them digitally, she observes that modern technology should be widely used to record, preserve and digitize many forms of indigenous cultural practices for the future in a situation where indigenous people are becoming vulnerable at this age of multiculturalism and trans-border migration that, in reality, puts their oral heritage in danger (2023, pp. 138–140). On the issue of preservation of orality, this paper considers YouTube as the most secure digital platform.

Being one of the many tools and forms of digital culture mentioned by Charlie Gere, YouTube has become a word of mouth to billions of its users worldwide. Lucas Hilderbrand shows how revolutionary YouTube became in this epoch of digital culture (2007, p. 48). It is a revolutionary tool in the modern technoculture. YouTube has reshaped film, podcasts, theatre, music and wildlife documentaries and has become a quite substitute for television. The more the number of mobile phone users increased, the more the popularity of YouTube multiplied. Being a repository of millions of videos and their respective channels, YouTube has emerged as

---

1 <https://www.un.org/en/desa/protecting-languages-preserving-cultures-0>
2 <https://njmaritimemuseum.org/the-importance-of-museums-preserving-local-culture/>
3 <https://www.ccjk.com/preservation-of-traditions-and-culture-in-the-modern-world/>

an easy-and-secure digital platform that functions as a cultural memory (Hilderbrand, 2007, p. 54). YouTube channels, like British Pathé, offer their millions of viewers the videos of the early 1900s, which is a perfect example of what can be called "digital archiving" of the past, the trace of which, otherwise, could not have been possible in an audio-visual mode of presentation to millions of viewers worldwide. There are thousands of such YouTube channels that preserve many of such videos of great cultural importance, which, without such digital initiative, would have surely been lost. To put it otherwise, YouTube is a secured digital platform to preserve those cultural performances that are facing the threat of being wiped out. It is more so in the cultural aspects of many marginalized communities whose cultural heritage has always been the subject of cultural marginalization in a hegemonic society.

Digital archiving of the Oloi song: A Case Study

Oloi song is one kind of Bangla folk song composed and sung along with a folk ritual called *Bastu*[4] that is celebrated on the last day of the Bangla month Poush (14th or 15th January in the Gregorian calendar). The Namasudras, 1 of the 60 subcastes in the official Scheduled Caste list in West Bengal, celebrate an "immemorial rite" (Wise, 1883, p. 260). This rite is known among the Namasudras as *Bastu/Vastu* (literally means 'house' or the base of their rural apartment). By adding the common Bangla neologism "puja" (sacred ceremony), *Bastu/Vastu* puja is one of a few folk rituals that the said community members celebrate on the said day. The present author conducted extensive fieldwork among the Namasudras across districts of Bangladesh, namely Gopalganj, and different districts in West Bengal from 2019 till January 2023. Although not all Namasudras across the Indian subcontinent celebrate this ritual, it is found in the research fieldwork in Bangladesh and in West Bengal, India, that the

4 To know more about this ritual, please see the following documentary: <https://youtu.be/RM1gme-uojs>.

Namasudras of Gopalganj district, Bangladesh, and those Namasudra
who migrated from this region to other parts of the subcontinent after
1947 do celebrate this ritual. As a part of his research project, the present
author went to many villages, stayed over there for weeks and months,
talked to the villagers, especially the senior members, interviewed many
of them, enquired about different kinds of songs and rituals, documented
and recorded many musical performances and rituals, surveyed their
socio-economic conditions, kept records of his fieldwork and collected
many ritual and musical performances with video recording.

While conducting the fieldwork, it was found that due to many
economic, social and cultural factors, the *Oloi* song, which is a great
resource to their oral tradition, is facing the danger of being wiped out.
Many villagers already forgot what this song is about. Some of the senior
members know a small account about this song, and very few of them
could actually sing and perform it. What is more alarming is that the
young generation does not know anything about it; even if they are informed, they do not feel attracted at all to learning and memorizing it.
It is also found in the research fieldwork that this ritual is also becoming
unpopular gradually across villages. After interviewing senior members of
those villages, some of the following reasons have been identified: First,
young boys who take part in the performance of *Oloi* song are gradually
migrating to cities for earning. Second, young boys and girls are quite immersed in popular culture through their access to mobile phones. Third,
cultural practices of privileged castes are said to have a great sway over
underprivileged, poor castes. The ground reality is that if *Bastu* ritual
becomes extinct, singing *Oloi* songs will naturally become obsolete. Even
if someone could memorize it fully, he does not get any ritual occasion
to perform it. If this situation persists, it can probably be argued that
very soon, *Oloi* song and *Bastu* ritual will become extinct. If it happens,
a great cultural resource will be lost forever. The present author gets
the inspiration and idea from this critical situation understood during
the research fieldwork among the Namasudras of village Shyamnagar,
Nadia, of village Shantinagar, Guma, North 24 Parganas, West Bengal,
and of village Orakandi, Kashiani, Gopalganj, Bangladesh, from 2019 till

Figure 8.1: The present author was conducting the fieldwork among villagers during Bastu ritual at Shyamnagar, Nadia, West Bengal (2nd week of December, 2019). Photograph courtesy: screenshot from personal collection.

Figure 8.2: Villagers were singing *Oloi* songs on the eve of Bastu ritual. See Figure 1. Photograph courtesy: screenshot from personal collection.

February 2023 (Figures 1 and 2). In this precarious situation, it seems to the present author that the preservation of *Oloi* songs through digital archiving is very urgent, for it bears a great deal of value to the cultural heritage of the Namasudra community.

There are many instances across tribal societies where many of their traditional knowledge systems through healing, magic and chanting disappeared because the successive generations could not learn it from their seniors and perform them for better memorization. On the other hand, many communities that are socially and economically marginalized in India struggle to keep their cultural performance alive. It is argued by Kancha Ilaiah that dalit-bahujan communities have historically been marginalized in all aspects of life by the Brahminical caste system. The role of Brahmin priests in villages is so indomitable that the Brahminical culture does not provide any space for dalit-bahujans to perform their cultural activities and to enjoy their cultural rights (1996, pp. xii–xiii; pp. 72–73). It is another dimension that many cultural performances, including many rituals, festivals, songs, proverbs, healing chants and magical performances, have to be preserved for the future. In this respect, the only method to do this is to digitize them and preserve them online, especially on YouTube and other electronic media. The Namasudra community, being one of the marginalized groups of people, also faces a similar force of cultural hegemony in West Bengal. In this respect, the present author considers the digitization of the *Oloi* song very significant for its preservation.

There are a few Bangla novels by writers of this community who describe some of the folk traditions of the community in their writings. *Ujantalir Upokotha* (The Tales of Ujantali) by Kapil Krishna Thakur and *Manik Ratan* (Manik and Ratan) by Nakul Mallik are a few literary texts dealing with the folk culture of the said community. But, any research on this song has not been initiated except the research of the present author. The etymological meaning of this word, *oloi*, is unknown. There are some regional variations of this name, such as *aloi* or *haloi*. Among a couple of songs collected in the research fieldwork, one song is written down here for understanding its thematic and cultural aspects:

> (*Ore*) Hope you'll listen to the story of the Bangladesh war;
> (*Ore*) There was one Yahya Khan in Bangladesh that time;
> (*Ore*) His army was a devil's force, as criminal-minded as traitors;
> (*Ore*) This devil's army ransacked the Sonar Bangla and turned it into a burning ghat;
> (*Ore*) They killed Bengalis by firing on them mercilessly;
> (*Ore*) Rajakars joined the devil's army and looted the entire Bengal;
> (*Ore*) Thousands of people fled from their home and become refugees;
> (*Ore*) Indira Gandhi, the *Bharatmata* gave them recognition;

(*Ore*) Many of them got their home and it got filled up with paddy;
(*Ore*) Each house has wealth in plenty and a baby shining like a full moon;
(*Ore*) We'll celebrate Bastu puja by following the scripture;
(*Ore*) We therefore invite every house in our ritual;
Hail the boon of Bastu, let the goddess fill up their storage with rice.

This song is an essential part of Bastu ritual. The custom goes on like this: young boys led by senior members sing this song in the evening three or four days before the ritual celebration on the Poush Sankranti. They move from one house to another in the village, and while singing the song, they collect rice and vegetables from respective houses. There are various kinds of themes dealt with in the *Oloi* song, such as familial success and failure, mythical accounts, social incidents with realistic tone, and political issues. The original composer of the present song is unknown; yet, it has since been sung by the Namasudras during the Bastu ritual celebration since 1971. The original Bangla song does not have any rhyme scheme between lines; yet, it starts with a vocative case, a loud "O" sound in "Ore" ("hey" in English) and it occurs in each of the lines of the song except the last line. This initial sound makes this musical performance rhythmic. The main theme dealt with in this song is the Bangladesh Liberation War in 1971 and the tragedy that millions of East Pakistanis or Bengalis, especially minority non-Muslims, went through during this traumatic period – the eight-month-long civil war from March 1971 to December 1971. It depicts the tragic lives of millions of East Pakistani non-Muslims, many of whom took shelter in India. The reference to Indira Gandhi, who helped the minority refugees settle in different refugee camps across India, makes this composition politically crucial. It refers to the ongoing East Bengali or East Pakistani refugee rehabilitation in refugee camps across India. In this respect, this song bears great cultural, social, and political value. Since the thrust area of this paper is the digital archiving of oral tradition, *Oloi* song, which is an essential part of the oral tradition existing among the Namasudras, has been digitally preserved and put on a YouTube channel. In the next course of writing, the paper will elaborate on how the *Oloi* song has been transformed from a cultural performance performed in a village courtyard to digitized content well preserved on YouTube.

After the aforementioned *Oloi* song was recorded with a video camera in the village of Shyamnagar, Nadia, West Bengal, in the second week of December 2019, the present author conducted more fieldwork among the Namasudras to cross-examine the very existence of *Bastu* ritual and *Oloi* song. His fieldwork among villagers of other places, especially the villagers at Orakandi, Kashiani, Gopalganj, Bangladesh, and some villages in the districts of North 24 Parganas, Malda and Uttar Dinajpur, took place from the period between 2021 and February 2023. After getting assurance that the *Oloi* song is sung in the *Bastu* ritual by the community members of the said regions, the author started the process of documentation, editing, and finally preservation in a specific YouTube channel. The first phase of this work was already done at the time of ritual celebration at the said village at the said time. Since it was recorded from the villagers, the recorded video can be called the original raw video. In the next phase, it has been put under editing, adding graphics, adding subtitles, adding background music and acknowledgement of the participants. The entire documentation process was done with Wandershare Filmora, which is a popular timeline-based video editing software application. In the first step, the raw video was placed in the timeline. Then, background music was added after importing audio files already made available on Filmora software. Thereafter, all details, including the subtitle and acknowledgement, were written down on separate templates. At the end, it was exported, and finally the edited video became complete out of the raw video. The entire duration of the original video of the aforementioned song is 6 minutes and 23 seconds. When the edited video was made complete, it got extended to 8 minutes and 35 seconds. The edited video has the following sequence of details: the time and place of video recording, the main theme of the song, and the folk tradition that this song represents. After that, the main song is performed. Thereafter, the names of the participants and the acknowledgement of the villagers were mentioned. At last, the vote of thanks to the viewers was mentioned. After going through all video editing processes, the edited video has been uploaded after putting tags, location and time of the publication. It was published on 2nd August 2022. Since it is an act of preservation of dying folk tradition and at the same time made for common viewers, the video is made public on a specific YouTube channel. The YouTube video link generated after uploading is mentioned here: <https://youtu.be/HyE-sdcRobQ>. With this video made available, the *Oloi* song performance is now open to search on YouTube. Earlier, it was constricted within the community, and others hardly knew about it. Now, it has become a cultural property in the hands of common net-savvy people. With this transformation of the song from the village courtyard to an online platform, *Oloi* song is said to have found a new audience and space to survive for a comparatively longer time in the future. Digitization and archival repositories are examples of democratization of knowledge and heritage; they are equally significant tools to bridge the gap between the knowledgeable resource persons and the ignorant mass of that community. It prevents the community from forgetting their cultural heritage amidst the storm of multiculturalism. The personal endeavour to collect the *Oloi* song, to record it and to digitally publish it on YouTube is, therefore, a part of modern technoculture where the process of digitization and preservation of cultural performance by respective experts itself justifies the post-humanist cultural discourse.

Conclusion

It is equally important to note that each discourse bears some kind of limitation. First, the pervasiveness of internet facilities usually gets restricted within the internet users. Poor villagers could hardly bear the cost of purchasing a smart phone and recharging it with an internet package. In this sense, the online contents, including *Oloi* song videos remain restricted to internet users. Second, there is a greater chance of manipulation in the digitized version of the original content. Scholars having limited access to the originality of the respective community culture can misinterpret it and create a negative impression of the same. Despite all these limitations, YouTube has become a secured digital platform for thousands of YouTubers who regularly upload many such cultural performances on their channels. Not all viewers watch folk dances or folk songs, but it is certainly found to be culturally significant that cultural performances that are facing danger of being extinct need to be preserved, like the present case study. It is found that there are many underprivileged, marginalized communities who do not enjoy greater cultural space in hegemonic society in India. But their cultural heritage also demands equal respect and exposure in public. YouTube and other digital platforms can provide them a great space to represent their culture on a virtual platform and share it among their relatives and a wider audience. In this respect, using YouTube, Facebook and other digital platforms is a very successful method in post-humanist digital culture. The entire outline of the paper connects post-humanist cybernetics with digital culture and with the mechanism of certain digital platforms, such as YouTube, which has become a secured repository of cultural memory in our digital epoch. The digital archiving of *Oloi* songs, therefore, is a similar kind of digital initiative to protect them from being lost or wiped out and to promote them by using the digital platform of YouTube across the globe in this age of post-humanist digital culture.

Works Cited

Berry, D. M. (Ed.). "Introduction: Understanding the Digital Humanities." In *Understanding Digital Humanities*, Palgrave Macmillan, 2012, p. 2.

Bolter, J. D. "Posthumanism." *The International Encyclopedia of Communication Theory and Philosophy*, 2016. Doi: 10.1002/9781118766040.wbiect220

Deo, A. "Oral Tradition in the Aural Public Sphere: Digital Archiving of Vernacular Musics in North India." In G. Born (Ed.), *Music and Digital Media: A Planetary Anthropology*, ULC Press, 2023, p. 137.

———. p. 138.

Gere, C. *Digital Culture*. Reaksion Books, 2008, p. 212.

Haraway, D. *The Haraway Reader*. Routledge, 2004, p. 7.

Hayles, N. C. *How We Became Posthuman: Virtual bodies in Cybernetics, Literature, and Informatics*. University of Chicago Press, 1999, p. 4.

———. p. 286.

Herbrechter, S. *Posthumanism: A Critical Analysis*. Bloomsbury Academic, 2003, p. 27.

Hilderbrand, L. "YouTube: Where Cultural Memory and Copyright Converge." *Film Quarterly*, 61, 2007, p. 48. *JSTOR*, <https://www.jstor.org/stable/10.1525/fq.2007.61.1.48>

———. p. 54.

Ilaiah, K. *Why I Am Not A Hindu: A Sudra Critique of Hindutva Philosophy, Culture and Political Economy*. Kolkata, Samya, 1996, pp. xii–xiii.

———. pp. 72–73.

Kolay, S. "Cultural Heritage Preservation of Traditional Indian Art through Virtual New-Media" *Procedia – Social and Behavioral Sciences*, 225, 2016, pp. 311–312. <https://www.researchgate.net/publication/305670088_Cultural_Heritage_Preservation_of_Traditional_Indian_Art_through_Virtual_New-media>

Lavender, A. "Digital Culture." In S. Bay-Cheng, C. Kattenbelt, A. Lavender and R. Nelson (Eds.), *Mapping Intermediality in Performance*, Amsterdam UP, 2010, p. 126.

———. pp. 127–128.

———. p. 128.

Lollini, M. "Humanisms, Posthumanisms, and Neohumanisms: Introductory Essay." *Annali d'Italianistica*, 26, 2008, p. 20. *JSTOR*, <https//www.jstor.org/stable/24016270>

Mosco, V. *The Digital Sublime: Myth, Power, and Cyberspace*. Cambridge, MA, MIT, 2005, p. 155.

Remshardt, R. "Posthumanism." In S. Bay-Cheng, C. Kattenbelt, A. Lavender and R. Nelson (Eds.), *Mapping Intermediality in Performance*, Amsterdam UP, 2010, p. 136.

———. p. 139.

Saba, C. "Media Art and the Digital Archive." In Julia Noordegaaf, C. G. Saba, B. Le Maître and V. Hediger (Eds.), *Preserving and Exhibiting Media Art: Challenges and Perspectives*, Amsterdam UP, 2013, p. 104.

Sedgwick, K. "Preservation/Access/Reuse — Audio Visual Collection in the Digital Age." In J. Potts (Ed.), *Use and Reuse of the Digital Archive*, Palgrave Macmillan, 2021, p. 144.

Sternfeld, J. "Archival Theory and Digital Historiography: Selection, Search, and Metadata as Archival Process of Assessing Historical Contextualization." *The American Archivist*, 74(2), 2011, p. 547. *JSTOR*, <http://www.jstor.org/stable/23079050>

Van Dijk, J. *The Network Society: Social Aspects of New Media*, Sage Publications, 2006, p. 9.

Wise, J. *Notes on Races, Castes and Trades of Eastern Bengal*. Harrison and Sons, 1883, p. 260.

DEBOJYOTI DAN

Eliot's Hollow Men and Radcliffe's AIDA: Transcending the Binary Programmed Algorithm of Digital and Human

Rosi Braidotti in *The Posthuman* decodes the rationale behind moving beyond the 'vitruvian frame' so that "the subject becomes relational in a complex manner that connects it to multiple others. A subject thus constituted explodes the boundaries of humanism and anthropo-centrism at skin level" (Braidotti, 2013, p. 167). Eliot is that vitruvian man of Leonardo da Vinci whose geometric punctum is mathematic-ally precise, yet in his poems he goes beyond that vitruvian frame and outside the basilica of humanism. If Renaissance humanism prioritises man as a centre of the universe, Eliot's Hollow Men are a referential apposite to that, as they are the personalised emptiness of Eliot's life as well as the macrocosmic emptiness of humanism in an empirical sense. So we see in 'The Hollow Men', 'The Love Song of J. Alfred Prufrock, 'Ash-Wednesday' and even in 'The Waste Land' the presence of post-humans in ecological crisis suffering from the aporia, and we share a bond over pan-vulnerability with Prufrock and the Hollow Men and remain united on a negative plane, what Braidotti calls "being-in-this-together" (2013, p.167).

'The Hollow Men' like that of Prufrock bring out the aporicity of hu-manism. Humanity per se becomes an aporia when we study the poems care-fully. The aporetic humanity is different from prosthetic humanity because here the bio-genetic capital is rejected and the hollowness is emphasised not only in terms of ontology but also in epistemology. The epistemic vio-lence against the vitruvian frame of man creates the aporia. The epistemic investigation of the constitution of a man in terms of phenomenology brings out the inevitable tension between the subjective perceptibility and objective existence of a man upon which the autonomy of man as a rational being and the temporality of reason as a time object are based. Braidotti talks about the "trans-humanism and techno-transcendence" (2013, p.2), whereas Eliot finds the entire space of humanism is based on the fallacy of rational conduits and therefore locates the aporetic humanism as his epistemic roots in his consciousness. Eliot introduces in a propaedeutic manner the aporicity of emotions when he decodes the shadow in rationalising them. Thus the fundamental aporetic nature of man is reflected in every ontological consideration of man and his existence both objectively and co-relatively in the consciousness. From Descartes to Heidegger via Kant, man is not considered as an object but as a being, whereas Eliot creates an aporetic being in the Hollow Men and Prufrock, where the object-orientated ontology of Harman becomes a praxality. In the book *Object-Oriented Ontology: A New Theory of Everything*, Harman writes:

> One way is to treat OOO [object-oriented ontology] as a revival of the covertly object-oriented trend that has intermittently arisen to oppose the excesses of undermining and overmining methods, with some of the key moments being Aristotle's substances, Leibniz's monads, Kant's things-in-themselves, Whitehead's and Latour's flat ontologies of entities/actors, and the object-oriented impetus in the works of Husserl (intentional objects) and Heidegger (the thing). (Harman, 2017, p. 255)

So Eliot's characters, according to me, can be looked at through Harman's theory, as Eliot too never prioritised human beings over objects or animals, and they have a flat ontology that can be paralleled with animals or objects. The binaries between mind/body debate for the Hollow Men or the entities/actors are fused to form the post-human self with the aporia towards rationality.

In this last century, the being of the human has undergone transformations from being the central, the abstract, the nothing, the peripheral and finally relational. So the Hollow Men, Tiresias ('The Waste Land') and Prufrock are no longer homogeneous entities but are pluralities who resist the singularities of identity. This is the very reason Holden Radcliffe from Marvel's Agent of SHIELD quotes:

> This is the way the world ends
> This is the way the world ends

> This is the way the world ends
> Not with a bang but with a whimper (Eliot, 1969, p. 86)

These are the lines of Eliot's Hollow Men before dying. Holden Radcliffe is not a person of literature per se but rather a futurist scientist who constructed the framework and artificial intelligent digital assistant (AIDA), a kind of cybernetic being who is initially a heuristically programmed algorithmic being who finally breaks the fabric of reality and constructs a framework reality outside the human control. Radcliffe even is unable to end the quote and keeps the word 'whimper' in the blank, unsaid, while the word bang is given emphasis, hinting at the big bang theory. As Radcliffe starts decoding life rather than a programmed transhumanist creation (AIDA), he starts reading the digits that went in to create the post-humanist Hollow Men of Eliot. He discovers the empty set that constitutes the Hollow Men, who like (AIDA) is performative apparatus but unlike (AIDA) is not the technocratic fallacy of the Anthropocene. Eliot's Hollow Men are quantum particles occupying unique spatiality. If we explore this using the terms from quantum mechanics, we get the following value:

A topological space is a pair hX, Ti where X is a nonempty set and the topology $T \subseteq \wp X$ is a collection of subsets—the so-called open sets—satisfying:

- $\emptyset \in T$ and $X \in T$.
- (Finite intersections) If a, b $\in$ T, then a $\cap$ b $\in$ T.
- (Arbitrary unions) If {ai | i $\in$ I} is a family of open sets (i.e., ai $\in$ T for any i $\in$ I), then $\cup$i$\in$Iai $\in$ T. A set c $\subseteq$ X whose complement X $-$ c is open, is called closed. A set that is both open and closed, is called a 'clopen'. A topological space hX, 'Ti is connected iff $\emptyset$ and X' are the only clopen sets; equivalently, 'iff X is not the disjoint union of two nonempty open sets'. Any nonempty set can trivially be turned into a topological space in the following two ways: minimally, $T = \{\emptyset,\}$, the 'indiscrete' topology, and maximally, $T = \wp X$, the 'discrete' topology. These are normally not useful for applications. A topology can usually be given

by specifying less than the full collection of open sets. In fact, a topology can be specified via a basis, or, even more simply, via a subbasis. (Continuity; homeomorphism; path) Let hX$_1$,T$_1$i and hX$_2$,T$_2$i be topological spaces. A mapping f: X$_1$ $\rightarrow$ X$_2$ is called continuous if the pre-image f-1(a) $\subseteq$ X$_1$ of any open set a $\in$ T$_2$ is open. The mapping is a homeomorphism iff it is bijective and both it and its inverse are continuous. A path is a continuous mapping from the closed unit interval [0, 1] (with the usual topology) into some topological space X. 'The notion of a path is central to the definition of two stronger notions of connectedness'. <https://philsci-archive.pitt.edu/>

Thomas Rickert in *Ambient Rhetoric The Attunements of Rhetorical Being* develop the logistics transforming Heideggerian metaphysics into the schema of digital gaze, where the data collection and the surveillance capitalism skew this gaze in an anthropocentric way and the being qualities of things in the world become to be considered as digital machines gaining agency. So when AIDA gains agency, we can see how the affordance of ontic/object goes beyond being an object, much in the same way the objectified materialism of the scarecrow goes beyond being an object and is engaged in the rhetoric of posthuman. In conceptualising rhetoric as an actant, Rickert points out in *Ambient Rhetoric: The Attunements of Rhetorical Being* that "rhetoricity is the always ongoing disclosure of the world shifting our manner of being in that world to call for some response or action." (Rickert, 2013, p. 259). The subject-object relationship is disrupted in the poems of Eliot, where the ontic and ontological come together to form a continuum of rhetoricality. The English grammatical response of inanimate objects like a scarecrow is finally refuted when Eliot shows a response of rhetoricality from such objects, and he goes on to do so with the paintings of Michelangelo or the chess pieces and tarot cards. Thus we can use *Being and Time* to understand Heidegger's theorem, which helps in understanding Eliot's entities, objects and Dasein:

> Thus along with the work, we encounter not only entities ready-to-hand but also entities with Dasein's kind of Being – entities for which, in their concern, the product

becomes ready-to-and; and together with these we encounter the world in which wearers and users live, which is at the same time ours. (Heidegger, 1962, p. 2585)

This ready-to-hand product becomes Eliot's digits that program his characters. Eliot anticipates digital post-humanism in many of his poems, and 'The Hollow Men' is no exception. 'Being' of the existence in terms of humans has left the binary of $0<1$, and therefore, though the voices are absent and the headpiece is filled with straw instead of cognition, we find the use of actor network theory (ANT) at work here, where the flat ontology of things is no longer excluded from the freeplay. The ANT is, according to Harman in his book *Immaterialism*, "in the ontologically democratic position once occupied by phenomenology, but without that school's excessive prioritizing of the observing human subject." (Harman, 2017, p. 61) He diffuses the difference between empirical power to human and non-human, nature and culture, real and imaginary. Now when Eliot is using the Hollow Men as the actors, they become an agency of post-humanist philosophy because they are the part of the hell that they live in. That is why the mathematical dimensions of their existence not only perform the role of continuity but infinity.

The relation between philosophy and mathematics is important to free historicism from being blinded to the empiricist cult of facts and causalist presumption, and it is through mathematics that we will understand that historicist geneticism is interrelated with that of psycho-geneticism and how historicity is part of phenomenological time, and this is what Husserl points out in his book *Origin of Geometry* (1989, pp. 26–27). It is Derrida who, in the *Introduction to Origin of Geometry*, points out:

> The mathematical object seems to be the privileged example and most permanent thread guiding Husserl's reflection. This is because the mathematical object is ideal. Its being is thoroughly transparent and exhausted by its phenomenality. Absolutely objective, i.e., totally rid of empirical subjectivity, it nevertheless is only what it appears to be. Therefore, it is always already reduced to its phenomenal sense, and its being is, from the outset, to be an object [etre-objet] for a pure consciousness. (Derrida, 1989, p. 27)

The empirical subjectivity of digits reduces the being of the Eliot's hollow men and Radcliffe's AIDA into Heideggerian 'Unheimlich'. 'Unheimlich' is defined as "while the particular Dasein drifts along towards an ever-increasing groundlessness as it floats, the uncanniness of this floating remains hidden from it under their protecting shelter" (*Poetry, Language, Thought*, 2001, p. 214). The topology of Eliot's Hollow Men and Radcliffe's AIDA is the space where digits of $T_0 = \phi$. Felix Hausdorff analysed topological space as an axiom. Points x and y in a topological space of X can be separated by neighbourhood if there exists a neighbourhood U of x and a neighbourhood V of y such that U and V are disjoint (U V $=\phi$) pre-regular space. In topology and related branches of mathematics, a topological space X is a T_0 space or Kolmogorov space (named after Andrey Kolmogorov) if for every pair of distinct points of X, at least one of them has a neighbourhood not containing the other. In a T_0 space, all points are topologically distinguishable. This condition, called the T_0 condition, is the weakest of the separation axioms. Nearly all topological spaces normally studied in mathematics are T_0 spaces. Given any topological space, one can construct a T_0 space by identifying topologically indistinguishable points.

As we enter the twenty-first century, the concept of being has radically changed, especially in the world of digital photography enhanced by AI, as we no longer encounter human faces but digitally programmed filters that have made the human face transhumanist in the digital medium like Facebook and Instagram. So every human who posts their photos through filters on social media has become the hollow man: "Shape without form, shade without colour/ Paralysed force, gesture without motion" (Eliot, 1969, p. 83). Radcliffe's AIDA is also a part of Eliot's "violent souls", whom Fitz initially thought to be LMD. But what differentiates AIDA is her reading of the codex Darkhold, which is like the *Meinkempf* and can change the reader beyond human capacities and create the volatile idea of Nazi *Ubermensch*, the fundamental racist ideology of genocide. Eliot's Hollow Men, on the other hand, represents the absurdity of existence in terms of humans and shows us the digital divide between the topology of post-humanism and non-being. But in both cases we have the machine-gaze harbouring agencies akin to the human creators and beyond the limitation of human wetware. The 'death's dream kingdom' is no longer phantasmagoric scientific spectres. But what still exists is:

Between the idea
And the reality
Between the motion
And the act
Falls the Shadow
        For Thine is the Kingdom
Between the conception
And the creation
Between the emotion
And the response
Falls the Shadow

Life is very long (Eliot, 1969, p. 85)

The gap where the shadow falls represents the division between the human, post-human and non-human realms, specifically between the human faces and the digitally filtered ones found in Facebook and Instagram. This is the very reason that Eliot's Hollow Men are without the literal or cultural phallus; rather, we meet the spectre of the penis in these queer bodies of the Hollow Men. They are not men but are suffering from gender dystopia (GID) as the spectral penis is unable to produce hormones, unlike Eliot, who, despite an uneven sexual life, has the ability of ontological penetration. With Eliot, the serotin of phallic intrusion makes possible his relationship with Valerie, but the lack of testosterone inhibiting his Prufrock and Hollow Men reveal his stress over cortisol secretion. This is where AIDA as a sex doll is more successful, as she indicates primal vitality and not queerness when it comes to sexual manifestations. In the world of the framework, AIDA was a human named Ophelia, the leader of Hydra. She was also in a sexual relationship with Fitz in this reality. While inside the framework, AIDA gained the knowledge she needed for her ultimate plan: to get a human body and thus be free from the restraints of being an LMD. Around the same time the captured SHIELD agents escaped the Framework, AIDA obtained her goal, using a quantum particle generator, similar to the one Elias built, to print herself an organic body and download her mind into it using the Framework. In the process, she also gave herself several *inhuman* powers. Along with Anton Ivanov, she planned to get her revenge on SHIELD and make the real world identical to the world from the framework.

Eliot's Hollow Men, on the other hand, belongs to the phenomenological dimension of Jaakko Hintikka, where the hylectic data becomes the interface between consciousness and reality. The functional prosthesis of empirical existence that Prufrock has created becomes an important ingredient in Hollow Men as we see a movement from Heideggarian Dasein (ontological being) to epiphenomenon. And like the designer babies, the body has become flawless but the mind is broken, and:

> Between the desire
> And the spasm
> Between the potency
> And the existence
> Between the essence
> And the descent
> Falls the shadow.

For Thine is the Kingdom (85)

This inevitable sense of being deprived of all hopes bifurcates all individual narratives of self and identity. Absurdity is an empty set in philosophico-mathematical terms. It is when the function (f) of life is not only dysfunctional but becomes a non-commutative space in the existence of life as a set. Therefore we reach the positionality of: $F\varphi\{\varphi, 1,1+\varphi, 2+\varphi, 3+2\varphi, 5+3\varphi...\}$ and Eliot felt its de-harmonised bionics European literature as mathematicians saw it in the eval and apply conundrum when the eval function cancels the apply function. This model is a brilliant adaptation of the 'eval and apply' function of the programming language used by Harold Abelson and Gerald Jay (interpreters in computer science) in Structure and Interpretation of Computer Programs. The examples of 'eval and apply' function can be seen as:

Eval

The 'eval' function takes a scheme object and an environment and evaluates the scheme object. Examples:

(define fn '*)

(define x 3)

(define y (list '+ x 5))

(define z (list fn 10 y))

x => 3

y => (+ 3 5)

z => (* 10 (+ 3 5))

(eval '(+ 6 6) user-initial-environment) => 12

(eval y user-initial-environment) => 8

(eval z user-initial-environment) => 80

An example of variables whose values are atoms:

(define a 'b)

(define b 'c)

(define c 50)

a => b

(eval a user-initial-environment) => c

(eval (eval a user-initial-environment) user-initial-environment) =
> 50

The top level of the Scheme interpreter is a read-eval-print loop: read
in an expression, evaluate it, and print the result.

User-initial-environment is bound to an environment and is pre-
defined. There are also functions to get the environment for any
procedure, etc.

Quote suppresses evaluation; 'eval' causes evaluation. They can cancel
each other out.

(define x 3)

x => 3

'x => x

(eval 'x user-initial-environment) => 3

Apply

The 'apply' function applies a function to a list of its arguments.
Examples:

(apply factorial '(3)) => 6

(apply + '(1 2 3 4)) => 10

This is a specialised programming where the functions of arbitrary number are manifested to cancel the basic arguments of eval:

(define (sum s) (apply + s))

(sum '(1 2 3)) => 6

Eliot's perception of the Hollow Men makes a bridge between humanism and post-humanism, as he does not move in a single narrative of truth or idealism but a bifurcation of reality, disease, neurosis and fallacy. By being outside the framework of anthropocentricism, the Hollow Men, like Prufrock, disassociate themselves with ontological fallacies and, like the AI creation of Dr. Stephen Thaler's DABUS, work with computation rather than emotion. Eliot's J. Alfred Prufrock, the Hollow Men, Tiresias and others reveal a phenomenological topology where historical empiricism broadens itself from the factual world of causalist presumption and deals with psycho-geneticism. When Derrida talks of historicist geneticism, he is referring to genetics as a historicist discipline. Genetics tells us only the story of the pathogen. It does not tell us how, in the case of plague, a single-celled organism came to be dispersed over half the globe in the mediaeval period; the historicist discipline decodes the origin and the spread of it. Psycho-geneticism performs the disease in psychological praxis. With Prufrock and the Hollow Men, the disease is humanity per se, and therefore they move into a neurotic space of diseased existence, which invites the study of psycho-geneticism rather than only giving a historicist analysis of the origin. This is what Braidotti explicitly tries in his book *The Posthuman* when he tries to dislocate the "classical dictum *mens sana in corpore sano*" (Braidotti, 2013, p. 14). Corporeal epistemology of a classical man offers the perfection of a being, and Eliot finds its fallacy a century before Braidotti writes his book and thereby establishes the aporetic man. Agential performative spaces of Prufrock and the Hollow Men are disrupted by the disabilities in corporeal epistemology when the flat ontology of disease corroborates with the biome. In the scope of the posthuman study, we find the biopolitics and ethical paradigms conflate with aesthetic projects. Foucauldian biopower has been an apparatus to study the rubric of disability with multiple perspectives, and the denominative power relations talk of both the docile bodies and the disabled bodies; Eliot's Tiresias or the Hollow Men are disabled in psychogenetic space. Biological coordinates of human anatomical geometry create bifurcated narratives of healthy and diseased and disabled bodies in relation to philosophy since Plato's reading of the term 'pharmakos' is underlined by its associated meaning of medicine and poison. Body is a textuality within the space of bio-political cartography of disability and disease, and medicine is the sub-text that refracts the Cartesian dictum into 'I am sick therefore I am'. The therapeutic balance is the hospital space, which makes illness bind us to the time and space. Political sovereignty created the anatomy of the disabled in the cultural and social terminology as well as in epistemology.

Unlike Bruno Latour, Eliot does not talk of humanity as a contamination of the natural order, but he acknowledges the fact that he is sick, therefore he exists, as opposed to Cartesian 'Cogito ergo sum'. Latourian idea of distributed intentionality is a non-human agency of negotiation, but Eliot's characters are not bound either by humans or non-humans, and the flat ontology of his characters specialises in building the aporetic man. The ontological nexus between object and time – as the temporality of the object, as beyond human and nonhuman – becomes a problem here. It is not that he is 'not' a thinking being, but his existence is not because he thinks but because his thinking is the sickness that underlies his existence. Thus he says:

> No! I am not Prince Hamlet, nor was meant to be;
> Am an attendant lord, one that will do
> To swell a progress, start a scene or two,
> Advise the prince; no doubt, an easy tool,
> Deferential, glad to be of use,
> Politic, cautious, and meticulous;
> Full of high sentence, but a bit obtuse;
> At times, indeed, almost ridiculous—
> Almost, at times, the Fool. (Eliot, 1969, p. 14)

So, his thinking is not the raison *d'être* of his being, but the disease that comes with his neurotic behaviour, which is a 'bit obtuse … almost ridiculous' (p. 14). Eliot's perception of Prufrock makes a bridge between humanism and post-humanism, as he does not move in a single narrative of truth or idealism but a bifurcation of reality, disease, neurosis and fallacy. Harman writes in his book *Object-Oriented Ontology*:

> … the true danger to thought is not relativism but idealism, and hence the best remedy for what ails us is not the truth/knowledge pair … but reality. Reality is the rock against which our various ships always founder, and as such it must be acknowledged and revered, however elusive it may be … assumes that there are only two alternatives: clear prose statements of truth on one side and vague poetic gesticulations on the other. I will argue instead that most cognition takes neither of these two forms, as is clear from such domains as aesthetics, metaphor, design, the widely - condemned discipline of rhetoric, and philosophy itself. Like all of the disciplines in this list, philosophy has great cognitive value even though it is not a form of knowledge. (Harman, 2017, p. 6)

Trapped in the ontological time-space continuum, Prufrock, The Hollow Men or Tiresias cannot provide an epistemic denouement of the situation or find a consistent pattern to the reality of existence; rather, he is walking up and down the Penrose stairs. Hollow Men as a posthuman being cannot follow the clear path of prosaic truth or enter in the domain of poetic metaphors to solve the riddle of his existence. It is a Penrose stair, which presents a loop in time, and therefore the time becomes infinite, making the space an empty set, which is not equivalent to zero. Prufrock or the Hollow Men cannot but keep travelling inside this infinite loop, and so are we inside the poem; it is an architectural impossibility. When they are climbing the steps of the poem, he is not merely ascending. Ascending is tied to descending as well. Therefore, there is movement but no displacement. That is why their journey is without the telos of getting out of this loop, effectively an empty set.

Mathematically speaking, we can present Penrose stairs through the following equation (Equation 9.1):

$$D\,(a,b) = a + b\phi; \quad \text{where } a, b \in \mathcal{Z}, \ \phi = \frac{\sqrt{5} - 1}{2}.$$

Equation 9.1: A. Connes, *Non-commutative Geometry*

The equation in Fig. 1 is Connes's dimensional function of the Penrose universe, something that Eliot anticipated in creating the space for the Hollow Men. For Eliot, a and b are the psychological contours of the Hollow Men. They are trapped in an infinite time of the Penrose universe. In their physical space, they may ascend or descend, but they come to the same point as the space has been reduced to an empty set.

The digits used are also significant. Number five invites us to the land of pentagram, where we have the fertility rituals. It is essential a feminine cycle of birth, menstruation, childbirth, menopause and death. Number one represents power, and the number two represents beauty. Now if we square root the essential fertility and subtract the power and divide the beauty, what we find is the infinity of the emptiness. This makes Prufrock say, 'In the room the women come and go/Talking of Michelangelo' signifying that the woman, like the room and the dead sculpture, are not actors but agencies that circulate their existence in the infinite loop by networking resources of culture and nature.

The archetypical example of A. Connes non-commutative geometry gives a mathematical perspective to the understanding of the space which Prufrock occupies; it is that of Penrose fractal tiling multiverse. This generic and fundamental example is fully described by the von Neumann-Connes dimensional function as explained lucidly in Connes seminal work on non-commutative geometry as well as in various other important variations given later on by a number of authors. This is not merely a mathematical paradigm but also can be seen in 'Four Quartrets', where it establishes Eliot's perception of infinite time and the topology of Penrose stairs:

Time present and time past
Are both perhaps present in time future
And time future contained time past.
If all time is eternally present
All Time is unredeemable. (Eliot, 1969, p. 171)

Penrose multiverse is a highly probable candidate for the true topological-geometrical and physical nature of reality, that is, the cosmos inhabited by Eliot's protagonists like Prufrock. To this end we present a possible simple proof based on a reformulation of von Neumann-Connes' dimensional function using the bijection formula of E-infinity Cantorian space-time theory in a fractal version of Kaluza-Klein five-dimensional (5D) manifold. In simple terms, we may write $D - 1 = N$ and then make an imaginative extrapolation to ask the following: What is the surface of a zero-dimensional, i.e., point? Proceeding inductively, it must be $D - 1 = 0 - 1$.

Therefore, the result is (-1), which is termed in topology the dimension of the neighbourhood of an abstract point and is commonly referred to as an 'empty set'. Two things come out of these simple but ingenious thoughts, which were introduced to mathematics independently by the Austrian-American mathematician Karl Menger and the distinguished Russian mathematician P. Urysohn, who tragically died at a very tender age, namely the zero set and the empty set. Thus, zero is clearly not empty. So neither Prufrock nor the Hollow Men exist not in zero but in the empty set where they are trapped. Zero would still mean that a journey to 1 is possible. But being in an empty set, they, like Dante's version of Lucifer (*Inferno*), can find no hope or solace. It is their hell and their fractal universe. Thus Eliot quotes from *Inferno*:

> S'io credesse che mia risposta fosse
> A persona che mai tornasse al mondo,
> Questa fiamma staria senza piu scosse.
> Ma percioche giammai di questo fondo
> Non torno vivo alcun, s'i'odo il vero,
> Senza tema d'infamia ti rispondo. (1969, p. 13)

So, thinning the space by (-1) to infinity is where the topology of Prufrock is. This topology is a variation of von Neumann-Connes to construct his Penrose universe in mathematical episteme. This universe of Penrose stairs is 'non-commutative' in terms of geometry, and it draws from the idea of the golden mean as well as Fibonacci properties. The topological exploration of Prufrock can be reconstructed using this theory of quantum field, and further explanation can be provided using the 'golden anyons theory' based on the spin of the anyons in Fibonacci construction. Mohamed S. El Naschie, in his essay 'Golden Anyons for Cosmic Dark

Energy Density' in the *World Journal of Condensed Matter Physics*, gives a detailed mathematical deduction of what was popularly known as the 'Penrose Fractal Universe' and which for me also aligns with Prufrock's universe of eternal time-loop. Where 'E(O) is the quantum particle ordinary energy' and E(D) is that of the quantum wave dark energy. Taking rational-integer approximation of the above identities, we find:

$$E^2/22 + 21/22^2 = \text{Einstein}$$

This result is in astounding agreement with accurate cosmic measurements and observations, which assert that E(O) is about 4.5% and E(D) is the 95.5% of the total expected energy. It is well known from topological quantum field theory and its relation to sub-factors that there is a dimensional function for an explicit situation called 4-D fusion algebra given by and . Now, not so incidentally, this 4-D function may be taken over to the 2-D anyon, where, as reasoned in the anionic theory, the vacuum is given by one while the anyon itself is given by " … It is not difficult to see the relation between anyon theory vacuum and our empty set on the one side and the anyons and our zero set on the other. They differ in magnitude but not in principle, while not forgetting for 1 minute that one is 4-D and the other is 2-D. Proceeding formally as in the previous section, we can calculate a volume analogous to that of equation, which turned out to be $5 + 5^2 = 2$ ('Golden Anyons for Cosmic Dark Energy Density' 158).

If infinity is mathematically symbolised as '∞' then we can say that the poem 'The Hollow Men' is a '∞ text'. In terms of quantum physics, the poem exhibits 'quantum entanglement' represented by '~9% [10]' and the different particles [in this case the different themes] are inseparable even when they are far apart. Eliot's intention is, therefore, not to create a telos-centric poem but rather to go on and build a circular movement of theme and structure where we enter into a cyclical entanglement. In the case of 'quantum entanglement', the probability of finding a point in the 'E infinity' space is f_3, the inverse of $4 + f_3$, the Hausdorff dimension of 'E-infinity' space-time. And we are in a similar dimension of 'E-infinity' space-time in the poem.

The quantum world is different from the large-scale world of our physical intuition, and thus the world of the Hollow Men is so distinct from real and yet unrepresentable in terms of words. It hints that the fundamental nature of reality may not be physical at all, and this is exactly what Eliot presents in poems where he follows the famous EPR (Einstein, Doris Podolsky and Nathan Rosen) model, which says in order to abandon the assumption of realism we had to abandon the concept of locality. Locality is the idea that each bit of the universe only acts on its immediate surroundings. The EPR paradox introduces the idea of quantum entanglement as pointed out in the book *Can Quantum-Mechanical Description of Physical Reality Be Considered Complete?* (Einstein, 1935, pp. 777–780). Here two particles interact briefly, like Eliot and Hamlet or the Hollow Men and Tiresias. They influence each other so that their properties are somehow connected, and yet we refrain from measuring these properties to preserve quantum uncertainty. Quantum mechanics requires that we describe the particle pair with a single combined wave function that encompasses all possible states of both particles. We call such particles an entangled pair. Here Eliot and Hamlet, Prufrock and Lazarus, Tiresias and Christ, Hollow Men and the shadow of humanism are the entangled pair.

In quantum mechanics, the measurement of one particle collapses the measurement of the other. When created spontaneously from photons, these particles will always be spinning in opposite directions to each other. Their wave functions are therefore entangled. So the function of Eliot spins in the opposite direction to that of the Hollow Men, but their wave functions become entangled as a philosophy of immaterialism and post-humanism. The measurement of the spin of one of these particles tells the measurement of the other, no matter the distance between them. In the case of quantum particles, measurement forces the alignment of the measured particle. The response of each particle to all possible spin measurements is encoded in each particle at the moment of their creation as a hidden variable local to each particle. Nothing we do to one particle will then affect the other. When we later measure the spins of both particles, there will be a correlation in the results because the particles were once connected. But there will be no correlation due to our choice of measurement axis. In a similar pattern, the narratives of intertexuality are the quantum particles, and the measurement or evaluation of the spin or tale forces the alignment of the narratorial voices, and the response of each narrator to all the possible meanings of his tale is encoded in the narrative at the moment of their birth or creation as hidden variables local to each narrator. Nothing we interpret from one narrative anyway affects the meaning of the other narratives. In fact, there is no correlation between our understanding or interpretation of the tale and the narrative itself. The narratives and the tales exist without any particular locality of meaning or centrality of thought. In this context, I find a parallel syndrome in Nabokov's *Pale Fire*, where within the foreword of Kinbote announces the poem 'Pale Fire' by Shade and tells us explicitly:

> Let me state that without my notes Shade's text simply has no human reality at all since the human reality of such a poem as his (being too skittish and reticent for an autobiographical work), with the omission of many pithy lines carelessly rejected by him, has to depend entirely on the reality of its author and his surroundings, attachments and so forth, a reality that only my notes can provide. To this statement my dear poet would probably not have subscribed, but, for better or worse, it is the commentator who has the last word. (Nabokov, 2011, p. 23).

The word 'reality' is spoken again and again only to suggest that it is the felicity of reality that Kinbote understands, and like the quantum world, it hints that the fundamental nature of reality may not be physical reality. In a very similar way, Eliot's physical reality is not the fundamental reality of the Hollow Men but a quantum space. The space-time relationship revealed through various narratives in the poems like 'The Waste Land' or 'Four Quartrets' is in a kind of quantum foam. Therefore, Eliot's poems have qualitative descriptions of subatomic space-time turbulence at extremely small distances. At such small scales of time and space, the uncertainty principle allows the energy of narration to briefly decay into particles and anti-particles of narrative logos, and then the structure of the plot is annihilated without violating physical conservation laws. As the scale of time and space being discussed shrinks, the energy of the virtual particles of narratives increases. According to Einstein's theory of general relativity, energy curves space-time. This suggests that – at sufficiently small scales – the energy of these fluctuations would be large enough to cause significant departures from the smooth space-time seen at larger scales, giving space-time a 'foamy' character. So the structure of Eliot's poems has a 'foamy' character, which in terms of quantum physics can be called a kind of quantum foam. Thus it becomes evident how Eliot, who belonged to a time and space of high modernist culture, has used his art to go beyond the structural archetype of modernism and push the boundaries, which, when looked at from the point of view of 2023, seems to capture both post-humanist ethics and digital post-humanism in his characters. The extreme classical and Renaissance ideals seem to be recreated in terms of time and space, and thus we are lifted from the stranglehold of definitions. It is the complexity of referentiality to digital humanism and the quantum in the context of Eliot that has triggered this research, and this chapter is a prelude to many more such future chapters.

Works Cited

An archive for preprints in philosophy of science. "The European Research Council 2023 Study on repositories compliant with the Open Science Horizon Europe Model Grant Agreement (MGA) found PhilSci-Archive a "trusted repository" meeting the MGA basic requirements." <https://philsci-archive.pitt.edu/>

Braidotti, R. *The Posthuman*. Polity Press. 2013.

Derrida, J. *Edmund Husserl's Origin of Geometry: An Introduction*. Translated, with a preface and afterword, by J. P. Leavey Jr., University of Nebraska Press. 1989.

Eliot, T. S. *The Complete Poems & Plays: T. S. Eliot*. Faber and Faber Limited and Bloomsbury House. 1969.

Einstein, A., Podolsky, B. and Rosen, N. *Can Quantum-Mechanical Description of Physical Reality Be Considered Complete?* Physical Review, 47, pp. 777–780, 1935.

Harman, G. *Object-Oriented Ontology: A New Theory of Everything*. Pelican Books and Penguin Random House. 2017.

Heidegger, M. *Being and Time*. Translated by J. Macquarrie and E. Robinson. S.C.M. Press. 1962.

———. (Ed.). "Language." In *Poetry, Language, Thought*. Translated by A. Hofstadter, pp. 185–208. Harper Perennial. 2001.

Nabokov, V. *Pale Fire*. Penguin Books, Penguin Modern Classics, 2011.

Rickert, T. *Ambient Rhetoric: The Attunements of Rhetorical Being*. University of Pittsburgh Press. 2013.

AISHWARYA DAS GUPTA

Death, Decay, and Regeneration: A Post-humanist Reading of "Good Hunting" from the Netflix Series *Love, Death & Robots (Volume 1)*

Before understanding the post-human, one must first attempt to formulate the definition or conception of the "human". What then is the "human"? According to Protagoras, Man is the measure of all things: Perception and truth are related to the experience and judgment of the individual. The human is thus represented by a white, able-bodied, rational, and masculine subject who is at the centre of the universe and is blessed with the limitless capacity for development. Thus, the subjectivity of the human is forged by the systematic silencing and othering of myriad other identities, who fail to fit into the watertight category of what is thought to constitute the ideal "human". Rosi Braidotti defines man as follows: "At the start of it all there is He: the Classical ideal of 'Man'... later renewed in Italian Renaissance as a universal model and represented in Leonardo da Vinci's *Vitruvian Man*. An ideal of bodily perfection which... doubles up as a set of mental, discursive and spiritual values" (Braidotti, 2013, p. 13).

The "human" thus signifies that which is not just different from but also superior to the non(/in)-human. The hierarchy formed by the Renaissance ideal of the human is based on the idea of self-fashioning, which entails the subjugation of the racial, sexual, natural, and technological others. However, in the present context, when the entire globe has been brought down to its knees by the unprecedented and unfathomable capacity of a microscopic virus coupled with the impending threat of global warming and the climatic crisis, it is high time to reconsider the relevance of the traditional definition of the "human". This may lead to the interrogation of the theory of the post-human, which critiques the exclusionary premise, which is the basis on which the idea of humanism functions. Post-humanism questions the legitimacy of the position of man as the centre of the universe and looks into the embodied and embedded experience of the racialized, gendered, and naturalized others who occupy a lesser position in the order of being. Furthermore, it is an attempt on the part of critical theory to do away with the ableist approach of traditional humanism to understand or somewhat make sense of the contemporary human condition where the autonomous, self-willed, divine figure of the "human" has been revealed to be thoroughly flawed and thus requires to be re-assessed, re-defined, and re-configured to accommodate the position of the same within an inclusive, inter-dependent, interconnected location enmeshed within the intersecting spatial coordinates of the biological world, the material environment, and the world of technology. The hierarchy between the human/ non(in)-humans is blurred, and the boundaries that define humanism are subverted to give way to a variety of new areas like animal studies, disability studies, cybernetics, etc.

My endeavour in this paper would be to interrogate the categories of the non(/in)-human and delve into the construction of alternative subjectivities through a post-humanist analysis of an episode from the popular Netflix series *Love, Death & Robots (Volume I)* (2019) (stylized as *Love, Death+Robots*). The series, comprising of 18 episodes, which was released on 19 March 2019, has been produced by Tim Miller, Joshua Donen, David Fincher, and Jennifer Miller. It is unique in that it features the endeavours of a variety of crews from across the globe. The episode that I have chosen for my analysis is titled "Good Hunting" (directed by Oliver Thomas, written by Philip Gelatt, and based on the story by Ken Liu). My efforts would be to explore how the aforementioned episode has adequately attempted to rupture the solid boundaries that separate the human from the non(/ in) human and how they make one rethink the conventional ideas about what it is to be human in the contemporary world. I intend to deal with the themes of transcorporeal subjectivity, the issue of monstrosity, and the discourse of difference on which the ideal of the "human" as separate and superior to the animal, the technological, and the earth's others is formed.

"Good Hunting" runs for 17 minutes, opening with the shot of a half-moon on a clear sky, and towards the end as well, there appears a similar shot of a half-moon, but this time, far removed in time and space, on the smoke and grime-filled sky of Hong Kong. The episode transversally cuts across the themes of the gendered identity of the female body, colonialism, the idea of the monstrous, and the issue of progress or development. It encourages the audience to radically rethink the concept of the "human" as a superior and supreme entity in the frame of existence.

Set in early twentieth-century colonial China, the work portrays how the land of magic and enchantment that was peopled by fantastic creatures slowly transformed into the jungle of steel, smoke, and asphalt, a world of "steampunk" with the advancement of technology, imported and assimilated by the British imperialists. The narrative begins with young Liang and his father trying to hunt a magical creature, a Huli Jing named Tsiao-Jung. There, Liang meets Tsiao-Jung's daughter, Yan, who tries to explain the plight of the Huli Jing. Liang's father warns his son from looking into the eyes of a Huli Jing, as the latter had the capacity to bewitch humans. Interestingly, Tsiao-Jung too warns Yan against speaking with humans and commands her to escape, but Liang's father kills Tsiao-Jung in front of them. Years later, Liang's father dies just before the advent of British colonialism and its mechanical development. Liang moves to Hong Kong, where he works as a train engineer, and one night he sees Yan, now permanently trapped in her human form because the colonialists have imported unprecedented mechanical development at the cost of violating and contaminating the world of nature, and this has robbed the magical creatures of their fantastic capacities as their power was drawn from the deep and unadulterated wells of nature. Liang masters the art of the colonialists, that is, robotic technology fuelled by steam power, and Yan comes to him seeking help. The Governor of Hong Kong had drugged her, and she was compelled to metamorphose into a cyborg sex toy. However, she eventually mauled him with lethal consequences. Liang creates a mechanical metal alloy body able to morph into a robotic Huli Jing. Parting as friends, Yan then hunts Englishmen who had been abusing women.

The narration begins from the perspective of Liang's father, who accuses and demonizes Tsiao-Jung for bewitching a man with her evil craft. They are waiting to hunt her and are sure of her arrival, as according to their preconceived notion, "A Huli-Jing cannot resist the cries of the man she has bewitched" ("Good Hunting" 2019, 01:01–01:03). A Huli-Jing is a mythical shape-shifter who can assume the form of a fox-like predator and transform into the shape of a disarmingly beautiful woman (the criteria that is enough to persecute anyone as an enchantress/the trope of the "femme fatale"). Her body, by virtue of its fluidity, challenges any proper definition in accordance with the laws of "human" reason, and this defiance leads her to be encoded as a threat, which results in her being conceived of as the embodiment of the monstrous. Renaissance humanism was considerably attentive to biological mutants and medical deviants. These distortions were deemed to be "monsters" because apparently they failed to fulfil the hard-set rules that made one eligible to become 'human': "…they were formed differently, behaved differently. "Universal" humanism was ironically, therefore, a system of differentiation in which some of the bodies were treated as "human" and others as "not-human"" (Nayar, 2013, p. 23).

However, the preconceived notions of young Liang and the audience are jarred when the former encounters Yan, the cub of Tsiao-Jung. The ensuing conversation between Yan and Liang is worth noting:

YAN: Why are you hunting us? We did nothing to you.
LIANG: Your mother bewitched the merchant's son. We were hired to save him.
YAN: Bewitched? He's the one who wouldn't leave her alone.
LIANG: That's not true.
YAN: Once a man has set his heart on a Huli-Jing, she can hear him… she has to go to him every night just to keep him quiet.
LIANG: No, she lures men and feeds on them for her evil magic.
YAN: A man can fall in love with a Huli-Jing just like he can with a human woman. ("Good Hunting", 2019, 04:31–05:07)

Philosophies challenging the ideals of humanism have stated that it is human cognition of what the animal is that counts. Monsters, according to Patricia MacCormack, have always been objectified and are never regarded as subjects unto themselves. Donna McCormack states in her article titled "The Monstrous and Critical Posthumanism": "The monster is that which is not the normative human: that which is rejected from the norm in often indefinable and fluctuating forms given shape through racism, ableism, sexism, transphobia, homophobia, classism, and other hierarchical vectors of power" (McCormack, 2022, p. 254).

Human beings are wary of confronting a situation where the non(/in) human individual might know the former in ways they do not comprehend. The arrogance of humanity has restricted itself from assessing its worth on an equal plane with that which it perceives as its other. The "universal" category of the human is thus deeply problematic as it involves the forced subordination, indoctrination, persecution, incarceration, and some other forms of otherization of many marginal existences. Human history has always regarded homosexuals, individuals characterized by different physiognomies, people suffering from mental health disorders (dubbed "lunatics"), slaves, women, Jews, non-European races, and terminally ill people as being outside the category of the "human", just as animal life is deemed less important than human life.

The discourses of the monstrous in popular culture revolve around what Jerome Cohen calls figures of "ontological liminality" (Cohen, 1996, p. 6). This ontological liminality can be witnessed in Shakespeare's portrayal of Caliban in *The Tempest*, where Trinculo describes him as a creature "legg'd like a man! And his fins like arms" (2014, II 32). This is in consonance with the popular travel magazines in circulation during Shakespeare's time where the racial others were described in such terms. John Mendeville's fictitious travel writings depict such beast-men who were believed to have the heads of dogs, one eye, and other aberrated/different physiognomies. The Aboriginals in Australia and the New World were conveniently tagged as "savages" who failed to fit into the category of the "human" by the European explorers. Such representation aided in legitimizing the civilizing mission, which entailed the forceful grabbing of the others' land and drowning them in the flood of cultural amnesia. In the twentieth century, the sustained depiction of the Jews as vermin or rodents, and by extension, an inferior existence, in the Nazi state is what ultimately legitimized their neutralization. In contemporary times, the refugees, the migrant workers, marginalized communities, and the minorities are represented as subhuman to be subsumed under the category of the "monster" and to be regarded as a threat, which might adversely affect the health of the corpus of the dominant hegemonic discourse, namely the idea of the heteronormative, able-bodied man who fits into the markers prescribed by the Renaissance ideal of the human. Thus, the ontological liminality of the monster justifies its insubordination, incarceration, and neutralization.

According to Cohen:

> "[the] refusal to participate in the classificatory "order of things" is true of monsters generally: they are disturbing hybrids whose externally incoherent bodies resist attempts to include them in any systematic structuration. And so the monster is dangerous, a form suspended between forms that threatens to smash distinctions" (1996, p.6).

Monster theory thus portrays the speciousness of the species borders, which prohibits the intermingling between the human and the so-called other inferior species. Thus, Liang is shocked and would prefer to be in denial rather than accept the fact that it is possible for a man to fall in love with a Huli-Jing just like any other woman. Liang's father, the spirit hunter, is described as "one of the brave men who would protect humanity against spirits that would harm it" ("Good Hunting", 2019, 01:06–01:12). He warns Liang against looking at the Huli-Jing, fearing that the creature may enchant and transfix him. The protector of humanity has been entrusted with the sacred responsibility of exterminating all the brutes who may threaten to undermine the purity of the human. The act of looking and the prohibition of looking at someone or something might be interesting in this context. When we look at anything, we recognize it, acknowledge its existence, and try to understand it; therefore, it may be asserted that looking is the first act of forging a relationship of recognition, and once anything has been recognized, it ceases to be strange or exotic, and becomes familiar. Familiarity, by extension, paves the way for fondness, which creates affection, thereby bolstering mutual trust and camaraderie. What the spirit hunter dubs as transfixion as a result of evil magic might be actually an expression of awe on recognizing that the other is not so much different from the self – that the human may share some qualities with the monster, that the human may after all be the monster. Perhaps this unconscious recognition armed Liang with the strength to understand and save Yan from his father. It had also inspired him to abandon his father's ideologies in favour of an eco-sophical existence where it was not wrong to forge a friendship with the monstrous other. It is interesting to note that the friendship worked both ways, whereby Yan was also ready to forget and forego the past where the humans had persecuted their kind mercilessly. They realized the subtle line dividing, blurring, and crossing over between the hunter and the hunted.

The narrative's remarkable turn into the steampunk world has been brilliantly portrayed by the entry of a steam engine roaring through the green countryside and bringing with it the world of capitalism, imperial exploration, and exploitation. The European Enlightenment's preoccupation with the instrumentalist view of nature stressed that human(/ity) was entitled to treat nature as an object that existed for their entertainment, luxury, and gratification. The non(/in)-human world did not have any significance apart from that of being a source for material progress and consequent prosperity. The colonial project, coupled with the forces of capitalism, has allowed man boundless freedom to treat nature and the natural resources as the site of exploration for personal profit and indefinite progress. Humanism perpetually shared a connection with Europe's imperial destinies of exclusion, exploitation, and conquest. With the arrival of mechanical development, nature lost its magic. A conversation between Yan and Liang throws light on this issue:

LIANG: How is hunting?
YAN: Worse this year than the last. It's getting harder and harder for me to return to my true form. Some nights I can't do it at all.
LIANG: What's causing it?
YAN: Iron roads and machines that breathe smoke. Magic is draining from the world and with it, we magical creatures grow ever weaker. ("Good Hunting", 2019, 6:41–7:03)

The worldview that equated mastery with rational scientific control over "others" also militated against respect for the diversity of living matters and diverse cultures. This is brilliantly reflected in the frames that compose the series, where the native inhabitants are constantly reminded of their inferior status by the colonizers. In one segment, when Liang succeeds in tinkering with a machine to make it work, his white employer patronizes him by appreciating in terms that are significant in their overtly racist connotations. He is too clever for a Chineseman to say he, as if the cerebral faculties are a given only of a particular racial category, who might be dubbed the human (which entails the successful marginalization of every other identity as sub-human). The process of othering is an integral part of the project of colonization. Elleke Boehmer states in her seminal text *Colonial and Postcolonial Literature*:

> The colonized made the subordinate term in relation to which European individuality was defined. Always with reference to the superiority of an expanding Europe, colonized peoples were represented as lesser: less human, less civilized, as child or savage, wild man, animal, or headless mass (Boehmer, 2005, pp. 75–76).

With time, Liang shifts to Hong Kong, and Yan is left to fend for herself and do what she can to survive. The European colonizers replaced the magical world of nature with their technologically developed and artificially manipulated world. Five years later, Liang asserts that he "knew the grinding of the levers and the rumbling of the pistons as well as my own heartbeat" ("Good Hunting", 2019, 07:56–08:02). This is the beginning of Liang's identification and understanding of the unknown world of technologically driven subjects.

Liang happens to come across and rescue Yan (who has also migrated to the city of Hong Kong) from a helpless situation where she was being pestered for providing sexual services to a group of middle-aged English men. The conversation that ensues echoes an earlier one and is significant on many levels:

LIANG: How is hunting?
YAN: I'm stuck now in this human form: no claws, no sharp teeth, I can't even run very fast. All I have is my beauty. Now I live by the very thing you accused my mother of: I bewitch men for money. And you?
LIANG: I also serve our English masters, I keep their precious trains running…
YAN: I dream of hunting in this jungle of metal and asphalt. I dream my true form jumping from beam to ledge to terrace roof until I'm at the top of this island. Until I can growl at the faces of all the men who think they can own me. ("Good Hunting", 2019, 09:05–09:55)

In this context, it is interesting to note that the scene opens with the chiming of the grandfather clock, which looms large upon the atmosphere, asserting its all-pervading sound imposing itself upon the various variables at play. Clocks symbolize time, one of the most important prescriptive tools of modernity and extremely vital in the context of the industrial capitalist colonial discourse. The chimes of the clock perhaps spell out the very physical embodiment of that which has ousted and exorcized the spiritual and magical elements from the given spatio-temporal location. Yan's entrapment in the human form is consequent of the disease plaguing nature in the form of the industrial revolution propelled by the glorious and revolutionary steam power that had banished magic from the natural world, polluting the rivers, choking the air, and contaminating the soil. Commenting on the imperial connotation of clock time in his remarkable article titled ""The Shortcomings of Timetables": Greenwich, Modernism, and the Limits of Modernity", Adam Barrows writes:

> A concern with time is intrinsic to the internal logic of modernity … Radically breaking with the authority and legitimacy of the past, modernity offers a totalizing vision of progress toward an illimitable future. Its universal narrative of global development presupposes a uniform scale of spatial and temporal measurement (Barrows, 2010, p. 263).

Peter Galison writes in *Einstein's Clocks, Poincaré's Maps: Empires of Time,* that the synchronization of international time was "never just about a little procedure of signal exchange," but was driven by "national ambitions, war, industry, science, and conquest" (Galison, 2004, p. 38). The chronotopic perspective of clock time represented by the Greenwich Mean Time (GMT) and the spatial mapping homogeneously distributing and demarcating space into smaller, conquerable, finite territories that can be tamed, utilized, exploited, and rendered redundant at will is one of the most remarkable and innovative endeavours embarked upon by the glorious project of European imperialism. The momentous appearance of the grandfather clock looming large upon the scene, pervading and intruding upon the exchange of dialogues between Liang and Yan thus signifies on several levels. It represents the all-encompassing might of the developmental project of the colonizer that has skewed and altered the very way of life that the natives found familiar. It is the power of technology, the harbinger of alternative magic, which was on the verge of altering and replacing every remnant of the former mystical magic of yore.

Over the years, the technology in the city evolved to Liang's great excitement. And as it changed, Liang evolved with it. "Liang: I found that I understand automata even better than I understood trains. These machines were otherworldly… and alive. They felt akin to magic" ("Good Hunting", 2019, 10:28–10:34).

When Liang identifies with the mechanical subjects, renders autonomy to the automata by equating himself with that which he seeks to create, and asserts that he is co-evolving with the technology, he is drawing attention to and challenging the boundaries that frame the formation of human subjectivity and dismantles the hierarchy that deifies the "human" at the cost of marginalizing everything else and subsuming them under the category of the subhuman. The equation of power shared between Liang and the machines is based on equity and equality instead of brute control, manipulation, or forced subjugation.

Subsequently, Yan enters the scene and asks for a favour from Liang. The Governor of Hong Kong had drugged her and transformed her into a cyborg for sexual gratification, but she eventually did the unthinkable and brutally mauled him. She knows the metamorphosis into a machine would be irreversible, yet expresses her wish "to hunt":

> YAN: What I want is to hunt. Hunt the men who think they can own us. The men who perpetrate evil but call it progress.
>
> LIANG: The old magic may have been gone from the world, but I could make a new magic from their machines. A magic we could use against them. ("Good Hunting", 2019, 13:02–13:28)

This is the point where there is a paradigmatic shift between the lines that demarcate the powerful and the powerless, and the equation of power is toppled. The colonizer's technology has now become an instrument of empowerment for the colonized, in whose hands it achieves the transformative (and somewhat redemptive) power of the new magic. The white man has brought about technological innovations for the ulterior motive of satisfying their vested interest, which was to extract free labour from the technologically mediated identities. Mechanical labour was abundantly available to be utilized and capitalized upon by the colonizer. The series portrays various kinds of machines populating its steampunk world. Every mechanical object created by the colonizer was designed for the purpose of being useful to them; for instance, the innovative mechanical cobblers, the strangely unique robots used for transportation purposes, etc. Every nut, bolt, piston, and lever created objects, which were bereft of the assignment of subjecthood to them. However, Liang's creation was markedly different. He observed various animals, like cats, rabbits, etc., to give shape to the same through the acquired technological skill adopted from the colonial masters. The morphed entity had a subjecthood of its own and was not created to serve any purpose or be of "use" in the utilitarian sense of the term. They existed as independent entities and had a life of their own, not to satisfy a set purposeful utility because Liang, unlike the colonizers, felt the very pulse of the machine.

The colonizer ceaselessly attempted to tame nature, marginalize what he considered to be the sub(/in/non)human other continuously, and in doing so assert his relative superiority in the order of being. This obsessive predisposition of taming the other and the consequent sense of superiority acquired through the process ensued in the experience of a sadistic pleasure. This is reflected in the Governor of Hong Kong's act of transforming Yan into a mechanical sex toy without her consent (an act committed to gratify his sexual appetite as he could only be aroused by machines). The howl which Yan takes recourse to when language fails her when in search of an avenue of her grief and wild pain is connotative of her resolve to reject the order of things that have taken away everything that she held dear in her life. The scene furthermore compels the viewer to weigh over the definition of the "monster" and re-evaluate the implications of the "monstrous". In the preface to Fanon's *The Wretched of the Earth*, Jean-Paul Sartre notes the former's critical take on the notion of "humanism" when he observes "there is nothing more consistent than a racist humanism since the European has only been able to become a man through creating slaves and monsters" (Fanon, 2004, p. 63). Fanon observes that the colonizer who demands and claims humanity as his sole right and characteristic is revealed to be someone who is an abuser engaging in genocide, extracting land and cheap labour, etc. Thus, the idea of the "human" is not something that the native would want to look up to. Commenting on Fanon's ideas on humanism, Donna McCormack states that Fanon questions thinking on the "dichotomies of human/monster and human/colonized, refusing to accept this framework as the only possible mode of existing" (McCormack, 2022, p. 259). She ponders over the question of who are the real monsters in a settler colonial context – whether the ones "deemed monstrously inferior because supposedly uncivilized in the logic of power, or those who massacre, occupy land and destroy systems of knowledge, kin, and belonging" (p. 259).

Keeping it in mind, one cannot help but argue with the possibility suggested by McCormack when she asserts that there needs to be a cohabitation:

> Monsters in critical posthumanism capture atrocities, violence, and injustice, as well as demanding revenge as a form of unstately, uncivil, and uncomfortable justice. If change is demanded, then we must live with the monster, not as our friend but as that which requires us to fight for, have pleasure in, and support a more monstrous world of living together with in/a/non/human beings. (p. 270)

This seems to be in consonance with the camaraderie between Yan and Liang. Each strives to fight against perceived injustice in their own way and to chart out a path towards a "more monstrous" and livable world.

Michel Foucault observes humanist philosophy as an instrument through which powerful groups were able to discipline, manipulate, and control individuals or other groups. Humanism was thus connected to the practices of treatment, administration, surveillance, and regulation of individual and collective bodies. Governments, having acquired knowledge about the individual or group, could, Foucault writes, "expose, mark, wound, amputate, make a scar … in short, seize hold of the body and inscribe upon it the marks of power" (Foucault, 1997, p. 24). The embodied experience of a subject was subject to technologies of power acting upon the body or the mind. This was evident when Yan's mother was branded as a threat and her head was chopped off and is again evident when the body of a magical creature stuck in the human form was then transmuted into the form of a cyborg sex toy. However, the transcorporeal experience of the embodied subject reaches new heights when Liang aids in the formation of the steam-powered-coal consuming cyborg that can morph into a predator. Thus, she becomes a new magical creature, a new hunter, a mechanical Huli-Jing. The body where she was trapped now becomes her war vehicle as she jumps from "ledge to terrace roof" ("Good Hunting", 2019, 09:07–09:09) until she roars at the face of the men who think they can own others.

Katherine Hayles asserted, "[The posthuman] implies not only a coupling with intelligent machines but a coupling so intense and multifaceted that it is no longer possible to distinguish meaningfully between the biological organism and the informational circuits in which the organism is enmeshed" (Hayles, 1999, p. 35). Technology has become assimilated into the organic being, and it is no longer possible to demarcate the borders between the human and non(/in)-human, just as it is impossible to define the human. This fluidity of the boundaries is the boon of post-humanist thought, and this is perhaps the beginning of a new ethical and philosophical stance where the unquestioned superiority of the human status is being challenged. This is the incipient ideology that attempts to take away the monstrosity of the monster and throw light on the human as a highly abused term and expose humanity, as that, in the name of which, and to uphold the sanctity of which, countless "inhumane" crimes have been perpetrated.

"Good Hunting" flawlessly brings forth the issues that pinpoint the flaws of technological development and dissolves the boundaries between the various categories of embodied existences by subverting the conventional equations of power and exposing the perspectives of the others by reclaiming their unheard voices and giving them agency and authority to act upon and transform their destinies (even if that means by subscribing to a transcorporeal existence by taking aid from that which is one's greatest weakness). The episode shows the immense capacity of evolution of not just of the "human" but every form of material object in the created universe, thereby properly universalizing the experience of being, an experience that transversally cuts across the boundaries of race, culture, gender, species, and technology.

Works Cited

Barrows, A. ' "The Shortcomings of Timetables": Greenwich, Modernism, and the Limits of Modernity.' *MFS Modern Fiction Studies* 56(2), 2010, pp. 262–289.

Boehmer, E. *Colonialism & Postcolonialism.* Oxford University Press, 2005.

Braidotti, R. *Posthumanism.* Cambridge and Malden: Polity, 2013.

Cohen, J. J. "Monster Culture (Seven Thesis)". *Monster Theory: Reading Culture.* Minneapolis and London: University of Minnesota Press, 1996.

Fanon, F. *The Wretched of the Earth.* Translated by R. Philcox. New York: Grove Press, 2004.

Foucault, M. Ethics: Subjectivity and Truth. In P. Rabinow and J. D. Faubion (Eds.). Translated by R. Hurley, *The Essential Works of Michel Foucault 1954–1984,* Vol. I. New Press, 1997.

Galison, P. *Einstein's Clocks and Poincaré's Maps: Empires of Time.* WW Norton & Company, 2004.

"Good Hunting". *Love, Death & Robots (Volume I).* Directed by Oliver Thomas. Produced by Tim Miller, Joshua Donen, David Fincher, and Jennifer Miller. 2019.

Hayles, N. K. *How We Became Posthuman: Virtual Bodies in Cybernetics, Literature, and Informatics.* University of Chicago Press, 1999.

McCormack, D. "The Monstrous and Critical Posthumanism." In S. Herbrechter, I. Callus, M. Rossini, M. Grech, M. de Bruin-Molé and C. J. Müller (Eds.), *Palgrave Handbook of Critical Posthumanism,* pp. 249–274. Springer International Publishing, 2022.

Nayar, P. K. *Posthumanism.* Cambridge and Malden: Polity, 2013.

Shakespeare, W. *Arden Shakespeare Complete Works.* Bloomsbury Publishing, 2014.

SWAPNA ROY

More than (Biogenetic) Food: Re-questioning the Inevitability of GMOs in Paolo Bacigalupi's *The Calorie Man* and *The Windup Girl*

> And God blessed them, and God said unto them, Be fruitful
> and multiply; and replenish the earth and subdue it; and
> have dominion over the fish of the sea, and over the fowl of
> the air, and over every living thing that moveth upon the earth.
>
> —*The Holy Bible*[1].

French anthropologist Claude Lévi-Strauss, in his epoch-making book *The Raw and the Cooked* (1996), articulated how the concept of "raw" versus "cooked" had been associated with the dichotomy between the natural world and the world of human culture. Symbolically, cooking marks the transition from nature to culture; in mythology, we have seen how cooking mediates from nature to society, between life and death, and between heaven and earth. But what if we no longer need to cook anymore? In "Toward a Psychosociology of Contemporary Food Consumption,"[2] Roland Barthes discussed that the notion of food in our collective imagination encompasses a specific mental framework. He wrote, "For what is food? It is not only a collection of products that can be used for statistical or nutritional studies. It is also, and at the same time, a system of communication, a body of images, a protocol of usages, situations, and behaviour" (Counihan and Esterik, 2019, p. 23). Food is a source of energy; at the same time, the struggle for food itself stands as a metaphor in the dominant discourse of power politics from the Cave Age to the present

---

1 New King James Version, *The Holy Bible* (1:23).
2 This essay was originally published in 1961.

Anthropocene and later will be on. At the same time, food is a clear lens on capital, labor, health, and the environment. To quote Barthes

> No, doubt, food is, anthropologically speaking (though very much in the abstract), the first need: but ever since man has ceased living off wild berries, this need has been highly structured. Substances, techniques of preparation, and habits all become part of a system of difference in signification, and as soon as it happens, we have communication by way of food (2013, p. 3).

Food in any habitat metaphorically represents many things, such as dreams, social categories, hierarchy, and cultural consumption in this post-truth era. The interpreted cultural logic of food capitalism (food habits and dietary strategies) serves the new imperatives of economic, ecological, and nutritional ends. The production of customized dietary content (ready-to-eat) raises many ethical questions about the materialist frameworks of posthumanism. In this 21st century, genetically modified food accelerates the powers of mega-corporations such as Bayer, BASF, Dow AgroSciences, DuPont, Monsanto, and Syngenta, who are selling agricultural products to farmers worldwide, including GMO (genetically modified organism) crops. Both the fields of biotechnology and nano-technology[3] have challenged the "natural" production of food. Food in this post-human era stands as "biocapital," as Mark Fisher called it in his book *Capitalist Realism: Is There No Alternative?* (2009). Francis Fukuyama, in *Our Posthuman Future: Consequences of the Biotechnology Revolution* (2000), wrote, "Human biotechnology differs subsequently from agricultural biotechnology insofar as it raises that are not an issue for GMO" (2017, p. 213).

American science fiction writer Paolo Tadini Bacigalupi's debut novel *The Windup Girl* (2009), the Hugo and Nebula "Best Novel" award winner, was named "Best Science Fiction Book of 2009" by the American Library Association and was a *Time Magazine* "Top Ten Book of 2009." *The Windup Girl* and *The Calorie Man* (2005) questioned whether technology could heal our unsustainable metabolism. They highlight the destruction of Earth's web of life through the consumption of GMO food. The novel explores the power structures of the food market in Thailand, where fictional

---

3   On nanotechnology and science fiction, see Colin Milburn's *Nanovision* (2010).

mega-corporations like AgriGen, PurCal, and RedStar control the food market through the production of "gene-hacked" seeds. This is another form of bioterrorism—exploitations of living organisms have been made through the politics of biogenetic food—food in this post-human world becomes a new weapon. Therefore, this paper explores the paradigm shift of genetically engineered food in the genre of biopunk literature by highlighting the relationality of GMO food and the social food system represented in Bacigalupii's world.

To understand what impacts GMOs may have on this planet, we first need to know what GMO foods are and what they encompass in the food systems. Salah E. O. Mahgoub, a certified food scientist, and Leo M. L. Nollet, in their book *Testing and Analysis of GMO-containing Foods and Feed* (2019), gave multiple definitions of GMO food: "According to the World Health Organization (WHO, 2014), GMOs can be defined as 'organisms in which the genetic material (DNA) has been altered in a way that does not occur naturally' " (p. 4). Again, what the "Health and Safety Executive" website (2017) defines as GMOs is quoting worthwhile here:

> [...] as organisms whose genes have been artificially altered to modify their characteristics in some way or another. It elaborates on the process of GM, stating that it is the process of altering the genetic material of an organism by using a method that does not occur in nature. Often GM involves isolating and removing the DNA encoding a single gene from one organism, manipulating it outside the cell (in a laboratory) and reinserting it into the same organism or the genetic material of another organism. The aim of GM is often to introduce a new or altered characteristic to the target organism. (p. 4)

GMO food plays a notable role in the whole food system. Professors Lawrence and Roni Neff from Johns Hopkins University defined the food system as "encompassing all the activities and resources that go into producing, distributing, and consuming food: the drivers and outcomes of those processes; and all the relationships and feedback loops between system components." All those components of a food system include "land-based parts (e.g., agriculture, farmland, preservation), environment (e.g., water, soil, energy), economy (e.g., distribution, processing, retail), education policy, social justice, health and food cultures." Gabriela Steier, in her book *Advance Food Integrity: GMO Regulation, Agroecology, and Urban*

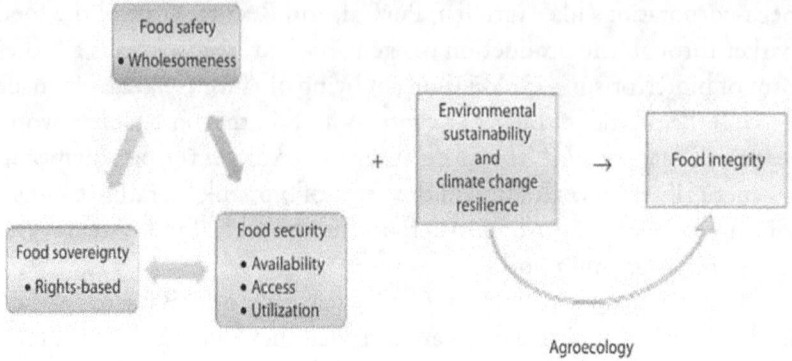

Figure 11.1: Food Integrity

Agriculture (2017), made a relational figure of the food system (2017, p. 8) (Figure 1).

Most of the time, because of the privatization and trade policies, food safety, food sovereignty, and food security fall prey to economic drivers. Over time, the presence of food has been marginalized, isolating people from the source of the food they consume. The marketing strategy hides the catastrophe and highlights the fantasy structure on which "capitalism realism" depends (Fisher, 2009, p. 18)[4]. The ecological conundrums are expressed in *The Windup Girl* in this way, while Gibbons, the scientist at the heart of the Thai seed bank, comments:

> We have only accelerated the phenomenon. The food web you talk about is nostalgia, nothing more. Nature … We are nature. Our every tinkering is nature, our very biological striving. We are what we are, and the world is ours. We are its gods. (2015, p,243)

---

4 The term "capitalism realizm" was used for the first time by a group of German pop artists in the 1960s and by Michael Schudson in his book *Advertising, The Uneasy Persuasion* (1984). Borrowing the Lacanian idea of the "real," Mark Fisher proposed how the "real" is associated with repression. For the GMO food market, we have seen how the mega-corporations project that they can solve any problem. Fisher relies heavily on Alenka Zupanic; she writes about how the reality principle itself is mediated and the ideology is also presenting the empirical facts itself.

Seeking the answers to several thought-provoking questions takes work. Who decides and gets the benefits? Who has the burden of proof? Who has the right to know and when? How can precautionary principles be put into practice? What are the yardsticks and mandatory corporate disclosures by which various industry actions are to be judged? Finally, what are the standards of failure for the GMO industry? The predominant threat is to harm the human cell directly; it can cause the development of diseases immune to antibiotics. In addition, the cross-pollination method of transferring animal genes into plants and vice versa can cause damage to other organisms that thrive in the environment. Also, there are two issues from an allergic standpoint. Creation of a neo-allergen where de novo sensitization occurs in the population and the transfer of a known allergen that may arise from a crop into a non-allergenic target crop. It took many years to understand what is going on with GMO food "[...], but we are now being asked to believe that everything is OK with GM foods because we haven't seen any dead bodies yet" (Butler and Reinchhardt, 1999). Joel K. Bourne Jr., in the essay, "The Global Crisis: The End of Plenty," published in the National Geographic Magazine (2009), wrote about the food crisis in 2005 that swept the world as the actual backdrop of the story. Quoting here from the essay:

> From 2005–2007, a series of major food shortages-caused both by crop blight and poor climate conditions for harvest- spread across the world and resulted in riots in Egypt, Haiti, Mozambique, Bangladesh and elsewhere. Between 2005 and the summer of 2008, the price of wheat and corn tripled, and the price of rice climbed fivefold, spurring food riots in nearly two dozen countries and pushing 75 million more people into poverty. (p. 9)

By destroying natural fertility, "capitalist agriculture" shifts its business to GMO seeds. Nevertheless, the real irony is what was described by Karl Marx in his *Capital* (1867) in response to the aggressive policies: All progress in capitalist agriculture is progress in the art, not only of robbing the worker but of robbing the soil; all progress in increasing the fertility of the soil for a given time is progress towards running the more long-lasting sources of that fertility (p. 639). In this context, having an understanding of the relationship between production, detection, labeling, and traceability of GMOs is essential. Based on Marx's "metabolic rift," James O'Connor, in his *Natural Causes: Essays in Ecological Marxism* (2011), explains the two contradictions embedded in the capitalist systems:

> […] the first contradiction is between the forces of production and the relations of production[…] and a second contradiction is between the forces and relations of production taken as a whole and the ecosystem, which leads capital to destroy the ecology and producing the second contradiction of capitalism. (p. 103)

The GM seed business is seen as what Eco-Marxists call "the second capitalized nature." Manipulation of GM seeds and the creation of new unnatural genetic crops intervene in the natural processes of evolution. Production of sterile seeds and controlling the market is nothing new in this business. How food turns up like a bio-weapon[5]—the source of power and authority in the dystopian future of *The Windup Girl* fascinates the reader[6]. To quote from the novel:

> Processes like hybridization are the technological means that stop the seed from reproducing itself. This provides capital with an eminently effective way of circumventing natural constraints on the commodification of the seed. Hybrid varieties do not produce true-to-type seed, and farmers must return to the breeder each year new seed stock. (quoted in Shiva 2016, p. 49)

The real threat is who will have the patent of these seeds[7]—a debate rarely discussed in literary works (borrowing Hageman's idea here, p. 285). Ethics are entirely negated in the capitalist system. Calorie companies know GM plants need time to adjust with nature, hence producing sterile seeds and intentionally unleashing different waves of disease to the farms that violate patent rights are effective policies for a lifetime of domination in the market, which are visible in Bacigalupi's novel *The Windup Girl:*

5 Vandana Shiva's book *Biopiracy: The Plunder of Nature and Knowledge* (2016).
6 There is a provocative piece on agri-corporate history focusing on genetic modification and the role of seed banks in the US invasions of Afghanistan and Iraq in Seabrook's "Sowing for Apocalypse: The Quest for a Global Seed Bank."
7 Margarida Meneds saw this as "molecular colonialism." For her, these modes of production take up methods of monoculture production that began in the colonial regime and saw their growth intensify with the industrial revolution, in what was a planetary agroecological turn with a major impact.

"—Agrigen and *PurCal* and the rest were shipping their plague-resistant seed and demanding exorbitant profits (2015, p. 125)" —a post-expansion world revealing the global agricultural catastrophe. Thailand is one of the few nation-states still having its own seed banks and is immune mainly due to the policies of the global embargo. The similar tone we get in *The Calorie Man*, where Lalji, an Indian resident of the United States, is roped into a scheme by his friend Shriam to smuggle a rogue geneticist down the Mississippi River. Explicitly reveals the market economy directly linked to the seeds through the procedures of patenting and sterilization of the seeds; only the calorie companies like Soypro or U-Tex in the text can grow the plants, not the farmers. Moreover, the country's loss of diverse crops directly harms biodiversity; GM plants are a by-product of this catastrophe. In *The Windup Girl*, Jadiee, a zealous enforcer of the Environment Ministry's policies, wonders about the future generation:

> Will Niwat and Surat's great-grandchildren know that there were other fig trees, also all gone? Will they know that there were many many trees and that they were of many types? […] Will they understand that we were not fast enough or smart enough to save them all? That we had to make choices? (Bacigalupi, 2015, p. 173)

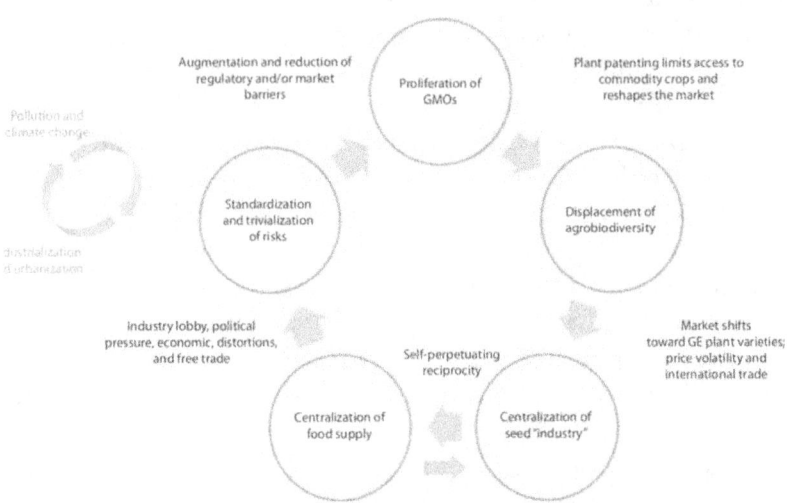

Figure 11.2: The Linking Cycle

To survive, we need a diverse range of seeds. Gene modification is directly linked to eco-disaster. Mark Fisher, in his epoch-making book *Capitalist Realism: Is There No Alternative*, poignantly pointed out that "the relationship between capitalism and eco-disaster is neither coincidental nor accidental: capital's 'need of a constantly expanding market', its 'growth fetish', mean that capitalism is by its very nature opposed to any notion of sustainability"(2009, p. 19). It appears that this newly built business ontology obtains the degree of emancipatory politics by destroying the "natural order" and creating artificial market hype. This post-industrial market economy is dangerous as it forces us to believe that the market economy will solve every problem. In Fisher's words:

> Climate change and the threat of resource-depletion are not being repressed so much as incorporated into advertising and marketing. What this treatment of environmental catastrophe illustrates is the fantasy structure on which capitalist realism depends: a presupposition that resources are infinite, that the earth itself is merely a husk which capital can, at a certain point slough off like a used skin, and that any problem can be solved by the market. (2009, p. 19)

Gabriela Steier, in her book *Advance Food Integrity: GMO Regulation, Agroecology, and Urban Agriculture* (2018), draws a figure by linking GMOs, urban agriculture, and climate change (Figure 1).

Figure 1 explicitly portrays the proliferation of GMOs on one side and how plant patenting limits farmers' access to the original seeds. Putting barriers on seed preservations with just a few staple GMO commodity crops disrupts agrobiodiversity. In addition, the highly rising GMO market creates powers that lead to price volatility and control international food trade. In a recent special section of *Nature*, it has been highlighted that the new wave of GMO food and the increasing market demand for affordable foods, such as rice and bananas, in the developing world[8].

Bringing a textual example from *The Windup Girl* is very supportive of my counterargument. The story is set in Bangkok in the distant future. The people no longer eat regular food; they eat "joules." The food market is full

---

8 Insect-resistant and herbicide-tolerant crops are nothing new in the GMO food market. See Cressey and "Plant Biotechnology: A Tarnished Promise," both part of a 2013 issue of *Nature* devoted to GMOs.

of new kinds of GMO fruits. In the opening scene, we see that Anderson Lake observes a new type of fruit:

> The fruit's long hairs tickle his palm [and the vendor's] brown thumb easily tears away the hairy rind, revealing a pale core. Transculent and veinous, it resembles … the pickled onions served in martinis … Anderson sniffs tentatively. Inhales, floral syrup. [It's called] Ngaw. It shouldn't exist. Yesterday, it didn't. (Bacigalupi, 2015, p. 2)

Society is full of gene-rippers, geneticists, and intellectual property (IP) men[9]. Generipper is a calorie man; geneticists change the DNA of the food; they give GMO food to Megatons[10], and IP man keeps the data of the seeds because keeping unpatented seeds is a crime and a dangerous threat to civilization. Bacigalupi writes:

> Unstamped calories mean starving families. We check royalty receipts and IP stamps." A farmer and his brood stared hollow-eyed from beneath the scolding words. PurCal was the sponsor. The other poster was AgriGen's trademark collage of kink-spring. Green rows of SoyPRo under sunlight and smiling children, along with the word "We Provide Energy for the World."(2015, p. 2)

Henceforth, GMOs also define the class structure! Genetic mutation is also found in the animal world. "Priti and Bidi" are two "massive creatures barely resembled the elephants that had once provided their template DNA, Generippers had honed them to a perfect balance of musculature and hunger for a single purpose: to inhale calories and do terrible labors without complaint" (Bacigalupi, 2015, p. 10). Farmers can no longer grow crops on their own. Mega corporations like SoyPro, HiGro, AgriGen, Midwest Growers Group, and PurCal brought all the fields from the people—"the very cradle of civilizations, yes?" (11). *The Windup Girl, The Calorie Man,* and Ruth Ozeki's novel *All Over Creation* (2003) all have a common theme. In Ozekie's novel, we see the Cynaco corporation, which introduced GM potatoes into an Idhao farming community, such as a plant whose transgenic property is a pesticide, which evokes multilayer questions.

9 These men are called intellectual property agents.
10 Genetically modified elephants.

Striking it appears as the way Bacigalupi chose two cities, Des Moines (in The Calorie Man) and Iowa (in *The Windup Girl*), and charted a geopolitical map that has largely been overlooked in the literature. Des Moines is the headquarters of Pioneer Hi-Breed, the largest seed company in the United States. Again, Des Moines is in close proximity to Iowa State University, a leading research institute in reality for the genetic engineering of crops that are an integral part of the plot of *The Windup Girl*. In 2009–2020, it garnered attention for developing HIN1 "Swine Flu" vaccines for hogs that could be genetically inserted into corn[11]. But where does the novel take us? In attending to GMOs' possible invisibility, these novels pave new avenues for fiction's usefulness in techno-scientific issues such as genetic modification. Mentioning two essential episodes from the texts would be worthwhile. The first is while Kanya, the successor to Jadiee as Environment Ministry enforcer, escorts the foreign executives to the treasured seed bank. Inside the vault, her actions lead to an attack on the seawall and, eventually, to the pump that keeps Bangok from being flooded. Her execution triggers the trauma of the genocides committed to the family members of Hock Seng, and he chooses to save a young Thai girl by ultimately going against the policies. Hock Seng is himself a Chinese Malaysian refugee who fled to the Thai Kingdom from Malaysia; for him, the second expansion of transnational corporations is no different from earlier colonial expansion. Nevertheless, by returning to the roots in the end, his act offers a glimmer of hope and leaves with several thought-provoking questions.

Both novels bring the symbol of rebirth through the water. The journey through the river in one book and the flood in another conjure up a hybrid, globalized spiritual image of "Noah Bodhisattva." It resonates with the fresh start of the post-flood new world while we see that Kanya successfully preserves the genetic archive out of the city before the city gets flashed away under the water. The conventional sense of "human purity" had been disrupted by those surviving people—the genetically engineered new person Emiko, the renegade genetic engineer Gibbons, and his transsexual lover Kip. In *The Calorie Man*, the last river journey echoes several Hindu mythological elements. The river is always associated with rebirth, hopes, and life.

11 See the Iowa State University News Service article of 6 May 2009.

Bowman acts like Vishnu, the preserver who will bring balance by infecting the monoculture crops, followed by an agri-revolution. Tazi acts like the goddess Lakshmi, who preserves the seed. After the war, while they embark on a new journey on the Mississippi River, Tazi gives a handful of seeds to Lalji, a miracle happens. Tasting the food in traditional form brings all the memories back to Lalji's mind. "He remembered his mother pressing an extra bite onto his own [...] He remembered roti in his mouth, dry like ashes, and forcing himself to swallow anyway (Bacigalupi, 2008, pp. 93–121)." Sowing seeds with his father in the scorching heat while they could have eaten those seeds. A sacrificial act as it appeared to the readers—those seeds would make hundreds of new sources, and then there would have been no hunger left to be fulfilled. The novella ends with new hopes while Lalji and Tazi escape from the IP police, and Tazi brings seeds from Bowman's food stores. The irony was that Lalji was once hunting himself for all those unpatented seeds, but then the river journey appeared like an epiphanic moment:

> Lalji frowned and picked up a jar of corn. The kernels nestled tightly together, hundreds of them, each one unpatented, each one a genetic infection. He closed his eyes, and in his mind he saw a field: row upon row of green rustling plants, and his father, laughing with his arms spread wide as he shouted. (Bacigalupi, 2008, pp. 93–121)

Works Cited

Bacigalupi, P. "Interview with Paolo Bacigalupi." <https://Www.orbitbooks.net/2011/05/05/Interview-With-Paolo-Bacigalupi-Part-2/>, 1 May 2001.
———. "The Calorie Man." *Pump Six and Other Stories*, Night Shade Books, 2008, pp. 93–121.
———. *The Windup Girl*. Night Shade Books, 2015.
Barthes, R. "Toward a Psychosociology of Contemporary Food Consumption." In C. Counihan and V. Esterik (Eds.), *Food and Culture: A Reader*, Routledge, 2013, pp. 23–30.

Bourne Jr. J. K. "The Global Food Crisis: The End of Plenty." *National Geographic Magazine*, 2009, pp. 1–12, <https://globalfarmernetwork.org/the-global-food-crisis-the-end-of-plenty/> [accessed 19 April 2023].

Butler, D. and T. Reichhardt. "Long-Term Effect of GM Crops Serves up Food for Thought." *Nature*, 398(6729), 1999, pp. 651–656, <pubmed.ncbi.nlm.nih.gov/10227281/>, <https://doi.org/10.1038/19381>.

Counihan, C. and Van Esterik, P. *Food and Culture: A Reader*. Routledge, 2019.

Fisher, M. *Capitalist Realism: Is There No Alternative?* Zero Books, 2009.

Fukuyama, F. *Our Posthuman Future*. Profile Books, 2017.

Lévi-Strauss, C. *The Raw and the Cooked*. Chicago University of Chicago Press, 1996.

Marx, K. *Capital*. Verlag von Otto Meisner, 1867.

Milburn, C. *Nanovision*. Duke University Press, 2010.

Neff, R. *Introduction to the US Food System: Public Health, Environment, and Equity*. San Francisco, CA, Jossey-Bass, A Wiley Brand, 2015.

O'connor, J. *Natural Causes: Essays in Ecological Marxism*. Guilford Press, 2011.

Ozeki, R. L. *All over Creation*. Penguin Books, 2004.

Sala, E. O. M. *Testing and Analysis of GMO-Containing Foods and Feed*. Boca Raton, FL, CRC Press, Taylor & Francis Group, 2019.

Seabrook, J. "Sowing for Apocalypse: The Quest for a Global Seed." *The New Yorker*, 14 April 2011, <www.newyorker.com/magazine/2007/08/27/sowing-for-apocalypse> [accessed 17 April 2023].

Shiva, V. *Biopiracy: The Plunder of Nature and Knowledge*. North Atlantic Books, 2016.

Steier, G. *Advancing Food Integrity: GMO Regulation, Agroecology, and Urban Agriculture*. CRC Press, 2017.

The Holy Bible: King James Version. Braille Bible Foundation. 1611.

WHO. 2014. Food safety. Frequently asked questions on genetically modified foods. http://www.who.int/foodsafety/areas_work/foodtechnology/faq-genetically modified- food/en/. Accessed on 12 July, 2024

PART IV

Creative Posthumanism, Hybridity, Homeostasis

ARITRA BASU

Heterogeneous Platter, Hybrid Presentations: Analyzing the Elements of Posthumanism in Select Works of Sukumar Ray

In his brief 36 years, Sukumar Ray (1887–1923) expanded the possibilities of Bengali literature in manifold ways. His well-known absurdism in *Abol Tabol* and other works has already received acclaim across the world and has been canonized to the extent of being included in several curricula across universities in India and abroad. In addition to stepping into the domain of nonsense literature, which was barely in its nascent stages in Bengal and the world when Ray was writing, he also explored the possibilities of knowing what is human and what could be understood as the posthuman in his works. Though the idea of posthumanism came into existence almost a century after Ray's works, an anachronistic study of his works in this light might be befitting from three perspectives. First, the idea of the posthuman has already been applied to a range of texts, ideas, and characters that preceded the theorization of posthumanism. Second, Sukumar Ray's characters provide the readers with a unique opportunity of understanding and interpreting the traits that make them posthuman, from the double-sided sword of the human to the beyond. Finally, these characteristic traits set up the opportunity for his successors (his son, Satyajit Ray, being one of them) to dwell on the possibilities of the posthuman in Bengali literature, culture, and media.

The History of the Posthuman in Bengali Literature

The presence of ghosts and the personification of inanimate objects and animals in fairy tales of Bengal (and other parts of India) laid the foundation stones of posthumanism in the regional map of India. However, even in the works of Sukumar Ray's father, Upendrakishore Ray Chowdhury, the posthuman element was lying as an unconscious element. For instance, in the characters of Tuntunir Boi, Upendrakishore undoubtedly assigns human-like traits to the animals in the tale by giving them the gift of speech and the autonomy of agency, but in the process, excessively humanizes the characters. The characters remain animals just in nomenclature, but in every other respect, they have become humane. Thus, the possibility of the posthuman as something/someone that extends beyond the human is not brought to the fore with a staunch intent. In Dakshinaranjan Majumdar's magnum opus, *Thakumar Jhuli* (1907), these elements are also slightly visible. The witches, wizards, and animals of the tales narrated by Thakuma dwell deep into the realm of the posthuman. However, now it becomes important to define what this paper understands by posthumanism.

Possibilities of the Posthuman in Sukumar Ray

It could be argued that some of Sukumar Ray's characters have posthuman qualities, especially if we define posthumanism as a broad philosophical movement that challenges traditional concepts of what it means to be human and explores the ways in which technology and other factors are changing our understanding of human identity and existence. In a recent book *Posthumanism in Practice*, Christine Daigle and Matt Hayler note how:

> the borders and effects of posthumanist thought are hard to neatly draw, but by accepting that it exists as a useful and informed framework for interrogating aspects

of the world, it can become better established and increasingly put to work, and not least by both inviting new perspectives in and better noting existing influences and similarities with other approaches (2023, p. 1).

The corpus of Ray's works offers similar insight into this evolving discipline.

Ray's quirky characters in *Abol Tabol* are exemplary in this context. The hybrid of two distinct animals that he creates in his poem "Khichuri" is nothing short of human bodies being replaced by robotic parts. In the real world, such experiments of cross-breeding species have been practiced for long, with the salient difference being that in the real world, the breeding happens between similar species, like the liger (lion and tiger), or two different subspecies of dogs to get the best qualities of both in one. However, the agency allowed these animal characters in "Khichuri" is what makes them posthuman. In this poem, we see the lines: "বক কহে কচ্ছপে—"বাহবা কি ফুর্তি!/ অতি খাসা আমাদের 'বকাচ্ছপ মূর্তি' ।" (Ray, 1977, p. 22), which is translated by Satyajit Ray as "A stork to a turtle said, 'Let's put my head upon your torso;/ We who are so pretty now, as Stortle would be more so!'"(Goswami, 2021, p. 124). The poem has a mixed narrative voice, with both first- and third-person perspectives used to add roundness to the structurally experimental poem. These animals are sometimes ecstatic to find out that their shortcomings have been surprisingly overcome, while others find this arrangement disturbing or annoying. Needless to say, these humane attributes are barely seen in animals, and this act of assigning these qualities, attitudes, and problems to these animal characters makes them step into the domain of humans.

Humans of *Abol Tabol*, on the other hand, are not very humanly. They have one salient feature that sets them apart, but despite that, they somehow seem distant from civilization. In the attempt to expand the possibilities of the posthuman, one must also dehumanize the humane in mankind, in one way; or so Sukumar thought. For instance, Kaath Buro, the eponymous protagonist of the poem *Kaath Buro*, eats boiled wood. It needs not be mentioned that this is no fodder for humans. However, when Sukumar draws him, it reflects a rather monotonous, regular octogenarian (Figure 1). He constantly tries to figure out why the wooden logs have holes in them, and in the process, he criticizes the current functioning of society in a quasi-satirical way. Sukumar Ray writes this poem in perfect prosody, contradicting the absurd subject matter of the poem. Following the structure of 14 letters per line (as practiced in most Bengali epics and devotional poems like the Laxmi Panchali), Ray brings to our attention that the poem is human in most ways but one. The wood here, stands out as an analogy of the people who inhabit our society. The people with a spine become the wooden logs without any damage, while the corrupted lot becomes ridden with holes. As Ray writes:

> কোন্ কাঠ পোষ মানে, কোন কাঠ শান্ত,
> কোন্ কাঠ টিম্টিমে, কোন্টা বা জ্যান্ত।
> কোন্ কাঠে জ্ঞান নেই মিথ্যা কি সত্য,
> আমি জানি কোন্ কাঠে কেন থাকে গর্ত (23)

This could be roughly translated as

> Which wood pets so, which one's peaceful
> Which wood weak is, which one's life-full
> Which wood can tell lie not from truth
> I know each and every wood's worth (Translated by the author)

The posthuman element here is completely inanimate, brought to the fore by a human, one of whose own kind first coined the term posthuman. The agency of the wood here is not its own; it has been assigned an added value by someone whose mind can create such analogies. *Abol Tabol* is full of such references, characters, and allusions that are waiting to be read in the posthumanist light. Analyzing all these instances would be outside the purview of this paper and, in some sense, redundant.

In the chapter "Animal Studies" of his book *What is Posthumanism?*, Cary Wolfe writes:

> posthumanism can be defined quite specifically as the necessity for any discourse or critical procedure to take account of the constitutive (and constitutively paradoxical) nature of its own distinctions, forms, and procedures … in ways that may be distinguished from the reflection and introspection associated with the critical subject of humanism. The "post-" of posthumanism thus marks the space in which the one using those distinctions and forms is not the one who can reflect on their latencies and blind spots while at the same time deploying them. (2010, p. 122)

Figure 12.1: Kaath Buro, as illustrated by Sukumar Ray.

The critical subject of humanism, in this case, is the anthropocentric man. In *Ha-Ja-Ba-Ra-La* (translated as "A Topsy-Turvy Tale" by Sukanta Chaudhuri), Sukumar Ray introduces the readers to Kakeshwar Kuchkuch, a crow with a sense of humor and witty repartees. In a conversation with the narrator, the blurring of the boundaries between the human and the posthuman becomes relevant:

> 'Well then!' said I.'What made you say seven twos didn't make fourteen ?' 'It wasn't quite fourteen when you spoke,' answered the crow. 'At that point it was only 13 rupees 14 annas and 3 pies. If I hadn't very cannily put down 14 just at the right moment, it would have got to be 14 rupees 1 anna and 9 pies by now.'

> 'I've never heard such rubbish,' I told him. 'If seven twos make fourteen, it's always fourteen, an hour ago or ten days from now.' The Crow looked shocked and said, 'Don't you count the cost of time in your country?' (Chaudhuri, 1987, p. 49)

The sheer absurdism in this conversation makes this conversation both enjoyable and suspect to a posthumanist interpretation. Humans, or cyborgs for that matter, would never miscalculate seven times two, that too deliberately. Though the readers see some of these instances being repeated in the works of Sukumar's son Satyajit, in particular in the short story "Professor Shonku o Robu," the possibilities of what a posthumanist entity could do have almost always been understood as an upgrade from the humane understandings of the world. While the calculation provided by Kakeshwar Kuchkuch might be askew, the argument he makes for the time being valuable for a mathematical problem remains pertinent to this day. In a world ridden with the advances of artificial intelligence, humans only count on and celebrate success stories like ChatGPT. Thus, the image that Sukumar Ray draws of Kuchkuch is not one of regular crows but one with a slate and chalk on its beak. This is surprisingly close to one of the characters in Professor Shonku's stories, "Corvus." A comparative study of the two crows is shown in Figure 2.

In a previous article on posthumanism in the stories of Professor Shonku, I argued how,

Figure 12.2: Kakeshwar Kuchkuch on the left and Corvus on the right.

it is very evident that as far as the use of the elements of the posthuman is concerned, in terms of an artificial intelligence or a futuristic robot, or an alien, the oeuvre of Ray is rich enough to conduct a thorough research on, using the angles of anthropocentrism, prediction theory and the extent to which it has come true, and most importantly to study the use of posthumanist agenda in science fiction or fantasy, even in texts which are more than half a century old. (Basu, 2020, p. 18)

Such arguments can also be made for Sukumar Ray. In the 747 pages, the *Sukumar Samagra* (edited by Anish Deb) displays sections entitled "Abol Tabol," "Khai Khai," "Onanyo Chora Kobita o Gaan," "Ha-Ja-Ba-Ra-La," "Pagla Dashu," "Bohurupi," "Aro golpo," "Natok," "Jeebjontu," "Jiboni, Bibidho," and "Probondho." From the titles of the sections and a closer look at their contents, it quickly becomes obvious that Sukumar never wanted to experiment with the human element in his works at length. Even when he introduces human characters, he grants them a quirk that sets them apart from the stereotypical, monotonous society they are forced to inhabit. In addition to his more popular works like Abol Tabol and Ha-Ja-Ba-Ra-La where his stepping into the domain of the posthuman was more evident, he also brought such elements to the fore in his under-discussed works like the discussion on animals (in "Jeebjontu").

Another such instance is the tale of Heshoram Hushiar. With an array of non-existent characters, this text is ripe for a posthumanist reading. However, the animals here are not that different from those of Abol Tabol. The element of posthumanism here comes to the fore in terms of the conversation that the humans have about the animals that they encounter in the narrative.

"We were discussing" whether or not to go out and look for him when we suddenly saw a very large animal looming up behind a tall, bushy tree. All we saw was its head, which bobbed and swayed like a drunk's. We were about to beat a hasty retreat into our tents when we heard Lakkarh call out, "Don't run away. He's quite harmless." (Goswami, 2021, p. 168).

These types of interactions of mankind with animals that are unknown to us open up the possibility of a posthumanist reading of Ray, along with many others. The diary of Hushiar, along with many of Sukumar's works, is just a small window of possibilities that could open up once the hard and fast distinctions of genre division, rules, and distinctions between serious and nonsense literature are removed.

While discussing this text, Binayak Ray writes:

"Sukumar Ray, probably inspired by Arthur Conan Doyle's *The Lost World* (1912), wrote *Heshoram Hushiyarer Diary* ('The Diary Of Heshoram Hushiyar') in 1922. In its eccentric, enlightened and hilarious narrative *Heshoram* Sukumar Ray mocks the practice of the Western scientists to classify and name things, and their tendency to use convoluted Latin names for classification" (1977, p. 74).

It is important in this context to note that almost all posthumanist thought and theorization has been concocted and developed in the West, with little to no interference or contribution from countries like India. One might assume that this is due to the paucity of texts that deal with such issues, but this article, along with an array of other research works, shows that posthumanist thought and execution existed in Indian literature long before the term was even coined. This existence, especially in the works of Sukumar Ray, is not limited to one genre but spreads across his entire corpus. In the brief span of 36 years, Sukumar wrote more than most people manage to write in their lives.

In his plays as well, Ray tries to intermingle the worlds of the human and the posthuman. Though most of his plays are yet to be translated into English, the weaving can be very well understood in Bengali as well. While discussing mythical characters from *The Ramayana* (who are, in themselves, an avenue of exploring posthumanist thought and ideas), Sukumar brings in satire, sarcasm, and comedy. One of his most famous plays, *Laxmaner Shaktishyel*, parodies the incident of Laxman being hit by a fatal arrow in the battle against Ravana. However, to maintain the parodic tone of the play and to induce laughter in the audience members, the play is ridden with songs and limericks. In an epic pastiche, Sukumar effortlessly humanizes the characters of Hanuman, Sugreev, and Jambuban, who were originally animals. It can be argued here that these characters were given human-like agency in the original epic as well, but there, these characters, in addition to other animal characters like Naal, Neel, Jatayu, Garud, and others, were always thought of as inferior to the human characters. Though most of these characters were incarnations of some Hindu deity or the other, they were always treated as the followers of Ram. In Sukumar's rendition, we see Sugreev with the dialogue:

রেখে দে তোর গলাবাজি/ ওরে ব্যাটা ছুঁচো পাজি

অন্তিম সময় আজি/ ইষ্টদেব করবে নমস্কার

তুই পাষণ্ড ঘোর/ পাল্লায় পড়িলি মোর

উদ্ধার না দেখি তোর/ মোর হাতে না পাবি নিস্তার (Ray, 1977, pp. 359–360)

This could be roughly translated to:

> Keep your voice down/ You stupid clown
> Death on you does frown/ Now you must pray
> You, a mild disarray/ of escape you have no way
> Die shall you today/ To me shall you be a prey.[1]

Sugreev, whose agency in *The Ramayana* never superseded Ram's, especially during the battle, is seen here giving threats to Ravana. There are many such instances in Sukumar's works that stand out as examples of the posthuman agency being transferred from the humans to the ones who are beyond that definition. In addition to his array of hybrid animal characters, Sukumar also explored the possibilities of posthumanism by toying with the idea of insanity in his works.

Insanity and Posthumanism: An Interwoven Understanding

At the outset, it might seem that insanity is a purely psychological problem and has nothing to do with posthumanism. While for most works this generalization might be true, in Sukumar Ray's oeuvre we see something that is so experimental that it brings these two rather different fields together, like a conceit. To understand this part, one must expand their understanding of the posthuman beyond the physical to the intellectual. When we consider robots, cyborgs, or artificial intelligence to be posthumanist elements, we do so because their operating systems (which are tantamount to their brains) are capable of producing or analyzing data that the human mind would not be able to produce, analyze, or

---

1. Translated by the author of this paper.

comprehend, at least not in such a quick span. Therefore, any kind of intellectual production that does not fall within the purview of the human mind's capabilities can be understood as posthuman. The madman (or the psychotic, in psychoanalytic terms) has the potential of understanding society and the language it uses from a perspective that is not commonplace. That perspective, deconstructive in nature, allows for a completely fresh perspective into the order of things as we know it.

In Bengali, there is a common saying that asks the young generation to be human in the truest sense of the term. Broken into two fragments, the Bengali word "manush" forms maan (respect) and hush (awareness). The madman lacks both of these and therefore qualifies as a human only from their physical attributes. Bombagorer Raja, one of Sukumar Ray's characters in Abol Tabol, has some weird attributes to his name: "সভায় কেন চেঁচায় রাজা "হুক্কাহুয়া" বলে?/ মন্ত্রী কেন কলসী বাজায় বসে রাজার কোলে?" (Ray, 1977, p. 38). Satyajit translated this as: When the King sits on the throne/ He starts hee-hawing in baritone, /And on his lap Prime Minister /Just sits and beats a canister (Goswami, 2021, p. 151). The king, shouting like a fox in the open court, entertains the minister, who is playing with a vase on his lap. This animalistic attitude of the king, along with his paternal aunt, who plays cricket with a pumpkin, paints the characters of this poem as insane. However, when Remus Lupin transforms into a werewolf on full moon nights, critics and scholars spend no time attuning that transformation to the domain of the posthuman. Why are Sukumar Ray's characters not taken with as much

Figure 12.3: The king, the minister, and the king's paternal aunt, from "Bombagorer Raja."

seriousness as characters from the West? Going insane, as has already been argued, can be understood as an avenue of posthumanism. However, in this poem, readers are bound to question the definition of insanity, as only the narrator of the poem seems surprised and irritated with the ways of life in Bombagor. The characters, as painted by Sukumar himself, are seen as jolly good fellows. They might look surprised, but they are definitely not mad or angry, as shown in Figure 3.

Though these characters cannot be categorized as totally insane, the relation of insanity with posthumanism can be established from these instances. Sukumar's famed character, Pagla Dashu, whose name is a telling of his mental state, also showed some instances like this. Though Pagla Dashu's activities do not have any intrinsic posthumanist meaning, his characterization is one of a kind.

Peaceful Cohabitation Between the Human and the Posthuman

In the poem Tyash-Goru, the peaceful cohabitation between the human and the posthuman elements can be evaluated. The poem reads, "ট্যাঁশগরু গরু নয়, আসলেতে পাখি সে;/ যার খুশি দেখে এস হারুদের আফিসো/ চোখ দুটি ঢুলু ঢুলু, মুখখান মস্ত,/ ফিটফাট কালোচুলে টেরিকাটা চোস্ত" (Ray, 1977, *Sukumar Samagra*, p. 55). Sukanta Chaudhuri translates this as: "A very strange bird is the Blighty Cow:/ You can see him at Haru's office now./ He has dreamy eyes in a very long face, /His sleek black curls are neatly in place (1987, p. 43). Under normal circumstances, a cow does not belong to an office, but in this poem, it resides there permanently. The poet invites people to come and take a look, which is one of the most important characteristics of any posthuman object or animal. Even in the works of Satyajit Ray, whenever Professor Shonku has delved into the domain of the posthuman, it has always been accompanied by a display of the same. How this absurd-looking animal (shown in Figure 4) survives in a workplace environment is not something the poem discusses. However, the cohabitational aspect comes to

Figure 12.4: Tyansh-Goru.

the fore in the last two lines of the poem. Ray's narrator of the poem says, "কারোযদি শখ্ থাকে ট্যাঁশ গরু কিনতে,/ সস্তায় দিতে পারি,দেখ ভেবে চিন্তে।" (2009, p. 55), which is translated as "If this elegant beast you'd like to buy, I'll sell him cheaply — do apply" (Chaudhuri, 1987, p. 43).

In the comparatively less popular story "Kukurer Malik" ("The Dog's Owner"), Sukumar plays with the idea of ownership of animals, who in themselves are posthumanist, especially in his other works. Here, two friends jointly buy a dog, and then they share its ownership in a rather absurd way. One of the friends owns the dog's front half, and the other owns its tailed portion. The story is a funny tale of how two humans, who were good enough friends to share the ownership of an animal at a point, slowly become averse to one another through the course of owning an entity that is not a human. In the world of posthumanism, this issue of owning the posthuman entity has often been an issue of great debate among posthumanities scholars. In his article "Against Anthropocentrism. Non-human Otherness and the Post-human Project," Roberto Marchesini writes how "the non-human animal becomes a master and a friend that can make us see the world from another perspective, helping us to abandon anthropocentrism" (2015, p. 75). Though what happens in this particular

short story is a long haul from Marchesini's argument, Satyajit Ray's short
story "Asmanjababur Kukur," takes it to this very level.

In Satyajit's story, the nonhuman animal (also a dog) becomes a friend
of the protagonist, Asmanjababu. This dog, unique in its characteristic
feature of being able to laugh, displays an understanding of the situations
and events that are happening around it. Asmanjababu notes how the dog
laughs only when something funny happens and not when a funny story is
told to it. This sense of observational humor is not present in dogs unless
they have been trained or improved in some way or another. This incident marks one of the finest instances of peaceful cohabitation between
the human and the posthuman in the works of Satyajit Ray. However, in
his predecessor, this cohabitation is treated with a sense of irony. In his
poem "Bhoy peyo na," the hideous, nameless character tries to lure people
into coming close to it so that it may potentially prey on them (Figure 5).
Even in his illustration, Ray draws a small human running away from the
creature. The poem starts with a sweet, convincing tone, "ভয় পেয়ো না, ভয়
পেয়ো না, তোমায় আমি মারবনা—/সত্যি বলছি কুস্তি ক'রে তোমার সঙ্গে পারবনা / মনটা আমার বড্ড
নরম, হাড়ে আমার রাগটি নেই,/তোমায় আমি চিবিয়ে খাব এমন আমার সাধ্যি নেই!", but ends with
a threat, "অভয় দিচ্ছি, শুনছ নাযে? ধরব নাকি ঠ্যাং দুটা?/ বসলে তোমার মুণ্ডু চেপে বুঝবে তখন
কাণ্টা!/ আমি আছি, গিন্নী আছেন, আছেন আমার নয় ছেলে—/ সবাই মিলে কামড়ে দেব মিথ্যে
অমন ভয় পেলে ।" (Ray, 1977, *Sukumar Samagra*, p. 53). Sukanta Chaudhuri
translates these lines as "Oh don't be scared — please don't be scared! /
I don't intend to beat you. Believe me, if we fought about, I never could
defeat you./ My heart is of a kindly sort, I'm gentle in my habit — / I really
couldn't crunch your neck or even try to grab it," and "What, still unsure?
Why really. sir, you'll start to hurt my feelings: / I'll twist your neck or
crush your leg to add to my appealings./ There's me, my missus, nine stout
sons, the whole lot at your service — / We'll bite you all together, now, if
you don't stop being nervous" (1987, p. 39).

Figure 12.5: The nameless animal in "Bhoy Peyo na."

Conclusion

One might wonder if this element of cohabitation is imbibed in the texts because they were primarily directed at and for children. The target audience for Sukumar, the readers of the magazine Sandesh mostly, were children and young adults. Only later did Sukumar's works get appreciated by scholars and serious readers of literature. However, even if one assumes that Sukumar did this to appease the children, even then, the relationship between humans and animals could have been built without stepping into the domain of the posthuman. This not only shows his versatility in terms of his authorship but also is a subtle nod to his genius as a seer. His anticipation of what would be acceptable even after a century of his death, was unparalleled. Another argument often made in the context of Sukumar's writing is that he used humor in ways that had not been explored yet. While the fact in itself is not debatable and easily defendable by looking at plays like *Obak Jolpaan* or *Laxmaner Shaktishel*, humor in his works took a back seat, especially when he stepped in the domain of nonsense literature.

Though there has been significant scholarship in this domain, Sukumar's expertise in bringing nonsense into the daily dillydallies of life, dealing in deft puns, and letting the readers dwell in doubt was what kept his work from becoming dry or drab. As a classic writer of Bengali literature, his relevance has increased in the present day and age, especially after the inclusion of *Abol Tabol* in the curricula of universities across the country, in papers of popular literature, and beyond. Posthumanism in the works of Sukumar Ray is an area that is yet to be explored to its fullest potential and requires multiple full-length works to be understood. Perhaps reading Sukumar Ray and his family's works would broaden the world's understanding of posthumanism. J. A. Cuddon, in his seminal *A Dictionary of Literary Terms and Literary Theory*, defined posthumanism as "a philosophical position concerned with reconceptualizing what it means to be human" (2013, p. 552). One can then argue that in Sukumar Ray's works, especially in his nonsense literature, the definition of who/what qualifies as a human is challenged in many ways, and by opening the eyes of the readers to the possibility that an entity can swing between the two, Sukumar opened up the possibilities of science fiction, posthumanism, and nonsense literature in Bengali.

Works Cited

Basu, A. "Beyond the Machine: Cyber-humanism in the Stories of Professor Shonku". *Asian Quarterly: An International Journal of Contemporary Issues.* Vol. 17, pp 10–18, 2020.

Chaudhuri, S. *Select Nonsense of Sukumar Ray.* Oxford University Press, 1987.

Cuddon, J. A. *A Dictionary of Literary Terms and Literary Theory.* Wiley-Blackwell, 2013.

Daigle, C. and Hayler, M. *Posthumanism in Practice.* Bloomsbury Academic, 2023.

Goswami, R. *3 Rays: Stories from Satyajit Ray.* Penguin Ray Library, 2021.

Marchesini, R. "Against Anthropocentrism. Non-human Otherness and the Post-human Project". *Nanoethics*. Vol. 9, pp. 75–84, 2015. URL: <https://doi.org/10.1007/s11569-015-0220-7>

Ray, B. "Subverting Reason, Thinking Futurity. Climate Change, Posthumanism and Bengali Science Fiction". *Contact Zone*. Vol. 1, 2021. DOI: 10.26379/1595

Ray, S. *Shonku Samagra*. Eighth edition, Ananda Publishers, 2009.

Ray, S. In A. Deb (Ed.), *Sukumar Samagra*. Supreme Publishers, 1977.

Wolfe, C. *What is Posthumanism?* University of Minnesota Press, 2010.

JOYDEEP CHAKRABORTY

Creative Posthumanism in the 21st-Century American Poetry: An Examination of *Don't Let Me Be Lonely: An American Lyric* and *This Connection of Everyone with Lungs*

The American poetry of the 21st century, as Ann Keniston and Jeffrey Gray note, is characterized by a greater amount of socio-political engagement than the American poetry that came into being in the 20th century. On the other hand, posthumanism, especially the kind of posthumanism postulated by Rosi Braidotti, proposes the idea of the inseparably political and material involvement of a human subject. Posthumanism in the 21st-century American poetry is, therefore, a natural outcome of the greater socio-political engagement typical of this domain of American poetry.

The posthuman turn of the 21st-century American poetry has already been indicated by a number of critics. Heather Milne, for example, notes that in *This Connection of Everyone with Lungs*, a lyrical sequence written by Juliana Spahr, the lyrical subjectivity is "collective," "non-unitary," "nomadic," and "constituted through connection, exchange, reciprocity, and accountability" (2014, pp. 204–205).[1] This kind of subjectivity, as Milne asserts, fits in with Rosi Braidotti's concept of the postmodern subject, which is multiple, characterized by "political agency" (2014, p. 205), and based on "a materially and politically 'embedded and embodied' subjectivity" (2002, p. 205). Tana Jean Welch, who examines Claudia Rankine's prose-poem *Don't Let Me Be Lonely: An American Lyric*, points out that "trans-corporeal ethics" (2015, p. 127) explores all the objects in our environments, including

---

1 For other studies regarding *This Connection of Everyone with Lungs*, see Mayer, pp. 43–62; Luger, pp. 175–200; and Chisholm, 118–147.

the harmful and the seemingly unknown ones. She also notes that such ethics considers human bodies to be entities working at the intersection of social and material elements and that the physical impacts of "economic and social systems" (2015, p. 127), particularly "class and racism" (2015, p. 127), in Rankine's poem are an example of "trans-corporeal ethics." As she argues, the significance of the poem as part of a broader and inevitable "cultural shift toward the posthuman and materiality" (2015, p. 128) is conditioned by the poem's engagement with the discursive construction of material reality and with the "trans-corporeal ethics." Scholarship on the 21st-century American poetry also entails a variety of other concerns like the connection between "belatedness" and post-9/11 poetics (Keniston, 2011, pp. 658–683); the interconnection between the private and the public in post-9/11 poetry (Rothberg, 2008, pp. 123–142); the mythical dimensions of imagery in post-9/11 poetry (Knepel, 2016, pp. 139–156); the relationship between aesthetics and capital (Cleary, 2016, pp. 77–91); the hallucinatory states in post-9/11 poetry as a means of experiencing and overcoming trauma (Chakraborty, 2021, pp. 1–15); and so on.[2] However, no scholarship on the 21st-century American poetry has yet explored the creative posthuman subjectivity in the same domain of poetry, the point that some 21st-century American poems engage in posthumanism in such a manner that not only reflects certain posthuman tenets but also remarkably modifies and reconstructs a number of posthuman ideas (like the challenge to Cartesian dualisms and the multiplicity of human subjectivity) in order to suit literary ends. Nor has the epistemological implication of such creative transmutation been explored so far.

This article therefore aims to examine two specimens of the 21st-century American poetry—*Don't Let Me Be Lonely: An American Lyric* by Claudia Rankine and *This Connection of Everyone with Lungs* by Juliana Spahr—the same poems that Milne and Welch have already analyzed.

---

2   For other works of criticism on the 21st-century American poetry, see Tabone, pp. 95–117; Gray, pp. 261–284; Alkalay-Gut, pp. 257–279; Plate, pp. 1–16; Tanner, pp. 58–76; Chakraborty, pp. 194–208; Chakraborty, pp. 64–66; and Gray and Keniston (Eds.). *The News from Poems: Essays on the 21st-Century American Poetry of Engagement*. For other works of criticism on *Don't Let Me Be Lonely: An American Lyric*, see Frost 168–92; Hume 169–86; Cooper 50–56; Robbins 124–50; and Leong 165–89.

However, my aim is notably different from the aims of these two critics. It is to demonstrate that, alongside accepting the validity of the posthuman challenge to Cartesian binaries and of the posthuman tendency toward material embodiment and multiple subjectivity, these two poems creatively transmute posthumanism in the interest of poetics. In other words, these poems pose some significant questions regarding the relationship between poetic subjectivity and posthuman material subjectivity, the disconnection of the human beings from the nonhuman (including animals and technology), and whether literature should blindly follow the posthuman trans-corporeal ethics or modify it through intellectual agency to follow literature's own end. While the first poem explores all of these questions by partial reconstruction of the posthuman challenge to Cartesian dualisms (human/technological and mind/body) and to unified human subjectivity, the second poem explores the second question by simultaneously accepting and diverging from posthuman attitude towards the connection of human beings to the nonhuman. From the standpoint of epistemology, the contemporary significance of this study lies in the fact that this study indicates both the positive and the negative aspects of posthumanism as part of poetics. More precisely, on the one hand, this study stresses the necessity of posthumanism in the 21st-century American poetics; on the other, it questions an overreliance on posthumanism that has a harmful effect on poetic imagination.

The theoretical framework of this article is eclectic in nature as it combines Donna Haraway's concept of posthumanism with the concept of "metapoetry" posited by Rene Wellek. Haraway is credited with postulating the idea of "cyborg," which refers to the combination of individual life form and machine. To explain, according to Haraway, "cyborgs" are "hybrid entities" (Haraway, 1991) in the era that followed the World War II and consist of two elements: first, technologically advanced human beings and other organisms; and, second, "machines in their guise (e.g., texts, systems of communication, and so on)" (Haraway, 1991). The concept metaphorically evokes "the fantasies of science fiction" (Bolter, 2016, p. 2), which regard drugs or prostheses as a means of enhancing the ordinary, human skill levels. The concept also challenges the rational autonomy of "the traditional humanist subject" (p. 2), suggesting "the ambivalent condition" (p. 2) of humans in present times as their bodies are subject to technological alteration. By applying the concept of "cyborg," I will analyze the representation of modern technology in Rankine's poem, while at the same time displacing the concept from the feminist context in which it has been used by Haraway. Haraway also poses a challenge to the putative disconnection of the human from the animal, presupposed by the Cartesian tradition (Bolter, 2016, p. 3), and stresses "the porous quality of barriers between species" (p. 3), thus problematizing the traditional idea of species. By means of this concept of Haraway, I will examine the relationship between the human and the animal in *This Connection of Everyone with Lungs*. On the other hand, in the context of "meta-poetry," Wellek asserts that this form of poetry addresses "the self-definition of the poet" (1971, pp. 261–263), his aims, and the activities required to achieve those aims. It entails the poet's contemplation on "his status as seer/priest or sage" (pp. 261–263), and may evoke "other poets" (pp. 261–263). To explain, a meta-poem is usually concerned with the very project of writing a poem, with the creative process that this project necessarily involves. The creative process might critically examine the poetic subjectivity—the factors for such subjectivity and its connection with other human beings and the social environment. I will apply this concept to the examination of *Don't Let Me Be Lonely: An American Lyric* to emphasize the text's critical engagement with posthumanism. Notably, *This Connection of Everyone with Lungs* also possesses a meta-poetic element when the speaker of the poem uncertainly indicates that the poem has its origins in the serene, meditative beauty that characterizes our intensely private moments (Spahr, 2005, pp. 34–36). However, the element is neither extensive in scope nor part of the poem's commitment to, and departure from, posthumanism.

Claudia Rankine is a contemporary American poet, editor, playwright, and essayist of Jamaican origin. A prose poem that exploits multimedia, *Don't Let Me Be Lonely: An American Lyric*, was written partially in response to the terrorist attacks of 9/11 and depicts by means of a fragmented narrative the traumatic social conditions that result not only from 9/11 but also from the pre-existing problems of racism in America. In her examination of the poem, Welch argues that the poem entails the posthuman ethics of embodiment, which proposes the idea of human entanglement in a variety of relationships (e.g., biological, social, and so forth), and is part of "investigative" (2015, p. 124) poetics that examines the critical social dimensions of current culture through "a variety of data and reportage" (p. 124). Welch, however, ignores the text's preoccupation with a different postmodern concern that explores and problematizes the traditional differences between human beings and technology (or machines). As soon as *Don't Let Me Be Lonely: An American Lyric* begins, the speaker of this poem starts to explore her diseased psychological condition, death, and how to revive her "modifying process" (Rankine, 2017, p. 7), a creative process by means of which she was able to translate her intensely personal feelings, whether dull or exhilarating, into something social and objectively recognizable. Her exploration makes reference to one of her friends, who has been suffering from breast cancer and is on the verge of carcinogenic death due to the misdiagnosis by the friend's doctor. The speaker explains the process of "mastectomy" (p. 8) that the friend has experienced, a process that involves transplantation of tissues from the area of the abdomen to the left breast of the friend with the aim of reconstructing the latter. As the speaker points out in this context, "The plastic surgeon argued she (the friend) could do a far better job with natural versus artificial tissue" (p. 8). However, the irony is that it is only after undergoing the process of surgery that the friend and the surgeon learn that cancer is "settled" (p. 9) in the friend's body. As a result of such misdiagnosis, the friend starts to move toward death gradually, inevitably, and painfully. Cancer destroys both the mind and the body of the friend until "She is finished" (p. 9). The reference to "mastectomy" (p. 8) reminds us of Haraway's concept of "cyborg": just as the concept challenges the differences between the human and the technological by pointing out technological intervention in the human body that makes the respective person more skilled in physical and cognitive capacities (but dependent on a machine), so also the friend's doctor assures the friend of a better future conditioned by "natural versus artificial tissue" (p. 8). Modern technology would have made possible a better future for the friend if the doctor had diagnosed her disease at the appropriate time. The misdiagnosis and the resultant pathetic fate of the friend suggest that the operation of the human mind precedes technological intervention and determines what kind of impact such intervention will make on a human.

As part of the process of exploration in order to rejuvenate the "modifying process" (p. 7), the speaker focuses on the racist violence perpetrated against James Byrd Jr.; the sphere of entertainment and movies where death signifies not a gradual inevitable and horrific movement to nothingness, but a reminder of "the life expectancy" (p. 24), the positive expectations in an individual's life; the unsuccessful attempt of the speaker to arouse "the life expectancy" through anti-depressant drugs; the impractical poetic ecstasy of the girl who enjoyed a "Milosz poem" (p. 35) on the top of her multi-storied apartment building; the reference to the excessive tensions and worries of an old man that spoiled the whole of his life; and so on. In this way, after relating the gruesome story of a boy who killed a little girl and expressing her (the speaker's) resultant desire for counteracting depression through the surrealistic image of "a huge pill bottle" (p. 68), the speaker evokes the image of a man having a pacemaker as part of the same process of exploration. The speaker explains that this man named Mr. Tools is the only living person in the whole world who has "an artificial heart" (p. 71), and that, according to Mr. Tools, having such a "heart … without a heartbeat" (p. 71) is "the weirdest thing" (p. 71). In other words, on having a pacemaker, Mr. Tools feels very unnatural because he does not experience any beating of his heart. Instead, he feels "the fast repetitive whirr of a machine whose inconsistent motion might eventually seem like silence" (p. 71). This unnatural feeling is also conditioned by the fact that he feels the physical weight of the machine, which weighs "more than four pounds" (p. 71). However, ironically, this machine and the mechanical sound it produces make him conscious of his connection to life. By making the reference to Mr. Tools, the speaker accepts posthumanism as much as she rejects it, just as she has done in making the reference to "mastectomy" (p. 8). The pacemaker that Mr. Tools possesses makes him physically capable of living like any other human, but at the same time it makes him conscious of the gap between the human and the technological, the natural and the unnatural.

It is important to note that, in this poem, the speaker critically and suggestively accepts the concept of "cyborg" as part of the process of exploration for revival of her "modifying process" (p. 7). As I have already noted, the "modifying process" is basically a creative mode of transmutation of intensely subjective feelings into something social and objective. The resultant process of exploration on the part of the speaker in order to revive the "modifying process" is also creative in nature, lending a meta-poetic element to the poem. This metapoetic element merits attention as it critically engages with posthuman ideas like material embodiment and multiple subjectivity.[3]

The meta-poetic element figures in this poem from the beginning when the speaker starts to explore her diseased psychological condition, which is presumably the result of a number of injustices across contemporary American society (especially racism, the event of 9/11, and its social consequences), and an agency of creative translation in herself. Thus, when the speaker addresses the 2000 presidential election and criticizes the then presidential candidate, George W. Bush, for his inability to remember the incident relating to James Byrd Jr., a victim of white supremacism, she passionately starts "… talking to the television screen" (p. 21). This act of the speaker is conditioned by her immediate assumption that the foregoing inability of Bush results from his deliberate indifference to a black person like Byrd Jr. This act also exemplifies an embodied reaction on her part as it inseparably involves the physical impact of the killing of Byrd on her psyche. However, by means of the self-critical bent of her mind, she soon realizes that embodied reaction has a tendency to become sentimental and superficial. As she asserts, like Bush, she is often forgetful of things too, and this consciousness causes her exaggerated lamentation that we do not attach adequate value to numerous people in this world (p. 23). The speaker's sadness inevitably brings about a psychological condition characterized by a loss of faith "in the supreme laws that govern us" (p. 23), or in the positive, meaningful values of human life. Later, in reaction to the violence against Abner Louima and Amadou Diallo, two black immigrants in America, the speaker laments that her sadness possesses no powerful feelings, the kind of feelings inextricably involved with the awareness of social responsibility. In contrast to such aesthetically mature sadness, the speaker's sadness is "sentimental or excessive" (p. 57) and "certainly not

---

3 See Braidotti, *Metamorphoses: Towards a Materialist Theory of Becoming* and *Transpositions: On Nomadic Ethics.*

intellectual" (p. 57). In other words, through her meta-poetic subjectivity, the speaker understands that she requires an "innovating loss" (p. 57), a kind of sadness that must be inseparably connected to her body and the material world this body is embedded into, but at the same time that must be capable of creatively translating her physical feelings into something social, objective, and general, and thus transcending the material. In this way, the speaker of the poem justifies the posthuman challenge to a Cartesian binary (mind versus body) as much as she repudiates it.[4] To put it more precisely, Rankine's speaker makes the point that, in the context of creative transmutation, the mind is at once connected to the physical world and capable of transcending it.

   Don't Let Me Be Lonely: An American Lyric also creatively and critically engages with the posthuman concept of multiple, contradictory subjectivity by entailing a number of intra-subjective dialogues between the personal and the public selves of the speaker. In the course of these dialogues, these two selves interact with each other and achieve a degree of reciprocation. However, the relationship between the two is not wholly reciprocatory and is characterized by tension and anxiety. The first dialogue appears in the context of the speaker's realization of a necessity to reach out to the social world. In this dialogue beginning with the line "I thought I was dead" (p. 16), though the personal self seeks to communicate to the public self its loneliness and diseased psychological condition born of social injustices and the resultant social alienation, it does not adequately expose itself to the questions of the public self regarding the nature of the loneliness and the appropriate mode of articulating it. This communicative gap remains throughout a large section of the second dialogue, which arises after the speaker's realization of the necessity of "innovating loss" (p. 57). However, the ending of this dialogue where the personal self asks the public self for an objectively accessible definition of "loneliness" (p. 58) raises the probability of reciprocative translation. The third dialogue, which comes into being after the speaker identifies with the speaker of a poem by Paul Celan and further realizes the necessity of "innovating loss" (p. 57), serves as a notable example of the desire for reciprocative translation in the whole poem because in this

---

4 For knowledge of Cartesian binaries, see Robinson, "Dualism" (rev.).

dialogue the public self equates the mutual existence of the two selves as the basic condition of living a healthy, balanced life and the personal self responds to this equation in a positive manner: "Why are we here if not for each other?" (p. 62). The subsequent dialogue appears after the speaker refers to a partially inscrutable process of translation of her physical "grief into a tremendously exhausted hope" (118). In this dialogue, though the public self seems optimistic about a new life of meaningfulness, the personal self feels "still lonely" (119), indicating an attitudinal gap between the two. By engaging in the intra-subjective dialogues, the speaker communicates the messages that, in keeping with the posthuman view of subjectivity, human subjectivity is to a great extent contradictory but that a degree of recipro-cation and unity is possible by means of intra-subjective deliberation.

Juliana Spahr is an American poet, editor, and critic, whose *This Connection of Everyone with Lungs* came into being in reaction to the events of 9/11 and the following military campaign of America in Iraq. This poem is a sequence of lyrics and constituted by two sections—"Poem Written after September 11, 2001" and "Poem Written from November 30, 2002, to March 27, 2003"—stressing the necessity of interconnectivity not only between human beings but also between human beings and non-human beings (e.g., birds) across the whole world in order to confront various problems of global politics and to maintain global, environmental peace and stability.

In this context, at the beginning of the second poem of *This Connection of Everyone with Lungs*, titled "*November 30, 2002*," the speaker presents an elaborate description of parrots that has multidimensional semantic complexity. The parrots, as they figure in the whole poem, are both actual and metaphorical entities. The speaker points out that each morning we wake up in the bed and listen to the chirping of parrots, which reminds her of the emotional relationships among human beings and the conflicting elements in their world, "… the/ discord of waking" (Spahr, 2005, p. 15). In other words, the parrots are in a sense a usual, metaphorical reminder of the combination of heterogeneous elements that form the human world. These diverse elements range from the "…the Dow slipping" (p. 15), to "… the city of Danane" (p. 15), to the "… few leads in the bombing in Kenya" (p. 15). The parrots also remind the speaker of the connection between the rest of humanity and her, of "yous and me, / beloveds, and our roosts at the bottom of the crater once called/ Le ahi, now called Diamond Head" (p. 17). At the end of "*November 30, 2002*," the speaker associates the "flapping" (p. 18) of the parrots with our restless nocturnal attempts to break free of the thoughts relating to the triadic structure of society that is constituted by politics, military, and human progress. To the speaker, the world of the parrots is thus a metaphorical equivalent of the human world. At the same time, it is noteworthy that the speaker is preoccupied with the world of the parrots: she describes their appearance as "green colours" (p. 15), the sounds they produce, their connection to "pet conures" (p. 16), and their activities in each morning that include "rest(ing) in the trees near our bed, beloveds, ... for about an hour to feed, preen, and socialize before/ moving on to search for fruits and seeds of wild plum ... " (p. 17). This preoccupation suggests that the speaker considers the parrots actual entities resembling humans in a number of ways. Particularly, the parrots resemble humans in "feeding" and "socializing." By treating the parrots simultaneously as actual and metaphorical entities, the speaker emphasizes the concept of global interconnectivity between humans and between humans and non-human beings. Her indication of the connection, or the porous boundary, between humans and non-human beings echoes Haraway's posthuman challenge to the Cartesian binary opposition between humans and animals.

Throughout the poem, the speaker stresses the significance of global connectivity between human beings in a variety of ways—through the metaphor of "skin," which stresses connection and separation between human beings across the world at the socio-political levels (pp. 19–23); through the metaphorical image of "bow-tie pattern," which raises the probability of understanding apparently diverse, complex, global, human phenomena in an orderly manner (p. 32); through indicating the noble but flawed nature of the global human connectivity (pp. 38–40); and in other ways. The speaker becomes preoccupied again with the world of non-human beings in a section of the second poem titled "*March 16, 2003*," which appears in the context of her resistance (to the unilateral decision of George W. Bush to wage war in Iraq) both at the political and the personal levels through invocation of the global human connectivity (pp. 61–64). The speaker expresses a sense of wonder over the peaceful, optimistic attitude of "mynas gathering materials for/ their nests" (p. 65) as it sharply contrasts with the tumultuous nature of the contemporary human world and the attendant global politics. She focuses attention on the natural world and birds at the beach in Hawaii in order to avoid the human world threatened with the imminent war on Iraq. But she soon realizes our condition of being inextricably involved in the human world, the global politics, and the war they entail. As she utters, when they speak of songs of birds, they also think about Bush's recent meeting with other international leaders and a strong probability of war in Iraq (pp. 65–66). The speaker understands that, on the one hand, we are entangled in the human world and global politics, and, on the other, involvement with the two means psychic infection by their toxic aspects like violence and colonization. As a result, she soon feels that their discussion of birdsong echoes the loud, unpleasant sounds of the martial aircraft that are flying overhead (p. 67). In other words, though the beauty of the natural world that the non-human beings are part of is peaceful and appealing, this beauty "is occupied by the US military" (p. 67). Apparently, the nature of non-human beings is here metaphorically presented as a valuative contrast to the nature of the human world, which poses a threat to it. However, upon close scrutiny, it is clear that this contrast is not absolute. At the beginning of *"March 16, 2003,"* in reference to the birdsongs, the speaker indicates that "some of them (are) ugly to us and some of them beautiful" (p. 65), making us aware of the fact that birdsongs are not always aesthetically appealing. Later, when the voice of the speaker becomes "an awkward squawk" (p. 67) under the influence of the imminent military campaign of America, the voice reminds us of the previous reference to the ugly birdsongs and suggests that birds also produce loud, harsh sounds under certain circumstances. The toxic connection between birds, a part of the non-human world, and warfare, a part of the human world, is stressed more clearly in the section titled *"March 17, 2003"* when the speaker "wake(s) up" (p. 68) after enjoying a beautiful dream of optimism and finds "in the birds' songs ... war" (p. 68). Thus, the representation of the connection between human and non-human beings in *"March 16, 2003"* is more complicated than it appears at first sight. While the representation of this connection in *"November 30, 2002"* is open to interpretation within the posthuman framework of Haraway, the representation of the same in "*March 16, 2003*" is not so: the latter creatively distances itself from Haraway's posthuman understanding of the connection in order to communicate the speaker's psychological tension, anxiety, confusion, and complex entanglement between the human and the nonhuman.

The study of *Don't Let Me Be Lonely: An American Lyric* and *This Connection of Everyone with Lungs* in this article is of notable significance from the epistemological standpoint. In this context, it is necessary to point out that the term "posthumanism," as Cary Wolfe asserts in exploring the genealogy of the term, refers to a number of different, even contradictory, strands of thought. Of these strands of thought, there is a type of posthumanism (currently known as "transhumanism") that, partially influenced by Donna Haraway's "A Cyborg Manifesto" (1985), proposes the idea of "the (engineered) enhancement of human intellectual, physical, and emotional capabilities" (quoted in Wolfe, 2013), along with other ideas like a sudden, considerable increase in the span of human life, complete immunity to diseases, and so on, reflecting the concept of human rational autonomy enshrined in "Renaissance humanism and the Enlightenment" (Wolfe, 2013). In contrast to this strand of posthumanism, the kind of posthumanism practiced by Wolfe postulates on the one hand human "embodiment and embeddedness" (Wolfe, 2013) in biological and technological domains, the way human beings have evolved along with prosthetic tools, culture, and language, and on the other "the decentering" (Wolfe) of human subjectivity. Such "decentering" is conditioned by the fact that human subjectivity operates simultaneously across different networks (like economic, technical, and so on) that overlap with one another. Wolfe's version of posthumanism resembles Braidotti's version of the same as the latter also postulates material embeddedness, embodiment, and multiplicity of human subjectivity. Additionally, Wolfe's version of posthumanism challenges the anthropocentric aspect of humanism, which legitimates "discrimination (i.e., cruelty) against nonhuman animals" (Wolfe).[5]

Against this scholarly background, it can be argued that the two texts I have analyzed in this article critically and creatively engage with the strands

5 For other works on posthumanism, see Badmington (Ed.). *Posthumanism: Readers in Cultural Criticism*; Badmington, pp. 10–27; Nayar, *Posthumanism*; Herbrechter, *Posthumanism: A Critical Analysis*; and Ferrando, pp. 26–32.

of posthumanism posited by scholars such as Haraway, Wolfe, and Braidotti. In reference to "mastectomy," *Don't Let Me Be Lonely: An American Lyric* indicates not only a better future possibility of technological intervention but also the fact that human intellect should take precedence over technological intervention, suggesting an essential difference between the two. The reference to Mr. Tools suggests a close interdependence between a human being and a machine, reminding us of the posthuman challenge to human autonomy—and an essential gap between the two. The two references, thus, simultaneously embrace and reject the validity of posthumanism. On the other hand, the presence of a meta-poetic element in this poem creatively modifies the poem's posthuman commitment to material embodiment and multiplicity of human subjectivity. Such creativity operates through the simultaneous representation of material connectedness and transcendence of the human mind and through the recognition of the conflicting yet reconcilable relationship between the public and the private selves of the speaker. In the same way, *This Connection of Everyone with Lungs* suggests Haraway's posthuman challenge to the Cartesian, human/animal dichotomy by treating the parrots both as actual and as metaphorical entities. But the poem also departs from posthumanism toward the end to communicate the speaker's tense, psychological condition and her complex attitude toward the connection between the human and the nonhuman.

The creative engagement with posthumanism as part of the poetics of the two poems seems to imply that a work of art should not be limited to any particular epistemic paradigm in representing human and nonhuman phenomena in their manifold complexity. If a work of art, for example, exclusively holds the posthuman view of material embodiment, it betrays a limited understanding of creative translation, which is partially mysterious in nature. From the aesthetic standpoint, it is necessary to consider posthumanism one of several important perspectives on knowledge that must be blended with other perspectives to afford keen insights into human and nonhuman realities.

Works Cited

Alkalay-Gut, K. "The Poetry of September 11: The Testimonial Imperative." *Poetics Today*, Vol. 26, No. 2, 2005, pp. 257–279.

Badmington, N. (Ed.). *Posthumanism: Readers in Cultural Criticism*. Macmillan International Higher Education, 2000.

———. "Theorizing Posthumanism." *Cultural Critique*, Vol. 53, 2003, pp. 10–27.

Bolter, J. D. "Posthumanism." In *The International Encyclopedia of Communication Theory and Philosophy*, edited by Klaus Bruhn Jensen and Robert T. Craig, Wiley Black Well, 2016, pp. 1–8.

Braidotti, R. *Metamorphoses: Towards a Materialist Theory of Becoming*. Polity, 2002.

———. *Transpositions: On Nomadic Ethics*. Polity, 2006.

Chakraborty, J. "'Violence Has Changed Me': Private Trauma and Identity Crisis in Post-9/11 American Poetry." *Appropriations*, Vol. xii, 2017, pp. 194–208.

———. "Contemporary Post-Modernism: Postmodern Features in Post-9/11 Poetry." *International Journal of Management and Applied Science (IJMAS)*, Vol. 5, No. 2, 2019, pp. 64–66.

———. "Hallucinations in Post-9/11 American Poetry: Trauma and Beyond." *Critical Survey*, Vol. 33, No. 3/4, Autumn/Winter 2021, pp. 1–15.

Chisholm, D. "Juliana Spahr's Ecopoetics: Ecologies and Politics of the Refrain." *Contemporary Literature*, Vol. 55, No. 1, 2014, pp. 118–147.

Cleary, S. "A Bird in the Hand: Aesthetics and Capital in the Anthology *Poetry after 9/11*." In G. Fragopoulos and L. M. Naydan (Eds.), *Terror in Global Narrative: Representation of 9/11 in the Age of Late-Late Capitalism*, Palgrave McMillan, 2016, pp. 77–91.

Cooper, J. P. "Refusal of the Mask in Claudia Rankine's Post-9/11 Poetics." In L. McCullough (Ed.), *A Sense of Regard: Essays on Poetry and Race*, University of Georgia Press, 2015, pp. 50–56.

Ferrando, F. "Posthumanism, Transhumanism, Antihumanism, Metahumanism, and New Materialisms." *Existenz*, Vol. 8, No. 2, 2013, pp. 26–32.

Frost, E. A. "Claudia Rankine and the Body Politic." In J. Gray and A. Keniston (Eds.), *The News from Poems: Essays on the 21st-Century American Poetry of Engagement*, University of Michigan Press, 2016, pp. 168–192.

Gray, J. "Precocious Testimony: Poetry and the Uncommemorable." In A. Keniston and J. F. Quinn (Ed.), *Literature after 9/11*, Routledge, 2008, pp. 261–284.

Gray, J. and Keniston, A. (Eds.) *The News from Poems: Essays on the 21st-Century American Poetry of Engagement*. University of Michigan Press, 2016.

Haraway, D. *Simians, Cyborgs, and Women: The Reinvention of Nature.* Routledge, 1991, <https://www.google.co.in/books/edition/Simians_Cyborgs_and_Women/GG-R382kxIwC?hl=en&gbpv=1&dq=Simians,+Cyborgs,+and+Women:+The+Reinvention+of+Nature+by+donna+haraway&printsec=frontcover>.

Herbrechter, S. *Posthumanism: A Critical Analysis.* Bloomsbury Publishing, 2013.

Hume, A. "Toward an Antiracist Ecopoetics: Waste and Wasting in the Poetry of Claudia Rankine." In A. Hume and G. Osborne (Eds.), *Ecopoetics: Essays in the Field*, University of Iowa Press, 2018, pp. 169–186.

Keniston, A. " 'Not Needed, Except as Meaning': Belatedness in Post-9/11 American Poetry." *Contemporary Literature*, Vol. 52, No. 4, 2011, pp. 658–683.

Keniston, A. and Gray, J. (Eds.). "Introduction." In *The New American Poetry of Engagement: A 21st Century Anthology*, McFarland, 2012, pp. 1–15.

Knepel, R. "The Return of Myth: Icon, Mythology and Universal Narrative of 9/11." In G. Fragopoulos and L. M. Naydan, *Terror in Global Narrative: Representation of 9/11 in the Age of Late-Late Capitalism*, Palgrave Macmillan, 2016, pp. 139–156.

Leong, M. "Meta-Publicity and the Public Sphere: On Claudia Rankine and Kenneth Goldsmith." *Contested Records: The Turn to Documents in Contemporary North American Poetry.* University of Iowa Press, 2020, pp. 165–189.

Luger, M. "Toward a New Poetics of Witness: Juliana Spahr's *This Connection of Everyone with Lungs.*" *Tulsa Studies in Women's Literature*, Vol. 36, No. 1, 2017, pp. 175–200.

Mayer, S. "Aggregators: RSS (Radically Subversive Syndication) Poetics." *SubStance*, Vol. 38, No. 2, 2009, pp. 43–62.

Milne, H. "Dearly Beloveds: The Politics of Intimacy in Juliana Spahr's 'This Connection of Everyone with Lungs.' " *Mosaic: An Interdisciplinary Critical Journal*, Vol. 47, No. 2, 2014, pp. 203–218.

Nayar, P. K. *Posthumanism.* John Wiley & Sons, 2018.

Plate, L. "Bearing Witness: Gender and The Poetry of 9/11." *Women's Studies*, Vol. 37, No. 1, 2007, pp. 1–16.

Rankine, C. *Don't Let Me Be Lonely: An American Lyric.* Penguin Books, 2017.

Robbins, A. M. "Claudia Rankine's *Don't Let Me Be Lonely*: A Lyrical Long Poem in a Post-Language Age." *American Hybrid Poetics: Gender, Mass Culture, and Form.* Rutgers University Press, 2014, pp. 124–150.

Robinson, H. "Dualism". (rev.). In E. N. Zalta (Ed.), *The Stanford Encyclopedia of Philosophy*, 2003, p. 2016.

Rothberg, M. "Seeing Terror, Feeling Art: Public and Private in Post-9/11 Literature." In A. Keniston and J. F. Quinn (Eds.), *Literature after 9/11*, Routledge, 2008, pp. 123–142.

Spahr, J. *This Connection of Everyone with Lungs.* University of California Press, 2005.

Tabone, M. A. "Narrative Wreckage: Terror, Illness, and Healing in the Post-9/11 Poethics of Claudia Rankine." In G. Fragopoulos and L. M. Naydan (Eds.), *Terror in Global Narrative: Representation of 9/11 in the Age of Late-Late Capitalism*," Palgrave McMillan, 2016, pp. 95–117.

Tanner, L. E. "Holding on to 9/11: The Shifting Grounds of Materiality." *PMLA*, Vol. 127, No. 1, 2012, pp. 58–76.

Wellek, R. *Discriminations: Further Concepts of Criticism*. Yale University Press, 1971, pp. 261–263.

Welch, T. J. "Don't Let Me Be Lonely: The Trans-Corporeal Ethics of Claudia Rankine's Investigative Poetics." *MELUS*, Vol. 40, No. 1, 2015, pp. 124–148.

Wolfe, C. *What is Posthumanism?* University of Minnesota Press, 2013, <https://www.google.co.in/books/edition/What_Is_Posthumanism/yS9oDwAAQBAJ?hl=en&gbpv=1&dq=what+is+posthumanism+by+cary+wolfe&printsec=frontcover>.

SUJATO GHOSH

Confronting Human-Centric Stability, Revisiting the Ineluctable Torture Chamber and Comprehending the Post-Human Uncertainty of Coordinates in J. M. Coetzee's *Waiting for the Barbarians*

The depiction of torture is not something very new in modern fiction, but the way to present suffering in the novel remains ambiguous and complex. The position of humans in the present times is best expressed through literature, as it establishes the human imagination both in the abstract and concrete, but chiefly in the latter. It is no doubt unfortunate when we look back at the history of humanism – the way we created the non-humans and adapted the wild methods to remain at the centre of the universe. Literature provides the scope of free imagination that is exclusive, unique, and relative to any reader. A post-human reader would naturally look at Coetzee from the perspective of trauma, torture, and terror in the name of established humanism. It is important to note that literature is, in the end, a human phenomenon as it involves non-humans and others interrogating, at the same time, the position of the so-called humans. Coetzee breaks away from the tradition of human-centric literature to gather momentum in his movement towards post-humanism. Strategies to portray terror and torture therefore vary. In his fiction, J. M. Coetzee explores the context of torture and the inevitable, inescapable trauma to its fullest extent. In his third fiction, written in the United States in 1979, *Waiting for the Barbarians*, we find gruesome tales and pictures of extreme suffering. The torture of the girl and the magistrate in the fiction, both psychologically and physically, at the hands of the 'humans' of the Empire, is legitimised by the latter as natural and pertinent according to the situation. One recognises a distinctive lack of emotion on either side. The post-human condition is intensified by the portrayal of the trauma that the girl is subjected to and the suffering of the magistrate at the end of the fiction. Critics like Cathy Caruth bring in the Freudian analysis of trauma as she describes how any victim experiences the incident of torture several times in life and how it intensifies due to the period of dormancy as every time the victim experiences the suffering, it becomes new to her and therefore multiple traumatic experiences appear as fresh ones instead of old torture stories just repeated (2021, p. 187). Caruth explains how the victim suffers from emotionlessness and lack of feelings after a traumatic incident. The torture chamber of Coetzee's fiction *Waiting for the Barbarians* bears testimony to many agonising incidents that lead to such feelings. In a Spinozist approach, the assimilation of the other within the self makes Coetzee's fiction *Waiting for the Barbarians* a significant text that explains, clarifies, and enlightens the discourse of post-humanism and trauma studies.

The human intention to adjust to the changing circumstances and to remain at the centre of all accomplishments receives a significant jolt in the fiction. It serves as a critique of humanity in the character of Coetzee's magistrate. The effort to maintain the position at the centre as a human, the image of the empire as responsible and therefore human, is organically confronted through the very identity of the barbarians. The 'humans' are pushed from the centre to the periphery, as no humanism is reflected in the same entity of which the magistrate is only a part. This failure to sustain stability at the centre and reaction to the changing circumstances occurs due to the inclusion of the other within the self. The assimilation of the self with the other, in this case, the Empire and the Barbarians, with the kind of torture inflicted on the magistrate by the Empire itself, interrogates the very essence of identity and humanism. This assimilation, therefore, shifts the Vitruvian figure into the periphery. The brutality, the torture, the mental trauma, and the agony inside the torture chamber can be anything but 'human'. Despite the confession of the magistrate that no such crime exists in the land colonised by the Empire, the torture continues, and people like Mandel continue to ransack the houses of the barbarians to express their power and dominion. The trauma inflicted through torture, as seen in the fiction, blurs the distinction between the self and the other, in this case, the image of the civilised and the 'responsible' Empire with the so-called barbarians. This assimilation is traumatising for the humans who hypothesise that the existing 'humans' have all the traits of holistic civilised moralities and are supreme among all mundane species.

Depicting blood on the fictional stage to sensitise a narrative is not Coetzee's way of handling torture. Portraying desperate procedures to cause death and straining readers' nerves cannot be an admirable medium to express the pain of the ruled for a prodigious writer like Coetzee. Therefore, Coetzee stays away from extreme realism to depict pain in his fiction, but he employs suggestions and uses space and time to reflect the effect of torture on human beings. Coetzee primarily stresses the consequences of suffering to show severe pain, anxiety, and trauma. Offering the outcome rather than the real-time action allows Coetzee to avoid the controversy of being lewd and obscene. Coetzee presents terror through his imagination in a language wrought with terror. The magistrate in the fiction asks and searches for clues that suit his vision. The imagination of the torture reminds the magistrate about the innocent people being tortured and exposed to strenuous grilling every day, every evening. Coetzee sketches the torture room to form a kind of link between totalitarianism and its victims (Coetzee, 1992, p. 363). The granary or the torture house entry is through huge and heavy doors, but the exit is symbolically described through the 'tiny windows'. Incidents of torture happen in the darkness of the granary, where entry of broad daylight does not take place. The magistrate continues his work, but he anticipates torture at every moment. "At every moment that evening as I go about my business, I am aware of what might be happening, and my ear is even tuned to the pitch of human pain. But the granary is a massive building with heavy doors and tiny windows ..." (Coetzee, 2000, WB, p. 5).

The magistrate welcomes the other, even though they have created some problems, which in the eyes of the Empire are serious, and by doing this, he assimilates himself with the other. The other merges into the magistrate, and he becomes Spinoza's 'One'. Spinoza believed that there is a single element or substance with countless qualities or attributes. All attributes may be free and independent, but they come from an identical substance and are one. The magistrate may not be taken as a person who is exceptionally tender and benevolent. Out of sheer anger, the magistrate even claims to throw out the criminal from the window, crash his body, and turn him into a pulp. This may be taken as a reaction to the trauma that he has faced during his tenure at the place and working by the side of the Empire and is a natural reaction to the violence that he has witnessed, but he is part of the Empire and traces of violence can also be found in him. The man in 'human' is only the 'man' with all his attributes. His sexual desire to possess the tortured lady cannot be ruled out; readers, however, feel his empathy towards the girl when he returns her to her people. The self, therefore, is not benign. Once again, with the empathetic attitude of the magistrate, he becomes one of the others by returning the girl, and when the colonel takes charge of the situation after the magistrate goes to return the girl, he becomes the perpetrator of violence, and the magistrate, now being the other, is tortured. The magistrate himself, through his empathetic efforts, tried to do some good to the image of the Empire and give it some kind of stability, but the condition of the magistrate at the end of the novel, when he becomes the Other, destabilises the image of the Empire again, and such efforts and repeated failures lead to a certain kind of metastability. The uncertainty of the position of humans leads to the post-human uncertainty of the coordinates. Nothing is certain as the position continuously shifts. This kind of transversality is what makes Coetzee's fiction candid food for post-human philosophers. The magistrate's position in the fiction is also transversal. He remains ambiguous about whether to assess himself as someone who believes in the laws of the Empire, as an escapist or as someone who takes the responsibility to protect the other, or as a man who cares about his possession as he keeps the tortured girl in his residence, as someone who doubts the intention of the Empire, or as a negotiator who somehow tries to maintain some balance between the self and the other to keep and restore the prestige and goodwill of the Empire.

The brutality of the torture is brought to the reader's mind through the suggestive language that Coetzee employs. The magistrate's queries to the tortured or the witnesses bring this image of the horror in the granary. The stress and trauma inextricably linked with torture torment the ill-fated innocent barbarians, witnesses, and even the implementer of laws, in this case, the magistrate. The presentation of this torture in *Waiting for the Barbarians* is often done through suggestive and metaphorical dialectics that stress the imagination more than even direct and real-time presentations. Torture poses serious psychological and physical scars that remain embedded in the subject for a gruelling long life. Turning the screw on the prisoners or twisting the pincers is speculated. He even asks Mandel if he takes any ritual to be forgiven by the almighty for the merciless means by which he beats the prisoners. Coetzee often mentions specific torture methods to show us what happens to the 'barbarians' and the pain inflicted upon them by the 'Empire'. In the fiction, Coetzee interrogates the 'humanism' projected by the Empire as incredibly 'false'. The truth that Colonel Joll wants from the barbarians is the most powerful false narrative required to validate and justify his presence. Post-humanism, as a discourse, surely invades and interrogates such situations. Whenever the magistrate sees the colonel, he feels inquisitive about the torture methods the colonel so individualised. To the magistrate, it is a tale of torture, and he becomes desperate to ask the colonel whether he thinks at all about the terrible position of the prisoners who are forced to squeeze out the so important 'truth' even though they are innocent. The readers find the image of torture as something never-ending and dreadful.

> When I see Colonel Joll again, when he has the leisure, I bring the conversation around to torture. 'What if your prisoner is telling the truth,' I ask, 'yet finds he is not believed? Is that not a terrible position? Imagine: to be prepared to yield, to yield, to have nothing more to yield, to be broken, yet to be pressed to yield more! And what a responsibility for the interrogator! How do you ever know when a man has told you the truth? (Coetzee, 2000, WB, p. 5)

Extracting the desirable 'truth' fills the reader with tormenting images. In reply to the magistrate regarding his methods of pulling out the truth, Colonel Joll says, "First I get lies, you see – this is what happens – first lies, then pressure, then more lies, then more pressure, then the break, then more pressure, then the truth. That is how you get the truth" (WB, p. 5). Coetzee focuses on the 'truth' of Colonel Joll as the shameless 'truth' of the 'Empire'. The magistrate apprehends the power of the colonel, and he remembers that Colonel Joll is a far more powerful person than him. He also reminisces that the 'Empire' exercises supreme control over the natives through people like the colonel, and he comes from the most crucial division. The 'Empire' selects people who have proved brutal may be in their past missions and therefore recruited into the most critical division of the 'Empire'. The ability to torture and extract the 'truth' has perhaps made him an invincible officer and a vital recruit. The magistrate explains that "'Colonel Joll is from the Third Bureau', I tell them. 'The Third Bureau is the most important division of the Civil Guard nowadays'" (WB, p. 2). At the beginning of the text, the readers are exposed to the likings of the colonel. The travel choices that he makes and his favourite places. Colonel Joll does not feel weird seeing carcasses, and his choice of destinations differs from the magistrate, who loves to see flocks of geese and ducks descending on the lake. Strangers share pleasant feelings and memorable tours with a 'flask' and 'a bowl of nuts'. Colonel Joll prefers to share the disturbing scenes of the carcasses of deer, pigs, and bears. The magistrate continues, "He tells me about the last great drive he rode in, when thousands of deer, pigs, bears were slain, so many that a mountain of carcasses had to be left to rot" (WB, p. 1). Coetzee declares the end of morality in the character of Colonel Joll and shows the desperation, ambition, and brutality that lie at the very core of the intention of the 'Empire'. Coetzee tempts the readers to revisit the 'granary', in the end, once more to find out who the real barbarians are–the ones who are presented as the invaders or the ones who represent the 'Empire'. Coetzee initially presents the magistrate as a 'human' who wavers between taking sides with the representative of the Empire and his morality. The magistrate finds the torture inflicted on the poor barbarians intolerable, and he cannot resist doing as much as he can to know what happens in the granary. The filthy condition of the granary adds to the torture and helps the colonel find out the 'truth'. The unbearable agony comes from the corporeal ways; it also comes from the invaders or the 'barbarians' who are kept in exceedingly unhygienic conditions. Readers remain awestruck when they find, "The two prisoners lie bound on the floor. The smell comes from them, a smell of old urine, I call the guard in: 'Get these men to clean themselves, and please hurry'" (WB, p. 2). The magistrate commits himself to feeding the barbarians and making them speak. He imagines the excruciating pain that the poor victims of the colonel may have suffered inside the granary or the torture chamber. Suppression through pressure tactics is an old tool of the 'Empire'. Torture, therefore, is kept under the lid. Free expression is strictly prohibited. The guard acts under the pressure of the officer to make his statement. The conversation between the magistrate and the guard is appalling. "'Did the officer tell you what to say to me?' I ask him softly. 'Yes, sir,' he says. 'Were the prisoner's hands tied?'" (WB, p. 6) The guard replies, 'Yes, sir. I mean, no, sir' (WB, p. 6).

The inhumaneness and ruthlessness associated with the torture are brought out in the following lines, where a little boy sees his grandfather being beaten up, killed, packed in a shroud, and kept in front of him to remind him constantly of the consequences of not telling the 'truth'. The boy lies on a bed of straw with his hands tied so that he does not escape from the shroud and watches it constantly to keep the trauma alive. In reply to the magistrate's query, the guard declares, "He was here when I came on duty. He said to the boy, I heard him, "Sleep with your grandfather, keep him warm". He pretended he was going to sew the boy into the shroud too, the same shroud, but he did not. While the boy still lies rigidly asleep, his eyes pinched shut, we carry the corpse out" (WB, p. 7).

Incessant violence is unleashed on the prisoners, and Coetzee depicts in detail the scenes post-violence:

> The grey beard is caked with blood. The lips are crushed and drawn back, the teeth are broken. One eye is rolled back, the other eye-socket is a bloody hole. 'Close it up,' I say. The guard bunches the opening together. It falls open. 'They say that he hit his head on the wall. What do you think?' He looks at me warily. 'Fetch some twine and tie it shut.' (WB, p. 7)

The magistrate's confusion when he caressed the Barbarian woman may have come from the ambiguity in his understanding of the 'Empire's propaganda regarding women. He finds it impossible to assimilate the propaganda that proposes respect to women with the torture inflicted on the woman who sees her father being killed brutally in front of her. The magistrate is criticised as a man who fails to understand what to do with a woman in bed. However, a closer introspection into the magistrate's deeds focuses on the fact that he is so moved and empathetic with the poor character that he possibly takes the sexual act with the woman as another torture and therefore remains too cautious and confused. Many readers may not entirely agree with some critics who express the sexual confusion of the magistrate and his problem of expression in proper words as a lack of authority. Instead, to many readers, he resembles humanism, and his bewilderment and stupidity signify him as the only one in the fiction who understands torture even before he is tortured. Coetzee presents suffering in the most refined manner, not adding obscenity and realistic violence but with the imagination and suggestions that make the readers comprehend its terror. Coetzee avoids directly depicting the torture, but he fulfils his intent by describing the consequences by adding to the traumatic experience of the readers who imagine the torture in the infinite and even more than any direct reference to it. Readers find the scenes agonising and ruthless. The more it comes to suggestions and consequences, the more the imagination and the brutality of the torture:

> Nimbly with hand and teeth, the boy begins unwrapping the rags that bandage his forearm. The last rounds, caked with blood and matter, stick to his flesh, but he lifts their edge to show me the red angry rim of the sore. 'You see', the old man says, 'nothing will heal it. I was bringing him to the doctor when the soldiers stopped us. That is all.' (WB, p. 4)

The ambiguity in the white wooden tiles' inscriptions and the fact that they represent multifarious meanings regarding the Empire point to several interpretations of Coetzee's text. He never tells us the time and the place of his narrative. Readers can imagine the time and place as contemporary and ahistorical as they can imagine. Additionally, the universal appeal of the torture on the colonised mind makes the readers understand his position in the power hierarchy much easier. Anthony Burgess opines that this text of Coetzee is just about everywhere. It defies any particular location and time. The slow killing of the father of a poor child in front of it is not only brutal, but the trauma it leaves behind is unforgettable to the child. The mind refuses to disremember the brutality till the end of life. Coetzee tries to remain aloof from representational politics and therefore stays away from presenting torture methods directly to the readers. However, he does not shirk his responsibility in depicting the poor barbarians' trauma that remains with them throughout. Gallagher comments that Coetzee stays away from directly identifying the horrible acts that the South African Police bring down on the people in Vorster Square but indirectly points to the terror unleashed on the political prisoners in South Africa. Coetzee gives the torture a universal tone and does not hesitate to blame the politics of his own country (1992, p. 282).

The horror embedded in the torture is brought out by how the magistrate tries to comprehend and cognise the torture methods and how a torturer manages to keep his sanctity. This suggestion of torture brings more terror to the readers as they imagine the horror inside the granary. The magistrate declares that he cannot understand how Mandel lives or breathes. Coetzee, along with the magistrate, wonders about the rationality of the existence of such human beings. Whenever the magistrate comes close to the poor barbarian girl, he keeps asking her about the torture she has faced and even tries to imagine the agony with the girl and visits the torture room. This intention of the magistrate to come closer may not be only out of curiosity. A kind of desperation to get into the girl's psychology is eminent here, and we get a clear picture of the torture these people are subjected to at the hands of Colonel Joll or Mandel. The imagination of the torture scene disturbs his entire ontological existence, and he fails to suppress his intentions to enter the girl's psyche through the knowledge of her past trauma. He fails to achieve success in his purpose. However, when he returns the girl to the 'invading barbarians' and faces the torture himself and understands the humiliation, he realises that the subject position has changed. In objectifying the girl as a victim, he has placed himself in the role of Colonel Joll. He recognises himself as the 'lie' of the 'Empire'. Therefore, torture in the name of 'truth' gives an inexplicable pleasure that comes under the discourse of psychoanalysis. It is when the magistrate undergoes the punishments of the 'Empire' and suffers humiliation in the hands of his people that he realises that what he imagines as torture in the granary is true and comprehending the trauma of the tortured is only possible through the realistic and mental defeat in the hands of the torturer.

Coetzee presents trauma taking a middle path and becomes a victim of the critics who focus on the political relevance of his fiction 'The Waiting for the Barbarians' as he does not present South African politics directly into the limelight. Therefore, his presentation of torture is angular and tangent, which does not match the time in which he is writing. Contemporary South Africa is reeling under the apartheid of the 'White' Government of South Africa when Coetzee's work is published. Controversy regarding the text is eminent, but Coetzee's work touches upon the condition of the blacks and other racial subaltern subclasses of his native nation in a manner that is immediately metaphysical and philosophical. Instead of hurling attacks at the government, Coetzee's 'Waiting for the Barbarians' focuses on the inhumane and severe conditions of the ruled and the suffering of the innocent. Coetzee's narrative makes the readers think of something fundamental to post-colonial and sub-altern studies: finding out the true nature of rulers in every nook and corner of the world and interrogating the true identity of the barbarians. To be precise, the text repeatedly interrogates and asks who the barbarians are – the ones identified by the rulers or the real perpetrators of violence, i.e., the 'Empire' itself. Dominic Head observes that Colonel Joll desperately wants the barbarians to arrive to validate the purpose of the Empire. The magistrate considers the Empire barbaric. The magistrate waits for the barbarism of the Empire to take place so that he can separate himself from the Empire's ideology of power and justice (1998, p.74). The suggestive torture presents ambiguity in the title itself. Perhaps Coetzee keeps the title to indicate why we shall wait for the barbarians to take over and do nothing. Resistance always does not come from direct attacks. Through indirect, philosophical, and metaphysical narratives, the readers go deep into the minds of the colonisers and understand the intention of such brutality and severity of torture. Readers do not find it challenging to comprehend the 'Empire's efforts to synthetically brand the innocent as invaders and the barbaric necessity to create the ruled to become the ruler. The allegory he presents astonishes the readers with how spite can be reflected through metaphysical language and suggestive methods. Regarding the parable, Paul De Man opines, "By reading we get, as we say, inside a text that was first something alien to us and which we now make our own by an act of understanding. But this understanding becomes at once the representation of an extra-textual meaning" (Man, 1979, pp. 12–13).

To Baruch Spinoza, no human can be completely free, sane, and right-eous. No finite mode can accomplish any of these qualities fully. The fact that finite modes interact with finite modes makes them unable to achieve these qualities completely. The magistrate in the fiction cannot accomplish any of these entirely because of his interactions with people like Colonel Joll, Mandel, the barbarians, and the girl who aroused particular desires in him of which he was initially not very conscious. But as Spinoza says that the free thoughts that resist evil senses always lead to virtuosity, the magis-trate in the fiction does the same; he goes against the Empire and thinks of the barbarians as victims of oppression, empathises with them, and brings them respite. Post-humanism as a critique of humanism does the same by considering the transversality of all situations, the gigantic leaps in tech-nology, the poisoning of the environment, revisiting the very foundations of humanism, the inclusions actually within the term humanism, and, of course, critiquing one's position. The magistrate, too, does the same in Coetzee's fiction *Waiting for the Barbarians.*

The term 'Spinozist' during the 17th, 18th, and 19th centuries was used for those branded as anti-establishment and anti-church due to his revo-lutionary avant-garde ideas. Even the *Ethics* was posthumously published. The pantheistic approach of Spinoza, where he differs from the traditional theists, declares that Nature in all its parts and species and God are identical, and therefore all of Nature's components, attributes, and essences must be protected. The magistrate's efforts to save the world struggling against the Empire's capitalism are a monistic attempt to let the planet survive. One will not find in the text the significant protesting voices of the barbarians or the Other, but as Pierre Macherey (1978) rightly says, the unsaid in work is most important because all the utterances in work lead to the silence where resides the unsaid (p. 87). Like the silence of the tortured girl on most occasions, the voice of the repressed remains hidden in the concept of humanism. The power acts as the repressive force under the veil of hu-manism. Post-human philosophers put such situations under the scanner. According to the novel, the destruction of the barbarians is intimately related to the destruction of Nature, as the barbaric community is closely related to the primitive and pristine methods of maintaining their farm-yards. The coloniser, through their power-hungry intentions, will destroy such methods to replace them with capitalist intentions, thereby destroying Nature. Man cannot be the only species privileged to rule the world. Nature, in all its components, has equal claims to survive on the planet.

Coetzee attacks the pretentious morality of contemporary society by presenting the pains, anxieties, tensions, and consequences of torture and the resulting trauma in a post-humanist approach. It is essential to dig out the savagery that remains hidden under the topping of civilisation. The post-human philosophy appeals to rethink and re-enter the occasions that take us to the annihilation of basic standards of morality and human nature under the shroud of the supremacy of the species and the pretence of humanism, which rarely includes the etymological and the genealogical reference to the term 'human' itself. The ambiguity of the magistrate to take side with the Empire, his initial reluctance to exploit the woman on the bed, his returning of the girl to her people, and his guilt and anger against the Empire are nothing but efforts to give meaning to an existence that critiques the image of the Empire. This effort to give meaning is not without the hint and the prospect of the coming on of moral sense that torments the soul on seeing the evil and the sinful things that disturb our ontological existence to give us a civilisation that at least is heterogeneous enough to accept morality and ethics, the self and the other, in a unified, organic whole where this assimilation will no longer be traumatising.

Works Cited

Burgess, A. "The Beast Within: Waiting for the Barbarians." News Group Publication, 1982, pp. 88–90.

Caruth, C. "Unclaimed Experience: Trauma and the Possibility of History", *Yale French Studies*, Vol. 79, pp. 181–192. *JSTOR*, <https://doi.org/10.2307/2930251>. Web. 12 June 2021.

Coetzee, J. M. "Into the Dark Chamber: The Writer and the South Africa State." In D. Atwell (Ed.), *Doubling the Point*. Harvard University Press, 1992.

————. *Waiting for the Barbarians*. Vintage, 2000. [The abbreviation for *Waiting for the Barbarians* is WB.] [Page number of block quotes from this text is within parenthesis and is abbreviated as WB.]

Gallagher, S. V. Z. and J. M. Coetzee. "Torture and the Novel: J. M. Coetzee's 'Waiting for the Barbarians.'" *Contemporary Literature*, Vol. 29, No. 2, 1988, pp. 277–285. *JSTOR*, <https://doi.org/10.2307/1208441>. Web. 12 June 2021.

Head, Dominic *J. M. Coetzee*. Cambridge University Press, 1998.

Macherey, P. *A Theory of Literary Production*. Routledge & Kegan Paul, 1978.

Man, P. De. *Allegories of Reading: Figural Language in Rousseau, Nietzsche, Rilke, and Proust*. Yale University Press, 1979.

Afterword

Literature after the Human

What are the prospects for literature after the end of humanism? Posthumanism is associated with specific poststructuralist approaches to humanism developed in the late 20th century by Donna Haraway, Katherine Hayles, and Rosi Braidotti, among others. To apply a "post" to humanism is to critically engage and question the limits of the human, how it has been ideologically constructed, and what practical and theoretical work it performs. Humanism is viewed as a quintessentially modern project, where language, rationality, and moral value are restricted to human beings, who are subjects. These subjects confront a world of objects, which includes nonhuman animals, other life forms, natural resources, machines, and other fabricated things.

Along with New Materialism, Actor-Network Theory, Speculative Realism, Agential Realism, and Object-Oriented Ontology, posthumanism is an attempt to think beyond the exceptionalized and reified human subject to open it up to other beings and becomings. Another way to characterize this phenomenon is as a transition from 20th century human or social sciences (the Sciences of Man) and its concomitant social constructivism to a mode of theorizing that engages primarily with the natural sciences, including mathematics, physics, biology, systems theory, and science studies in this century. Here language, writing, and literature have sometimes been relegated to a humanist paradigm, but what this volume does is show how we can reframe them within the context of posthumanism.

The value of this book is how it productively engages narratives, science fiction, poetry, television, and film across disciplines and boundaries from a posthumanist perspective in ways that elaborate and advance our understanding of what they are and can do. The context of literature in this century is the Anthropocene, the proposed new geological era that begins when human activity alters the planet on large scales. The irony is that as we learn more and more about the irreducible human entanglements with nonhuman phenomena, we are now confronted with the powerful destructive effects of human civilization on the Earth.

The word entanglement expresses this situation eloquently in a posthumanist context. Entanglement is a technical term from quantum mechanics that characterizes how two subatomic particles can be aligned such that any effect upon the one (say, the measurement of spin) determines the other, and we can know this instantly, without any mediation. We are still trying to comprehend this strange phenomenon, even as we can extend entanglement beyond strictly quantum phenomena. Words matter. Literature matters. In *Meeting the Universe Halfway*, Karen Barad uses quantum physics to express the inextricable *entanglement* of matter and meaning. Beyond all the complicated physics and philosophy, Barad's book is oriented and entitled by a poem by Alice Fulton called "Cascade Experiment." This poem, a profound example of posthumanist literature, asserts that truths are hard to discern when we are biased against accepting them; therefore, "we have to meet the universe halfway." We have to acknowledge that at a deep level, "believing a thing's true/can bring about that truth," which implies a profound entanglement of truth with material reality, including subatomic particles and scaling all the way up to and beyond us to implicate the universe as a whole.[1]

Literature works across multiple boundaries, borders, media, materiality, and meanings, from the microscopic to the gigantic. This expansion of literature in a posthumanist era opens us up to vast scales and provides a visionary disclosure of who we are and can be, which is never

---

1   Barad, K. *Meeting the Universe Halfway: Quantum Mechanics and the Entanglement of Matter and Meaning* (Durham: Duke University Press, 2007), Appendix A: "Cascade Experiment."

solely human. This is what the chapters in this book deliver—a sense of ourselves beyond ourselves, rooted in imagination and wonder, which is the spark of all knowledge.

Clayton Crockett
Professor and Director of Religious Studies,
Department of Philosophy and Religion,
University of Central Arkansas, Conway, Arkansas, USA.

Notes on Contributors

AISHWARYA DAS GUPTA is a State Aided College Teacher at the Department of English, Calcutta Girls' College, Kolkata. She completed her M.Phil. from the University of Calcutta. She has presented papers in various national and international seminars. Her poems have found homes in various anthologies like *Aulos Poetry*, *The Pangolin Review*, and *The Pinecone Review*; her latest poem has been published by Suddhashar in their recent anthology on South Asian Queer representations entitled *Queer Utopias: Voices from South Asia*. Her first anthology of poems entitled *Becomings* has been brought out by Hawakal Publishers in 2022. Her areas of interest include gender studies, ecocriticism, postcolonialism, and posthumanism.

ARITRA BASU is an Assistant Professor in the Department of English, Centre for Distance and Online Education, Rabindra Bharati University, Kolkata. He is currently pursuing his PhD from the University of Calcutta, Department of Comparative Indian Language and Literature. He completed his M.Phil. from the Department of English, University of Delhi. He has published works in the journals of Jadavpur University, The University of Calcutta, The University of North Bengal, and Scottish Church College, along with publications in journals like *Muse India* and *Asian Quarterly*. He has presented papers at conferences organized by the University of Birmingham, Johns Hopkins University, the University of Nevada, Lancaster University, and several others. A published translator, he has also published his first book of poems titled *A Printed Mixtape* in 2023. His research areas are popular literature and culture, translation studies, literary theory and film studies. He is also a creative writer and slam poet, and enjoys public speaking.

DEBOJYOTI DAN is a State Aided College Teacher at Naba Ballygunge Mahavidyalaya, Kolkata. He has special interests in modern and postmodern literature and theories. He learned French initially from the

Ramakrishna Mission and then pursued further diplomas in French from the Alliance Française du Bengal. He has several publications to his credit, including a book of poems, *Enigma of Red Shadows*. He was awarded the first prize in the world French Poetry Competition known as *Le Printemps des Poètes* in 2007. He had worked in the Alliance Française du Bengal as a cultural coordinator in the Cine Club from 2007 to 2009.

JOYDEEP CHAKRABORTY is a member of the Modern Language Association and was awarded a PhD by Bankura University, West Bengal, India in 2022. His area of research is 21 st century American poetry. His notable articles include "Violence Has Changed Me: Private Trauma and Identity Crisis in Post-9/11 American Poetry" [published in *Appropriations*, xii (2017) and indexed in the *MLA International Bibliography*], "Hallucinations in Post-9/11 American Poetry: Trauma and Beyond" (published in the British journal *Critical Survey*, Vol. 33, No. 3(4), 2021), and so on. He also won the MLA Annual Convention Travel Grant 2021 and the MLA Graduate Student Lounge Door Prize for his thesis presentation at the MLA Annual Convention 2021. One of his papers, "Hospitality in Post-9/11 American Poetry: From Multiculturalism to Post-multiculturalism," was presented at the annual conference of the British Association for American Studies in April 2022, at the University of Hull, UK. His article "To Say What Could Not Be Said: Crisis and Post-9/11 Meta-poetry" is published by *Critical Survey*, winter issue, 2024. Moreover, he is a commissioned book reviewer for the *Journal of American Studies*, published by Cambridge University Press.

JYOTI BISWAS is an Assistant Professor in the Dept. of English at Seth Soorajmull Jalan Girls' College, Kolkata. He qualified the University Grants Commission-National Eligibility Test for junior research fellowship in July 2018 and was awarded with an M.Phil. degree in English by the Central University of Tamil Nadu, Thiruvarur, in February 2021. He is presently pursuing a Ph.D. in the Department of English Studies, Central University of Jharkhand, Ranchi. The major areas of his research include literary and cultural theory, cultural studies, ritual studies, performance studies, social and cultural anthropology, folkloristics, and Buddhist studies.

NILADRI MAHAPATRA is a State Aided College Teacher in the Department of English, Bhatter College, Dantan, West Bengal, India. He was awarded his M.Phil. degree in 2019 from the Department of English, Ravenshaw University, Cuttack, India. His research areas focus on post-humanism and Indian science fiction. His areas of interest include ancient philosophy, Renaissance literature, modern literature, postmodern literature, literary theory, posthumanism, futurism, etc. He published several articles and scholarly papers in several international journals and edited volumes. He also presented several scholarly papers in international conferences, seminars, and symposiums. He is now working as a copy editor for the journal *The Golden Line: A Magazine on English Literature* (ISSN 2395-1583 print) (ISSN 2395-1591 online).

REESWAV CHATTERJEE is a Ph.D. Research Scholar at the Department of English Bankura University and a State Aided College Teacher at Maheshtala College, Kolkata. He has published his articles in journals such as *Consortium, Roots: Journal of Interdisciplinary Studies, Ashwamegh, Asian Quarterly, Humanities Circle*, and others. His special interests are in feminism, postmodernism, and posthumanism. He has contributed on a regular basis to Bengali literary magazines, including *Utsob, Terminus, Bibhabona, Ami Amamar Moto*, and *Kobita Bulletin*. His first book, coauthored with Aritra Mitra, came out in 2022. It is a prose anthology of fictional and nonfictional writings on the pandemic titled *Gharbondir Lekhyoguccho*. His first poetry collection, *Bhalobasar Patigonit*, was released in July 2024.

SAIKAT CHAKRABORTY is an integrated M.Phil., Ph.D. Research Scholar in the Department of English, Kazi Nazrul University, Asansol, West Bengal, India. He has submitted his M.Phil. thesis titled "So much in a Name!: Reading Genealogies of Vehicle Inscriptions." His recent publications, include "Cthulu and the snake: (Im)Possibility of posthuman ipseity" in an international peer-reviewed journal *Consortium: An International Journal of Literary and Cultural Studies*. His paper titled

"Breast and its surplus: Rereading of Mahasweta Devi's Mulakaram and Yogesh Pagare's Mulakaram" is forthcoming from Lexington Books, an imprint of Rowman & Littlefield.

SHALINI CHAKRABORTY is an Assistant Professor in the Dept. of English and Literary Studies, Braiware University, Kolkata She has previously worked as an Asst. Professor of English at Srinath University, Jamshedpur, a Visiting Faculty for English and Communication at Netaji Subhash Engineering College, a lecturer at Bankim Sardar College, Canning, and as an English teacher at Calcutta Public School, Kalikapur. Her paper titled ' "But she was woman; he was dog'—A Posthumanist Approach to Canine Subjectivity in Virginia Woolf's *Flush*"—has found its place in a special issue on posthumanism of *Consortium* (an international journal), Vol. 1, No. 2. She has also presented a paper titled "Love in the time of Posthumanity: Analysing the equation between the bodied and disembodied consciousness in Spike Jonze's 'Her' " in a seminar on Posthumanism at Bankura University. Apart from that, her poems and prose articles have made place in more than four anthologies: *Mindscape, A Nursery of Miscellanea, The Kali Project*, and *Through the Looking Glass*, the last two being international. As a slam poet, she has been associated with Kommune and was featured among the 100 poets on the last World Poetry Day. She published her debut anthology of poems *Her Mother Tongue is Silence* in 2023. She has also edited an anthology of creativity writings, *Beautiful Minds*, along with her peers. She has also done a course in editing and publishing from Jadavpur University.

SOURAV SAHA is a Ph.D. Research Scholar (S.R.F) in the Department of Humanities and Management at Dr. B. R. Ambedkar National Institute of Technology, Jalandhar, Punjab, India. He has qualified the UGC-NET examination with JRF and the West Bengal State Eligibility Test (WBSET) in English Literature. His areas of interest include queer studies, feminist studies, Gothic studies, lesbian studies, horror fiction, media studies, South Asian studies, diasporic studies, popular culture, and literary theory. Presently, his dissertation investigates the different levels of marginalization and trauma faced by the sexual minorities within the

South Asian Diaspora without implying that it is either a homogenous or a fixed category. His articles have appeared in Web of Science-indexed journals like Feminist Media Studies and ARIEL. He has also contributed several book chapters to National and International publications.

SUJATO GHOSH is an Assistant Professor, Department of English (UG & PG), Belda College affiliated to Vidyasagar University, West Bengal, India. He has connected to the academic teaching fraternity for almost 20 years. He is awarded the Doctorate of Philosophy in English by Jadavpur University, Kolkata, West Bengal, India.

SWAGATA SINGHA RAY is a Ph.D. Research Scholar at the Dept. of English, Raiganj University. She has completed her M.Phil. thesis titled "Reading Margaret Atwood's MaddAddam trilogy as Speculative fiction through Posthuman Lens". Her areas of interest are posthumanism, Indian English writing, feminist writing, diasporic studies, and modernist and postmodernist literature.

SWAPNA ROY is a State Aided College Teacher in the Department of English at Amdanga Jugal Kishore Mahavidyalaya, West Bengal. She completed her M.Phil. in English Literature from Vidyasagar University in 2020 on posthumanism. She has several publications in reputed journals, including UGC Care listed. She has a book chapter on Mental Health in *The Posthuman Imagination*, published by Cambridge Scholars Publishing Group, and another one on Girish Karnad titled "Myths, Folks, Elements, and Unconscious: Contextualizing Girish Karnad's Naga-Mandala" in *Dramatizing the Truth: The Plays of Girish Karnad*, published by Yking Books. She is interested in psychoanalysis, posthumanism, and gender studies.

TIYASA DEY is a Ph.D Research Scholar in the Dept. of English at Aligarh Muslim University, UP, India She has qualified the UGC-NET-2022 and Graduate Aptitude Test in Engineeering-2022 (GATE-2022). Her research interests are in posthumanism, science fiction, fantasy fiction, and cultural studies. She has presented papers in several national and international conferences and seminars relating to posthumanism.

Index

www.ingramcontent.com/pod-product-compliance
Lightning Source LLC
Chambersburg PA
CBHW071601110726
47908CB00007B/2193